THE FREEDOM TRAP

THE FREEDOM TRAP

Reclaiming Liberty and Wellbeing

Dr CRAIG HASSED

Other Books with Exisle Publishing

Illuminating Wisdom: Words of wisdom, works of art by Deirdre Hassed and Dr Craig Hassed

The Mindful Home: The secrets to making your home a place of harmony, beauty, wisdom and true happiness by Dr Craig Hassed and Deirdre Hassed

Mindful Learning: Reduce stress and improve brain performance for effective learning by Dr Craig Hassed and Dr Richard Chambers

Mindfulness for Life by Dr Stephen McKenzie and Dr Craig Hassed

ABOUT THE AUTHOR

Craig Hassed is an Associate Professor at Monash University, where he has taught in the Medical Faculty since 1989. He is also coordinator of the faculty's mindfulness programs. His teaching, research and clinical interests include mindfulness-based stress management, mind-body medicine, meditation, health promotion, integrative medicine and medical ethics. Craig consults widely with other universities and is regularly invited to speak and run courses in Australia and overseas in health, professional and educational contexts. He was the founding president of the Australian Teachers of Meditation Association and is a regular media commentator. Craig has written regularly for medical journals and has authored and co-authored twelve books and featured in the documentary *The Connection*, for which he also wrote the companion e-book. With Richard Chambers, he co-authored the online Mindfulness course in collaboration with Monash University and FutureLearn.

First published 2017

Exisle Publishing Pty Ltd
PO Box 864, Chatswood, NSW 2057, Australia
PO Box 60–490, Titirangi, Auckland 0642, New Zealand
www.exislepublishing.com

A CiP record for this book is available from the National Library of Australia.

ISBN 978-1-925335-46-0

Designed by Mark Thacker, Big Cat Design.
Typeset in Minion Pro 10.75 on 14.5pt
Printed in China

This book uses paper sourced under ISO 14001 guidelines from well-managed forests and other controlled sources.

10 9 8 7 6 5 4 3 2 1

Disclaimer
While this book is intended as a general information resource and all care has been taken in compiling the contents, neither the author nor the publisher and their distributors can be held responsible for any loss, claim or action that may arise from reliance on the information contained in this book. As each person and situation is unique, it is the responsibility of the reader to consult a qualified professional regarding their personal care.

CONTENTS

Prologue 1

1 **The freedom trap** 3

2 **In praise of freedom** 11

3 **So free we seem** 21

4 **Contemporary freedom — where are we now?** 47

5 **The philosophy of freedom** 65

6 **Freedom under the law** 87

7 **Liberté, egalité and fraternité — the politics of freedom** 113

8 **The science of freedom** 131

9 **The psychology of freedom** 147

10 **The ethics of freedom** 165

11 **Child rearing and education** 193

12 **Freedom of speech and privacy** 213

Epilogue 231

Endnotes 233

Index 256

PROLOGUE

The interest in freedom and the motivation for writing this book arises from personal experience and from working with many people over many years who have been oppressed by stress, life-threatening and debilitating illness, pain, fear, addiction and many other problems — in short, the human condition which we all share in our own unique ways. Such problems are often seen as individual issues but they have much to do with the society we live within. Although suffering has been as perennial as existence itself, today it is as if we live in a world that is breeding discontent and, well intended though our attempts may be, we are struggling to deal effectively with these problems.

How did we get into this situation in the first place? How can we stop multiplying our problems? How do we free ourselves individually and collectively from our burdens? What is freedom and how do we find it? This book aims to explore these and related questions from first principles. It aims to inquire into the nature of freedom itself and then to look at particular issues in light of insights gleaned from that inquiry. Freedom will be explored philosophically, psychologically, politically, socially, legally, ethically, scientifically and neurologically. We will reflect on historical and modern perspectives. Contemporary issues and many modern assumptions about freedom will be examined and questioned. The answers we come up with and the philosophical assumptions we make have profound ramifications for us as individuals and for the wider society. They will largely determine whether we reduce our burdens or multiply them. Hopefully, through questioning, we might come to a deeper understanding of freedom and how to promote it; real freedom, that is, and not just a shadow of freedom.

To aid us in our search, at the end of each chapter there will be reflective topics and practical exercises that we can explore for ourselves.

If we enter into this inquiry in an objective and impartial way, if we ask hard questions and are not too attached to any particular point of view, hopefully some illumination may arise along the way. We may change our views, or we may not. We may come to understand our own views even more deeply than before. Whichever way we see it, it is a basic premise of this book that these questions need to be asked and that answers need to be held up to scrutiny and not taken for granted just because we live in an age where certain assumptions about freedom are widely accepted without question. If we come to understand freedom more deeply then we should, individually and collectively, also grow in happiness, peace, health and harmony. If we don't understand what freedom really is then, no matter what we think, we may, individually and collectively, find ourselves in a kind of prison of our own making. For the purposes of this book, this is what will be called 'the freedom trap'.

CHAPTER 1

THE FREEDOM TRAP

The pitfall

There are many species of carnivorous plants — plants that eat insects and very small animals. Gruesome as they are, they use a variety of ingenious, effective but simple ways of trapping their prey, which is not so easy when your prey can fly and you can't move. One group, the pitfall (or pitcher) plants, are particularly interesting. They have a long, vertical, funnel-shaped and cavernous flower with a pit of digestive juices at the bottom and a wide opening at the top that curves forward. On the front lip of the flower is a landing pad of sorts covered with a little sweet nectar that attracts flying insects. The insect lands on the lip of the flower and begins to taste the sweet nectar. So far, so good as the insect seems to be getting a free lunch. But the nectar slowly gets more abundant and sweeter the further inside the plant's mouth the insect goes. While the insect's attention is totally consumed by the increasingly sweet taste of the nectar, it neglects to notice a few other relevant things are happening. Firstly, the slope of the wall becomes steeper and steeper the further the insect goes inside the flower.

Secondly, the wall is becoming more and more slippery and precarious with downward pointing hairs. Soon the insect gets to a point of no return. It loses its footing and falls into the sticky digestive juices at the bottom from which it can't escape. There was really no free lunch at all. The insect has become lunch.

It's interesting to marvel over the efficient, effortless and beautiful design of these plants, but possibly they represent a metaphor for the human condition. Are we, as it were, distracted and sipping the sweet nectar, all the while blithely inching our way closer to a pit we know not of? Are we one moment free and the next moment trapped? If so, what is the nectar? What is the slippery slope? What is the pit? What is it that distracts us? What is the trap and how do we avoid it? Upon what does our continued freedom depend?

> **The fox condemns the trap, not himself.**
>
> *William Blake*[1]

Perhaps the trap is hidden from sight by self-deception, false beliefs, a lack of awareness, conflicted internal motivations and a lack of reason. If so, non-attachment, self-honesty, the rule of reason, awareness and integration of the psyche may be the ways to avoid the trap or to find a way out of it. Perhaps for us the trap is made up of things that we find sweet and attractive, things such as desires and attachments to pleasure and possessions, but they have the potential to lead to addictions and unhappiness where we thought we might find satisfaction. Perhaps our hunger for ever-greater freedom draws us ever closer to the tipping point. Perhaps we misunderstand what freedom really is and so, rather than liberation, we find ourselves in what we might call the freedom trap.

So free we seem

It would be easy to think that a book called *The Freedom Trap* is in some way anti-freedom. Nothing could be further from the truth. This book is unequivocally, unapologetically, unhesitatingly, unambiguously, unflinchingly and unashamedly pro-freedom. It would also be easy to think that if a book raises concerns about the direction in which society is progressing then it must be anti-progress. That is also far from the truth. Progress there must be. Time and the world move forward; the decision lies as to which direction actually leads towards lasting freedom and happiness.

The main problem may be that we do not know as much about freedom as we think we do. We may be labouring under the burden of unquestioned assumptions. There are undoubtedly people who proclaim to have the answers as to what freedom is and how to promote it. They may give political speeches about it, write newspaper columns on it, protest in defence of it, fight wars for it, become activists to promote it and, dare I say, write books about it. However, speaking vociferously about something is not necessarily a mark of wisdom if this Tibetan proverb is anything to go by: 'Goodness speaks in a whisper, evil shouts.'[2]

There are clues all around us that we are not quite as free as we take ourselves to be. As Robert Browning wrote, 'So free we seem, so fettered fast we are.'[3] The first step in knowing what something is sometimes lies in discovering what it is not. In the tradition of Socrates, 'the man who knew nothing', it might be useful not to assume we know what freedom is at all.

If it is hard to be happy, at peace and in harmony with the world, if we are not free, then if we grow in freedom it stands to reason that we also enjoy all that comes with it, like greater happiness, peace and harmony. But there is too much in the modern world to suggest that the opposite is the case. Rising rates of mental illness, addiction, social isolation, conflict, inequity and endemic corruption suggest that we are missing something. Do we have the wrong idea about what freedom is? Are we barking up the wrong tree? Where are the answers going to come from? Hopefully from ourselves, but why not also ask the few wise people who promoted freedom in the wider world and also made a useful contribution to the wellbeing of others. People, for example, who were just in the face of injustice, truthful in the face of deception, compassionate in the face of hatred, and wise in the face of ignorance. What have they got to say about freedom? Perhaps the adversity they faced taught them a thing or two about it. Mind you, the answers wisdom gives are not always the ones we want to hear, which might explain why so many wise people have been criticized, put in prison and even executed.

To find answers we could also refer to evidence from modern science. Evidence, however, is just information. The problem is that it needs to be interpreted in order for it to be useful and there are a lot of things influencing how we interpret or distort information.

The other main way of exploring freedom is through direct personal experience and honest reflection. At the end of the day, it is for you, the reader, to make up your own mind about what freedom is and how you want to pursue it. The proof, as they say, will be in the pudding. It doesn't matter so much what other people say, or what the evidence is, or how it is interpreted. What matters is what we can discover for ourselves.

Where did our freedom go?

Let us consider our state of freedom throughout our life. For a baby, although totally dependent on its parents, its existence is also one of purity, innocence and freedom from ego and preoccupation with future and past. We may not remember much about what it was like to be a baby but we may remember a slow diminution in freedom as we grew out of the uncomplicated, bright and happy existence that was childhood and into the complex, murky and discontented state we tend to call adolescence. It's not so much that the world changed but more that the state of mind and being changed. Suddenly the fleeting worries or concerns of one's childhood begin to linger, elaborate on themselves and take up residence — worries about oneself, others, relationships, the world, the future, uncertainty, hopes, desires, regrets and on it goes. Perhaps the most perplexing thoughts and feelings were about discontent and unhappiness even when there was no good reason to be discontented and unhappy. At times we may have felt that we were living in an internal private prison without any real understanding of how we got there or how to escape. If we were lucky we may have come out the other side as a 'well-adjusted adult', whatever that may be, but for most of us the adolescent angst simply makes way for a more subverted kind of adult angst as most of us 'lead lives of quiet desperation' as the revered American author and transcendentalist philosopher, Henry David Thoreau, wrote in his classic book, *Walden*.[4]

Life may go on well enough, but there is something inside us that knows there has to be something better than this. If the adolescent gets tyrannized by an inner world of insecurities then the adult is likely to be tyrannized by a range of external burdens as well — burdens like family responsibilities, workload, buying a home, attaining financial security, staying healthy and then contemplating our mortality. Of course, as time goes on, most of us forget to live life consciously and deliberately, so preoccupied are we about getting to some mythical future place and time where we will be happy and content. Perhaps we forget to follow our passions in life. Perhaps we get subtly steered off course and find ourselves on a treadmill without ever making a conscious or discerning decision to get on it in the first place. Instead of truly living a life, we feel trapped by it. Again, to quote Thoreau: 'I went to the woods because I wished to live deliberately, to front only the essential facts of life, and see if I could not learn what it had to teach, and not, when I came to die, discover that I had not lived.'[5]

If we are lucky, and we don't settle for a life of quiet desperation, we may ask ourselves a number of fundamental questions about happiness and freedom. For example, with regard to freedom, which is more important — what is going on around us or what is going on within us? Are our greatest problems in our circumstances or in our minds? Can a person walk the street without any external hindrance and yet not be free? Can a person be in a prison cell and be free at the same time? If we weren't attached to things would we be both happy and free? Is it really true that truth is whatever we think it is and that one person's opinion about freedom and happiness is as valid as anybody else's? By not knowing ourselves can we be oblivious to what is conducive to our wellbeing?

These are questions humankind has pondered for as long as recorded history but they are just as important today, not just in a theoretical or academic sense but in a practical, immediate and very real way. Within the answers to such questions may lie the solutions to many contemporary problems. Whether we are conscious of it or not, we all have assumptions about questions such as the ones above. Maybe we haven't taken the time or effort to intentionally consider them but our assumptions declare themselves by how we live and what we pursue in life. Maybe we have unconsciously adopted the prevailing attitudes of the society, peer group or family we were raised in. Maybe we are just blown along by the winds of popular opinion and circumstance. Maybe we have consciously reflected on such questions and come up with answers radically different to the prevailing ideas. Maybe our assumptions have been tested and have not stood the test leaving us dispirited and giving up asking questions altogether. Maybe we didn't give up but asked the questions again with renewed enthusiasm and, after much effort, have made discoveries that have stood the test. Maybe those insights even aligned with what a few wise people had discovered before us.

SOME THINGS TO REFLECT ON:

- Are you living the life you feel you are meant to live?
- Do you feel that your life is being steered by external forces and circumstances rather than your core values and calling?
- What can you/should you do about it?
- Do you take time to cultivate wisdom and to understand yourself better?

SOME THINGS TO PRACTISE:

- Learn, perhaps through meditation, to stand back from and observe your thoughts without taking them as facts just because they are passing through your mind.
- Take time to read a little of what some of the world's great wisdom traditions[6] have had to say about freedom.

CHAPTER 2

IN PRAISE OF FREEDOM

If there is one word, one motivation, one principle that is more revered, one cause more worth fighting for than any other it would have to be freedom. Countries go to war for it, citizens plot uprisings over it, numerous movies are made about it, and individuals fiercely defend it whenever it is threatened. It is therefore fitting early on in *The Freedom Trap* that we give homage to some great examples of humanity's legitimate struggle for freedom.

It's in our nature

The pursuit of freedom is indelibly etched into our nature if observation of human behaviour is anything to go by. First, there is the raw, primitive cry for freedom given by a toddler at the supermarket checkout grasping with all its might to some shiny bauble or tasty treat. Then there are the discontented rumblings and extended debates that teenagers have with their parents over why they should be allowed to go to a particular party or stay out all night. There is the longing for freedom of subjugated people who deeply desire to throw off the physical, economic, political, social or religious shackles they endure. There is the struggle for freedom of the employee wanting to have flexible work hours or choose for themselves what work they will or won't do. There is the longing for liberation from work altogether of a work-weary person in anticipation of retirement. Then there is the longing for freedom from disease and suffering of a person in the final stages of life. Depending on the level of subjugation, people will not bear for long conditions under which they are not their own masters. Of course, in order for the longing for freedom to stir within us, we first need to be conscious of the fact that we are not truly free.

Whether or not we respect the freedom of others has a direct impact on ourselves and society. If an employer abuses or neglects workers' rights by underpaying them, it is a harbinger for further and greater abuses to come. Racial discrimination against someone in ways that are easy to ignore — even just thinking negatively about someone on the basis of their race — creates fertile ground for discrimination to flourish. Whether we cast our votes for politicians appealing to self-interest, or the interests of the country, or the interests of all humanity, sets the scene for the political system and discourse in which we find ourselves. As sweet as self-interest seems to be, it soon becomes a bitter and isolating trap within which we find ourselves sooner or later as illustrated by the following story.

A student of wisdom asked his teacher to show him heaven and hell. His teacher agreed and inquired as to which he would like to see first. The student replied, 'Hell'. He was duly transported to a beautiful mansion set amid the most magnificent and bountiful countryside. Entering the mansion, the student was taken to a banquet hall of extraordinary opulence where spread out was the most sumptuous feast he had ever laid eyes on. The student quickly perceived, however, that the room was also filled with the most excruciating misery he had ever seen. Despite this opulence the people were crying out piteously, sick and starving. He wondered why this was so and, taking a closer look, he noticed that the people were compelled to eat their food with forks which were too long to get the food into their mouths. The student wondered who could have been so cruel as to play such a macabre joke on these poor souls. He then asked to be taken to heaven. His teacher dutifully took him to an identical mansion set in an identical countryside. On entering he was shown to an identical banquet hall with the same feast laid out that he had seen before. The student noticed that the people were also compelled to eat with the same long forks and yet, to his surprise, everyone was healthy, happy and well fed. Wondering why, he again looked closely. The only difference he could see between heaven and hell was that in hell people starved because they could not feed themselves. In heaven they thrived because they fed each other.

Historical examples of the struggle for liberation

It is not too difficult to see why there is such a strong preoccupation with freedom nowadays. History, ancient and recent, is littered with abuses of freedom, some of which were begrudgingly tolerated for many years, such as miners enduring unsafe working conditions, and others which were more extreme and intolerable such as Cambodians living under the tyranny of Pol Pot. The former are tolerated because they may not have created misery extreme enough to galvanize resistance. The latter only survive by virtue of a massive power imbalance and the most extreme use of force, otherwise nobody would willingly be held in such a state. The following examples are all indicative of the perennial struggle for freedom. It is all human nature playing out.

Slavery

It almost boggles the mind to think that, around one and a half centuries ago, slavery was entrenched in the economic and social fabric of many of the world's leading political and economic powers — democracies no less. As unnatural as it was, it was construed as the natural order of things and so needed to be justified religiously, socially and economically if the societies perpetrating it were to have their consciences sufficiently blinded to what they were doing. There was even pseudo-science to make it appear as if slavery was a part of the natural order. No doubt, as William Wilberforce, the English politician and anti-slavery campaigner noted, it only took a moment's unbiased observation of the brutality and misery of the slave trade to have that view turned 180 degrees.

That people would die trying to escape slavery, and that social reformers would risk their reputations to have it repealed, is entirely understandable and admirable. What could a society possibly be thinking in order to justify that one person could own, buy and sell another human being? What kind of dogma or perverted logic could possibly justify it and make a person blind to the misery and suffering it caused? Possibly unfettered self-interest, delusions of superiority, and a total lack of compassion might have had something to do with it.

Apartheid and racism

Although slavery, by and large, passed into history the racist attitudes that allowed it to flourish didn't. They merely found expression in a watered down form. Oppressed races may no longer be in physical shackles but they could still be in economic, social and legal ones. Restrictions on the mixing of races, freedom of movement and association, education and work opportunities all meant that races would be unable to reach their potential or rise to positions of influence no matter what their merit.

Many of the most inspiring and universally admired figures in recent history — such as Mahatma Gandhi, Martin Luther King Jr. and Nelson Mandela — fought peacefully, courageously and unwaveringly to overturn such forms of injustice. King's famous speech delivered on 28 August 1963 at the Lincoln Memorial, Washington DC is one of the most revered proclamations for freedom ever spoken.

> **Five score years ago, a great American, in whose symbolic shadow we stand today, signed the Emancipation Proclamation. This momentous decree came as a great beacon light of hope to millions of Negro slaves who had been seared in the flames of withering injustice. It came as a joyous daybreak to end the long night of their captivity. But one hundred years later, the Negro still is not free. One hundred years later, the life of the Negro is still sadly crippled by the manacles of segregation and the chains**

> **of discrimination ... And this will be the day — this will be the day when all of God's children will be able to sing with new meaning: My country 'tis of thee, sweet land of liberty, of thee I sing ... And if America is to be a great nation, this must become true ... And when this happens, and when we allow freedom ring, when we let it ring from every village and every hamlet, from every state and every city, we will be able to speed up that day when all of God's children, black men and white men, Jews and Gentiles, Protestants and Catholics, will be able to join hands and sing in the words of the old Negro spiritual: 'Free at last! Free at last! Thank God Almighty, we are free at last!'[1]**

Economic injustice

In the natural scheme of things, wealth is generated by people providing physical labour, services and products that other people need. This generally requires access to land, services, labour and the marketplace in order to be productive and profitable. To be deprived of fair opportunity or access is an economic injustice. There are many historical examples of disenfranchisement, land enclosure, abuses of workers' rights, and deprivation of employment. There are also examples of the idle wealthy living off the hard work of the working classes. The settlement of North America by people looking for economic opportunity, the American and French Revolutions where the poor rose up against their economic and political masters, the struggle against the English class system, and in Australia the rising up of abused miners at the Eureka Stockade, are all examples of people seeking freedom from oppressive economic systems.

In the modern economic scheme of things, much income is earned by profiting from the useful work that others do while not doing anything useful oneself. It is one thing to invest money for a return by financing industry and opportunities for others to work. It is another thing to generate wealth via the convoluted, speculative, obscure and dishonest manipulation of money, markets and tax systems. The global financial crisis (GFC) is an example of the inevitable effects of an unjust economic system making some people fantastically rich on the back of other people's hard labour but with no accountability. Debt is played off against debt, hard-working people have their life savings lost in speculative schemes, and many people are manipulated into debts they cannot afford to repay. Like a house of cards, such an economic system cannot stand for long and it only takes a fiscal puff of wind to blow it over.

Naturally, people have an understandable desire to be free of parasitic economic systems that allow such abuses to flourish, although currently the economic pain does not seem to have yet been strong enough in most developed countries to mobilize the wider community into a modern revolution. But who knows, unless steps are taken we may see it happen again in the not too distant future and the results will not be pretty.

Political

One only has to consider the hardship being endured by tens of millions of refugees currently fleeing armed political conflicts around the world to see how strong the yearning for freedom is. History is littered with unjust political systems from whose tyrannical tentacles citizens wished to liberate themselves. Nazism was a recent but pertinent example. The wider European community passionately wanted freedom as did the just and good-hearted German citizens who could see fanaticism, intolerance, hatred and censorship becoming ingrained within the German social and political system. The Nazi government was elected by a largely angry, deluded and misled citizenry. Once ensconced the Nazis became almost impossible to remove as their stranglehold on power became total. It took a most gruesome war and many years of suffering to bring about its downfall. The tyranny of Stalinist Russia is another case in point, as is the rise of the brutal Pol Pot regime in Cambodia. Similar but less graphic cases could be made for many other people living under unjust political systems around the world. Whether democracy is the best form of government will be explored elsewhere, but there is little doubt that democracy is comparative freedom when it liberates people from the oppression of tyranny.

Liberation of women

Historical examples of women being denied access to education, the right to work, the right to vote, promotion based on merit, or the right to equal pay for equal work gave credence to the suffragette movement and its later incarnation, the women's liberation movement. Furthermore, the expectation that women should be required to continue to live at home under domestic abuse or violence was a case of old-fashioned womanly devotion and dutifulness gone too far, so divorce laws were liberalized. That the political and economic power traditionally rested in the hands of men, and that the power corrupted many men to the point of oppression or abuse of their duty of care to women, led to an understandable struggle to promote women's rights and address social wrongs.

Religious oppression

Considering the ubiquitous presence of religion in human civilization, it would be reasonable to assume that there is an inherent spiritual or philosophical longing within the human psyche. Spiritual insights and truths, however, soon formulate themselves into religious systems and then dogmas. Although religion is meant to be the vehicle for spiritual and philosophical truths it often gets in the way when it degenerates into mere dogma. Conformity to a religious institution and dogma can no doubt promote social cohesion, but it is not too long before the essential truths that the religion was originally designed to promulgate become secondary to the promotion of power and conformity. Furthermore, rather than the spirituality of different religions and cultures being seen as complementary they soon become competitive and threatening. This is fertile ground for xenophobia, superstition, religious oppression and fanaticism.

There are numerous examples of religious intolerance and discrimination. In Christian countries there is historical discrimination against Jews and within Christianity itself there is infighting and discrimination between Catholics and Protestants. In India there have been long periods of cohesion between Hindus and Muslims but also episodes of conflict. More extreme forms of oppression include the brutal so-called Inquisition in Europe during the Middle Ages and the suppression of scientific inquiry that was a part of Catholicism during the Renaissance, which later led to the Protestant Reformation. Today, there is the fanaticism of a vocal minority of self-labelled followers of Islam generating extremism, terrorism, intolerance of other faiths, and all-out war in some places.

With a love of freedom of thought and worship, it is entirely understandable and desirable for people from various faiths and cultures to fight to free themselves of such oppression in the name of religious tolerance.

In praise of freedom

History is full of noble examples of human beings promoting freedom. The central players in those events deserve to be revered and their stories taught in schools so that following generations can learn from them, be inspired by them, and follow their example. And, because history has a habit of repeating itself, there is also the need to learn to read the signs and recognize the conditions that led to the suppression of freedom in the first place.

The point is to affirm that people of many and varied cultures around the world will, sooner or later, fight for freedom whenever natural justice is oppressed. This chapter merely makes the point that there is a kind of true and substantial freedom that can and should be defended, so long as defending one's own freedom is not at the expense of justice, freedom and rights for others.

But here we are praising freedom when we haven't yet defined it or explored what it means to be free, truly free. We are on shaky ground indeed because we might make the common mistake of promoting and arguing for anything that flies under the banner of freedom but which may not be true freedom at all. So let us turn to that question now — what is freedom?

SOME THINGS TO REFLECT ON:

- In what ways does the struggle for freedom manifest itself in your life?
- Are you motivated more by self-interest or by the interests of others?
- What is the effect on yourself when you do things for others?
- Are the things you do and the decisions you make in your personal life the ones you would like to see society governed by?
- If not, why not?

SOME THINGS TO PRACTISE:

- Do a random act of kindness and observe the effect on yourself and the other(s) involved.
- See what effect it has when you don't go against your principles even if it is expedient to do so.
- Put somebody's interests above your own and notice what effect it has.

CHAPTER 3

SO FREE WE SEEM

Having considered some admirable examples of the advancement of human freedom in the previous chapter, one might expect that in the modern day we are enjoying the fruits of this progress — fruits like happiness, wellbeing, social equity and cohesion, and tolerance. Unfortunately, there is much to suggest that the opposite is happening, which should give us pause to reflect. Is the escalation of a variety of modern problems a wake-up call? Is all so-called 'progress' positive or are we also inadvertently taking a few wrong turns along the way? Let's consider these and related questions now.

What is going well?

If we use measures such as affluence, the abundance of food, labour-saving devices, medical advances, increase in life expectancy, comfort, convenience and increased choice as our yardsticks, it would be true to say that people living in developed countries now have a better life than they would have had at any other time in history. Just consider the hardships, illnesses and discomforts that people bore a century ago, let alone two millennia ago. Technological advances have made modern life unrecognizable to someone from the past. But are we freer, happier and more at peace with ourselves as a result? Today, do we have more cause for optimism than pessimism?

As James Branch Cabell, the satirical American author, wrote in *The Silver Stallion* in 1926: 'The optimist proclaims that we live in the best of all possible worlds; and the pessimist fears this is true.'[1]

Let's consider a few contemporary social and global problems into which we are pouring huge amounts of resources — problems such as poor mental health, substance abuse and chronic illness. In such domains, we are really struggling to 'turn the *Titanic*' at the moment. We hear the sound of icebergs scraping along the side of the good ship 'Civil Society' as we take on water but we are unable to take a different course. It almost seems like half of society is trying to turn the wheel one way and the other half the other way. The result? A lot of effort is being expended for little benefit.

The enemy without and the enemy within

Before we consider some problems that modern, developed countries are grappling with, let's consider a few propositions. First, if we are not free, even if unconscious of it, then although we might appear happy on the surface we cannot be truly happy. Second, we would not consciously and intentionally do something to harm ourselves. Yes, we might harm ourselves inadvertently, we might do it through compulsion, or we might trade a small or superficial harm for a greater good, but surely we would not harm ourselves consciously and intentionally.

Sometimes we need protection. For example, governments and lawmakers, through external agencies like armies and law enforcement officers, have a clear duty to protect the community from malignant forces from within and without. Benevolent and reasonable third parties are also required to play protecting roles in the case of people who are very young, incompetent or incapacitated. Hence, we have laws such as those granting power of attorney, where another party takes control if a person is not in a fit state to make their own rational decisions.

But what about people who we would otherwise say are competent? What about the many self-destructive behaviours that are common now, for example, smokers, gamblers, or the obese? Environment and socio-economic issues can have a major negative effect but when attempts are made to control or regulate such behaviours cries of 'nanny state' are generally heard far and wide. Fiercer resistance can arise in response to gun-control measures despite the massive harm that firearms cause in many countries. Does the community have a duty to protect us from ourselves? Are there malignant forces within us whereby we abuse ourselves? Can we and should we be protected from those internal tyrannies and, if so, how can government and lawmakers appropriately protect us from ourselves? Let's hold these considerations in mind as we consider the following issues.

Mental health

Since decent data has been collected, surprising trends have emerged in relation to mental health. Rather than growing in happiness the opposite seems to have been occurring. Since scales were developed there has been a notable 45 per cent increase in daily stress from the 1960s to the 1990s.[2] Data from the World Health Organization in 1996 predicted depression to be a leading burden of disease.[3] By the year 2000, depression caused the largest non-fatal disease burden, accounting for almost 12 per cent of all total years lived with disability worldwide.[4] Predictions estimate that by 2030 depression will be way out in front as the number one disease burden in developed countries.[5] Over 20 per cent of adults are expected to have at least one major depressive episode throughout their lives.[6,7] Predictions estimate that the problem is escalating[8] independent of the secondary effects that poor mental health has on physical health like increasing the risk of heart disease, cancer and poor immunity, and predisposing people to unhealthy lifestyles and substance abuse. Surprisingly, since the early 1960s — a period of relative economic affluence and global stability — suicide rates among the young have tripled in many affluent countries,[9,10] particularly among males. In the United States, for example, data shows that nearly 43,000 people die from suicide annually, that males complete suicide at 3.5 times the rate of females and that whites are the ethnic group most at risk.[11,12] The annual age-adjusted suicide rate in the United States is 12.9 per 100,000 individuals; in the United Kingdom it is 10.8; in Germany it is 10.3;

in France it is 14.6; in Australia it is 12.6 and in Hungary it is an astounding 21.0.[13–15] Around the world these rates have been rising.

By and large, the biomedical approach to depression, anxiety and stress is to throw antidepressants and sedatives at the problem, which for most patients is little better than providing an expensive placebo if major reviews of the research are anything to go by.[16–18] Depression is now being diagnosed and pharmacologically treated in younger age groups, but serious concerns about the ineffectiveness and danger associated with this strategy[19–20] and the skewing of drug trial evidence by industry[21–22] have been raised. The underlying causes of depression, like social isolation, overwork, poor sleep, lack of meaning in life and unhealthy lifestyle, are not being dealt with and yet we think that throwing a few psychoactive drugs at the problem is the solution. It may be a convenient solution from the pharmaceutical industry's point of view, but it is very inconvenient for the rest of society.

Materialism

A materialist view of the universe is far more common in the community now, especially since the decline of the influence of religion in many people's lives. Materialism as a scientific theory is that nothing exists except physical matter. As a philosophy of life materialism comprises a set of values and goals focused on wealth, possessions, image, and status. As such it stands in conflict with aims concerning the wellbeing of others and one's own personal and spiritual growth. According to an extensive review of the research,[23] people who place a high priority on materialistic values and goals:

- **consume more products**
- **incur more debt**
- **have lower-quality interpersonal relationships**
- **act in more ecologically destructive ways**
- **have adverse work and educational motivation**
- **report lower personal and physical wellbeing.**

Even if you experimentally activate materialistic aims in otherwise non-materialistic people it produces similar outcomes. Such data suggests the need for policies that diminish contemporary culture's focus on materialism, consumption, profit, and economic growth.

Addiction

Addiction has been a part of human life ever since people started experimenting with naturally occurring psychoactive substances, but trends suggest we are becoming a more addictive society than in times past for a variety of reasons. For example, more people self-medicate to manage stress and poor mental health. There is greater exposure and access to drugs of addiction. Many hold an unquestioned assumption that various substances can provide happiness and lasting relief of pain.

Alcohol has been around for millennia and then cigarettes came along. Some parts of the world used opium for centuries before it came to the West. Now there is a profusion of addictive substances available, many of which, like crack cocaine and ecstasy, are more quickly and strongly addictive than what has been available in the past.[24] Furthermore, the mode of administering illicit drugs by injecting them has produced many other problems, not least of which is the proliferation of infectious diseases like hepatitis B and C and HIV/AIDS.

When the modern drug problem gathered momentum in the 1960s and 70s, it was associated with freedom, the flames of which were fanned by increasingly liberal social attitudes in the so-called 'turn on, tune in and drop out' era.[25] Drugs were seen as a form of protest and a refusal to conform. For many vulnerable people, using drugs seemed to be a convenient solution for personal and social problems. Now, drug use is increasingly normalized and seen as a modern rite of passage for young people. Nightclubs, rave parties, and music festivals are just some of the environments in which young people are introduced to drugs. In more recent years, the freedom of the Internet has made the exposure to and purchase of addictive substances just a few clicks away. Suppliers are having a bonanza and struggle to keep up with the voracious demand.

Although stress and mental illness lead many people to self-medicate with substances, the reality is that using substances in this way tends to perpetuate the problem. For example, stimulants like ecstasy lead to a large release of the brain neurotransmitter, serotonin, and a resulting rapid but short-lived elevation in mood. Although this appears to produce happiness and freedom, the unfortunate reality is that such drugs then leave brain cells depleted of serotonin, producing a trough in mood, sometimes lasting for days afterwards.[26] Over time, the brain cells that produce serotonin become damaged so this trough deepens and prolongs itself, resulting in the person ending up with a perpetual depression. Such drugs also lead to other forms of brain damage. The person may be attempting to increase happiness or free themselves from their emotional suffering but the reality is that they become trapped in a downward cycle that initially seemed sweet and pleasurable.

Other than illicit drugs, there are many other types of addiction that have become increasingly common. These include addictions to gambling, food, pornography and social media to name a few. They all have a common neurological basis, which, like the pitfall plant, involve pleasure-seeking. These will be explored in more depth later.

At the tobacco industry's zenith, approximately half of men and a third of women smoked,[27] but because of the massive cost of smoking-related illnesses we have since come to accept strict anti-smoking laws. Thankfully, rates of smoking have declined significantly in recent decades. The harm wreaked by smoking is not just to the smoker themselves but also to those around them through passive smoking. Smoking is a widely promoted addiction that was shrouded in a smokescreen of misinformation and legal wrangles by the tobacco industry for far too long. The war has largely turned, with smoking rates dropping significantly over the last few decades. This has caused the rates of smoking-related problems to diminish. How autonomous is a smoker with an addiction to cigarettes? Not very. Paradoxically, in order to help free people of the scourge of smoking there is a need to impose strict laws limiting the use of cigarettes. This has done an enormous amount to liberate smokers and prevent new generations from being trapped by a habit that companies profited from for decades.

The rate of daily alcohol use among the young has declined in most developed countries,[28] although binge drinking remains a significant problem and predicts substance abuse as an adult.[29] The drop in tobacco and alcohol use has been as a result of extensive education programs, legislation, limiting advertising, heavy taxation and other restrictive laws. Although such interventions could be construed as limiting people's freedom, they have paradoxically promoted it by helping many people to be free of addiction. There is no current solution to the escalating use of heavier drugs, in fact, there is a drive to decriminalize them and liberalize their use. Although well intentioned, at least on the surface, only time will tell whether this is a valid solution or just another step down a very slippery slope into a drug-fuelled abyss.

Gambling addiction also causes a huge amount of harm. Key data about gambling includes:[30]

- **up to 3 per cent of the population are at risk of becoming, or are, problem gamblers[31] with far higher rates with saturation exposure (e.g. Nevada)[32]**
- **problem gambling costs the community billions of dollars a year**
- **the actions of one problem gambler negatively impacts the lives of between five and 10 others (e.g. friends, family and employers)**
- **only around 15 per cent of problem gamblers seek help**
- **problem gamblers are six times more likely to be divorced than non-problem gamblers, and are four times more likely to have problems with alcohol and daily smoking than non-problem gamblers[33]**
- **children with parents who are problem gamblers are up to ten times more likely to become problem gamblers themselves than children with non-gambling parents.[34]**

The negative impact of gambling rivals that of smoking but, interestingly, attempts to rein in gambling and easy access to things like poker machines, sports betting, online gambling and gambling advertising have thus far met with enormous resistance. 'Freedom' is the convenient and attractive refrain from industries that profit from 'legal addictions'. This rhetoric is sold to the punters and makes someone attempting to introduce responsible gambling laws look like someone who has a perverse desire to control others. But does promoting gambling have anything to do with promoting freedom? Which part of the self rules a problem gambler and which part of the self rules a society that leaves people vulnerable to gambling addiction? Governments and clubs are themselves now also addicted to revenue from gambling and political parties are seduced by funds from gambling industry lobbyists, making it well-nigh impossible to galvanize the community and political will necessary to act decisively on this matter. Surely the aim of limiting addictive practices like gambling and related advertising is not to oppress people but to help them to be free of the addiction that fires off the little pleasure/reward centre in the brain every time a coin is put in a machine or a ticket is bought at a gambling outlet.

No doubt the gambling industry profits hugely by drawing people in and increasingly uses advertising and the Internet to groom a new generation of potential gamblers in a way never seen before. Now there are many 'free' gambling sites on the Internet doing just that. Perhaps one day we will view the gambling industry and its tactics in a similar way to how we view the tobacco industry now.

The prohibition and criminalization of various addictions comes with its own problems including pushing the addictions underground. This approach has been expensive and only marginally effective. Clearly other strategies are needed. There are calls from some quarters for legalizing drugs of addiction but in the long run that may merely normalize pathological behaviour without addressing the social and emotional conditions that perpetuate it. The problem won't go away merely by regulating it or minimizing the harm associated with it. People will still be addicted and therefore not free and somebody somewhere will still be profiting from someone else's misery. The big question is how do we reduce demand for addiction so that people are less vulnerable to being played upon by negative influences? If we do that then maybe there won't be a problem.

Lifestyle-related illnesses

Some medical advances have been successful in dealing with major health challenges of times past but by far the largest increases in life expectancy came with the widespread introduction of sewerage, better housing and clean, reliable sources of water in the nineteenth century. Overnight, a whole range of common infectious diseases became uncommon. If such amenities are threatened, as happens in a natural disaster, then the health of a community quickly becomes imperilled.

Although making a less significant contribution to health and longevity, important medical discoveries include the introduction of aseptic techniques in surgery, antibiotics, vaccination and better emergency care. By the middle of the twentieth century it seemed that we were freeing ourselves of the burden of illness.

Strangely, the health problems confronting developed countries now are related to two main things. First, modern healthcare has become so complex, invasive and interventionist that it is a major health problem in itself. For example, a study in the British Medical Journal estimated that somewhere between 250,000 to 400,000 people die annually in the United States due to medical errors, making it the third most common cause of death after heart disease and cancer.[35] Second, the affluence responsible for delivering us from the evils of times past has now made us, as it were, victims of our own success. People in developed countries tend to be too inactive and consume too much food, and much of the food we do eat is processed thereby significantly reducing its nutritional quality and putting in empty calories. *La dolce vita* — the sweet life — as Italians say. We have become accustomed to what would have, at one time, been viewed as luxuries. Perhaps this is a perennial problem. As Samuel Johnson, the noted eighteenth-century English man of letters, wrote: 'The chains of habit are too weak to be felt until they are too strong to be broken.'[36]

A sedentary life

Unfortunately, this sweet and pleasant march towards the trap that is chronic illness is so seductive that we hardly know we are on it. We seem less ready to take the harder path towards a healthy and long life. We rely on modes of transport, labour-saving devices and desk-bound jobs to the point that most people have become extremely sedentary. These days, we tend to live indoors in front of a screen and receive relatively little fresh air and sunlight. The last Australian census to report on levels of physical activity reported, 'In 2004-05, 70 per cent of Australians aged 15 years and over were classified as sedentary or having low exercise levels.'[37] According to the State of Victoria's Children Report 2013–14, by the age of 15 to 17, only 14 per cent of males and 6 per cent of females are meeting the Australian Physical Activity Guidelines.[38]

Just a bit of regular exercise as we age is enough to markedly reduce the risk of chronic illnesses associated with ageing. As one study found, being sedentary before and in the eight years after retirement is associated with a nearly eightfold increased risk of chronic illness like heart disease, stroke and diabetes compared to those who were physically active before and after retirement.[39]

Obesity

Another example of the interesting tensions between the need for regulation being met by resistance in the name of freedom has to do with obesity, particularly childhood obesity. In the United States, over one-third of people are now obese.[40] Childhood obesity rates have tripled in Australia since 1985 to the point that up to 30 per cent of Australian children are overweight or obese.[41] Obesity levels in the United Kingdom have more than trebled in the last 30 years and it is estimated that more than half of the population could be obese by 2050. The United Kingdom is leading Europe's obesity league tables on 24.9 per cent, with France doing best with only 15.6 per cent of the population being obese.[42]

The costs of obesity to the community in the future will be enormous because of how it affects the person's own health and the health of generations yet unborn.[43,44] The modern obesity phenomenon is largely due to the increase in consumption of energy-dense foods driven by over-activating the brain's pleasure or reward-seeking centres. Such foods negatively change the expression of genes regulating metabolism and these changes can be passed on to the next generation.

Advertising for energy-dense food is ubiquitous in children's television and, as one expert wrote, 'Children are trusting, and hence vulnerable, to food advertising, influencing their desires and purchase requests to parents.'[45]

Poor nutrition has increasingly found its way into schools, making it all but impossible to control. Addressing the problem requires action on many different levels including patient- and family-focused interventions, like promoting healthy nutrition and physical activity, reducing television viewing, and using behaviour modification.[46] Another possible avenue is via the legislative bodies that regulate food production, content and sale, and create the economic and political policies directly affecting the food supply and the type and quantity of food made available to children.[47] Legislatively enacted federal programs such as the National School Lunch Program[48] in the United States provide opportunities to promote healthy nutrition and turn this problem around but there is enormous resistance to restricting food choices to healthier options or taxing unhealthy food. It is as if such policies are an abuse of a person's rights, and a person abusing their health is an expression of their rights. How perverse.

The final frontier for controlling childhood and adult obesity is through litigation. It is often employed as a means to protect public health when government regulation is absent or ineffectual. For example, litigation has been successfully employed to control asbestos and tobacco exposure.[49] Unfortunately, attempts to rein in the 'free market', limit children choosing the food they want, or curtail advertising unhealthy food are generally met with cries of 'nanny state'. Yes, we can make decisions for ourselves but the environment is making it difficult, not easy, for children and parents to make healthy food and lifestyle choices.

The scourge of chronic illness

Paradoxically, the poverty that we tried so hard to free ourselves from and the affluence we strived so hard to achieve throughout the nineteenth and twentieth centuries is now killing us. And now, the means we are trying to use to deal with the problem — modern biomedicine — is far less effective than many realize and it comes with its own set of problems.

As the twentieth century rolled on, we increased the incidence of a range of chronic illnesses caused by unhealthy lifestyle. The major causes of death in developed countries now are lifestyle-related, like heart disease, stroke, dementia and various cancers. Type 2 diabetes is a common lifestyle illness and predisposes a person to poor circulation, heart disease, stroke, cancer and dementia among other things. A generation ago it was only found in older people, hence its original name — maturity-onset diabetes. Now, such is the state of nutrition, obesity and inactivity, the early stages of type 2 diabetes are being seen in pre-teens.[50] In Australia over 10 per cent of diabetes in those under 18 is now type 2, with indigenous Australian children and adolescents being over six times more likely than their non-indigenous counterparts to be diagnosed with it.[51] Emerging economies like India and China aspire to adopt the Western lifestyle, which they associate with affluence but this will leave them equally at risk.[52]

With the prevalence and cost of type 2 diabetes rapidly increasing worldwide, it is increasingly important to understand the causes for this. Genes by themselves only explain about 3 per cent of the heritability of type 2 diabetes. The rest is explained by lifestyle changing how our genes express themselves. Lifestyle factors, like a lack of exercise and eating a calorie-dense diet, increase obesity and change the functioning of genes that regulate fats, sugars and insulin.[53] These effects are handed down to succeeding generations. Things like weight loss and exercise have the opposite effects.[54]

The biomedical approach struggles to make a significant difference to the outcome of lifestyle-related chronic illness — heart disease and cancer being the most common — once those conditions are well established. For example, the widespread prescribing of cholesterol-lowering drugs is aimed at reducing mortality from heart disease. They cost developed countries billions of dollars per year.[55] A review of their effectiveness published in the *British Medical Journal* showed that taking them for six years at best provided four days longer life expectancy.[56] This is despite the fact that the natural alternative, omega-3 fatty acids, are far more effective, safe and less expensive.[57] The medical management of type 2 diabetes provides equally unimpressive results according to a major review paper in the *Journal of the American Medical Association*. 'Among adults with type 2 diabetes, there were no significant differences in the associations between any of nine available classes of glucose-lowering drugs (alone or in combination) and the risk of cardiovascular or all-cause mortality.'[58]

The reported longer survival rates for common cancers are largely contributed to be the effect of screening programs identifying and treating low-level malignancies from which the person wouldn't have died anyway. Reporting these as a long-term 'cures' distorts the statistics and ignores the harms associated with over-diagnosis and treatment.[59] Survival statistics for patients diagnosed with more aggressive malignancies have remained relatively static for decades and many treatments are not as effective as many people assume. For example, the absolute five-year survival benefit of chemotherapy for the 22 most common adult cancers is approximately 2 per cent — that is 2 per cent more likely be alive in five years if you have it compared to if you don't.[60] There are a few less common cancers that are exceptions, like some childhood cancers, testicular cancer and some blood-related cancers, and the statistics for breast cancer have improved somewhat over the last decade, but nevertheless it is not so impressive despite such drugs being very toxic and expensive.

The biomedical approach is clearly not adequate by itself for dealing with the problem of chronic lifestyle-related illnesses because the underlying causes are not addressed. We commonly perceive that letting ourselves go and doing what we like is a happy life rather than happiness meaning being liberated from our unhealthy lifestyle habits. Making healthy change for ourselves takes much more effort than being the passive recipient of medical treatments being done to us. For some reason, we view effort as a far less attractive option despite the costs and side-effects of oftentimes marginally effective medical treatments that we seem to be prepared to bear. In the long run, however, making healthy changes costs far less,[61] significantly increases quality of life, and actually reverses the disease process even as indicted by evidence from various studies on illness like heart disease[62,63] and cancer.[64–66] Such changes have even been shown to slow down the ageing process as measured on a genetic level.[67,68]

Life expectancy in the future

The implications of lifestyle for future health and longevity are enormous. A commonly held assumption is that the increase in life expectancy seen over the last two centuries is going to continue into the indefinite future. But we should remember that people living on average into their eighties now were born into a totally different age, with different eating, exercise, leisure and work patterns. It will only take another few decades for the appallingly unhealthy lifestyle prevalent among many present-day children, adolescents and young adults to translate into chronic illness. When it does, modern medicine, with all its technology and drugs, will be largely powerless to do much more than eke out a little longer life while expending a huge amount of resources in the process. Unless we rein in our unhealthy lifestyle habits then life expectancy will likely plateau within the next generation and then go into an inevitable decline for the generation after that.

We need a major shift in the way we live. What will produce that shift? How are we going to bring this about? Personal discipline is ultimately in our own hands but this is not so easy. We also have to consider the impact that socio-economic status, environment and upbringing have on our minds, genes and brains. We have to do this together and via a wide variety of means that change the environment and influences on us. We also need to own our personal responsibility for our health.

Being driven to distraction

> **Neither plenitude nor vacancy. Only a flicker**
> **Over the strained time-ridden faces,**
> **Distracted from distraction by distraction,**
> **Filled with fancies and empty of meaning,**
> **Tumid apathy with no concentration**
>
> TS Eliot, *from* Burnt Norton

Now, perhaps more than ever, we live a distracted existence, skimming over the surface of life with little depth. The coming of modern information technology has, to some extent, freed us from the tyranny of distance, isolation and limitations in accessing information. We have more choice and more of the world at our fingertips than ever before. But has this also come at a cost we did not foresee?

It was reported in a Microsoft Canada marketing paper that the average attention span of humans has dropped to 8 seconds, ranking us behind goldfish (9 seconds).[69] This, they wrote, needs to be taken into account in advertising and marketing for the modern generation. Attention spans have been dropping significantly over recent decades, a phenomenon made worse by multitasking and the overuse of screens[70] and social media. We suffer from what some have called 'attention deficit trait', a tendency to have shorter attention and to be more distractible.[71] Contrary to popular opinion, the human brain — male and female, old and young — does not complex multitask, it does not pay attention to multiple complex things at the same time.[72] Multitasking does, however, increase the rate of errors and accidents, impairs memory, increases stress, negates empathy and reduces the level of engagement and enjoyment.

From limited to unlimited choice

In 2004, an influential book came out called *The Paradox of Choice: Why more is less*. In it the author, Barry Schwartz, argues that the desire for ever-increasing choice, rather than making us more free and happy, has made us more anxious, overwhelmed and paralysed with fear of missing out, also known as FOMO. Consumerism, marketing, online shopping, social media and online dating are just some of the ways in which our world has been filled with endless options, decisions and comparisons with others. Careers used to be more straightforward but now, for many people, there is endless mobility and always wondering if there is a better opportunity or greener grass over the next hill.

If 'choice is good' then we commonly think that 'more choice must be better'. The paradox of choice is that it seems to increase our range of options, freedom and happiness, but in reality this abundance of choice leads to wasted time, indecision, anxiety about making the wrong decision, and oftentimes paralysis through analysis, unless we are very confident and clear about what we want, adept in making decisions, and able to leave behind what we don't need. Freedom of choice is almost becoming a prison and an obsession. To use another metaphor, rather than modern life resembling a fine-dining experience with a well-chosen menu, it more resembles an all-you-can-eat buffet.

The 'equality' of women

Women in modern, developed countries are clearly freer than in times past but this may also come at a cost. For example, women are beginning to equal men in many undesirable ways. At one time, it was very uncommon for women to abuse alcohol and drugs, commit crimes, engage in acts of violence or commit suicide. Men still lead in all these areas but women are catching up quite quickly. In relation to substance abuse, population data suggests the gap between men and women has narrowed in recent decades.[73] In the early 1980s, the male/female ratio of alcohol-use disorders was 5:1 whereas more recent surveys report a ratio of approximately 3:1.[74] In fact, the most recent and extensive review of this subject suggests that women born in the late 1900s are virtually on parity with males as far as alcohol abuse and related harms.[75] US Department of Justice figures suggest that since the 1980s there has also been a significant increase in violent crime among young women.[76] Similar trends have been noted in Australia,[77] Canada[78] and the United Kingdom.[79] Is this really the equality and liberation women aspired to? Is this the new image of 'strong' and 'independent' women or is it merely women becoming as stupid as men? Are we, in the name of equality and liberation from stereotypes, socializing out of girls and young women qualities women excel in that the world desperately needs — like compassion, emotional intelligence and co-operation — because they are seen as undesirable to modern ideologies? Are the virtues of womanhood merely being replaced by the vices of manhood in the name of equality? Can we cultivate the upside of women's emancipation without the downside?

Sexually transmitted diseases and unwanted pregnancy

There were many things not to like about the stuffy, repressive Victorian era attitudes to sex that made out as if it was not to be enjoyed, at least not by women. So the pendulum started to swing, or should that be it began to 'rock'n roll' in the 1950s, but has it gone too far? With the 1950s came a change in music and, as Plato said, with that comes a change in society. Barriers and taboos started dropping away and social change gathered pace especially with the coming of contraception in the 1960s. Sex ceased to be something that was, according to nature, primarily for the reproduction of our species, and it became, according to us, primarily for pleasure. Reproduction was a nasty inconvenience that needed to be done away with.

The downside is that much of what has come as a result of the liberalization of sexual attitudes and practices has not been so pleasurable. There are sexually transmitted diseases (STDs), and not just the old ones like syphilis and gonorrhoea, but new ones like chlamydia, herpes, human papilloma virus, hepatitis B and C and, of course, HIV. Yes, there are harm minimization strategies, strenuous attempts to prevent STDs, and expensive drugs being developed to treat them, but they do play havoc with the individuals and communities that are affected by them.

The other issue is that many young people are engaging in sexual relationships before they have either the sufficient emotional maturity or the ability to deal with the potential fallout of unwanted pregnancy. Thankfully, teenage birth rates have dropped but this has been as a result of contraception and abortion. Now, it is not uncommon for children as young as twelve to ask for and be given contraception even without their parents' consent because 'if we don't they'll just go and do it anyway'. In the United Kingdom, widely reported figures that over 75,000 underage children were given contraception in 2011 — a rise of 50 per cent in the last decade[80] — created quite a stir. Despite the concern, the response has been largely to prescribe more contraceptives rather than turn around rates of underage sex as children are being sexualized at earlier and earlier ages.

In Australia, half of teen pregnancies end in abortion.[81] The rate of teen childbearing in the United States has fallen steeply since the late 1950s, from an all-time high of 96 births per 1000 women aged 15 to 19 in 1957, to an all-time low of 49 in 2000.89 Over that time, the rate of unmarried teenage births has increased from 13 per cent to 79 per cent because of changing attitudes to marriage and single parenthood. Most unwanted pregnancies occur in women and girls on contraception but without the self-discipline to take it strictly as prescribed and men commonly don't have the motivation or discipline to take preventive steps like wearing condoms. The unwanted cost of abortion will be explored in more detail later but suffice to say that it is not as simple a surgical procedure as is often made out. Then, of course, there are the battered emotions and self-esteem of people going in and out of superficial relationships where they are largely being used as a means to somebody else's end. And the sexual revolution was meant to be a particularly sweet and pleasurable thing.

Social isolation

Another surprising modern phenomenon is that, despite the majority of people living in crowded urban environments, there are escalating rates of social isolation and a diminishing sense of community. More people live alone and more families are fractured by divorce. Is living alone and not having to compromise our wishes making us freer or sadder? More young people are having virtual relationships on social media rather than real ones, and, for many, life is increasingly being lived in a world measured by the dimensions of the screen of a smartphone. Rather than being more connected with people through the use of social media there is a profound disconnection with the place and community we actually live in. As the extended family becomes a thing of the past, more elderly people live alone or feel lonely living in aged-care facilities.

Despite an increasing number of young people seeing technology as their way of connecting, in reality, the opposite may be happening. Interestingly, a Danish study of 1059 people looked at the effect of unplugging for a week. Half of the group unplugged from Facebook and at the end of the week they were asked what moods they were experiencing. The Facebook-removed group said they felt happier, less sad and lonely, more decisive, less angry or worried, more enthusiastic, less depressed. They also experienced an increase in satisfaction with their social lives and were more likely to be present in the moment. 'People on Facebook were 55 per cent more likely to feel stressed than their unplugged counterparts, and 39 per cent more likely to feel less happy than their friends.'[82]

Another study of pre-teens who had just five days at a nature camp and away from screens, phones and social media showed a far greater ability to recognize and respond to emotional cues,[83] which is an important part of social and emotional development.

Despite the popular mythology, the negative effects of an over-reliance on social media may be even worse than previously thought. A study on young adults in the United States showed that compared with those in the lowest quarter of social media use, individuals in the highest quarter of social media site visits per week and those with a higher total frequency of using social media had triple the odds of depression. This association had a strong, linear, dose-response trend — the more it was used the stronger the effect. As the authors concluded, 'Social media use was significantly associated with increased depression. Given the proliferation of social media, identifying the mechanisms and direction of this association is critical for informing interventions that address social media use and depression.'[84]

So, is this modern obsession with information technology really expanding horizons and liberating us, or is it, for the majority of people, narrowing the world until we live imprisoned within a dark, lightless room whose only illumination comes from a screen? Are we becoming trapped and isolated by the very things we thought would liberate us?

Crime

Depending on how you look at it, crime data is either getting better or worse. Some crimes that were on the decline— like car theft, largely because of technology like car engine immobilizers —are now on the rise again.[85] Other crimes are on the rise, particularly cyber-crime, drug offences and organized crime. Just like dealing with physical illness, the social illness that is crime cannot be effectively dealt with unless the underlying causes are identified and addressed. Such causes include social alienation, deprivation, unemployment, poverty and racism. It makes sense to address these underlying issues before law enforcement agencies become fatigued, overwhelmed or corrupted.

From a freedom point of view, we are increasingly using technological approaches to deal with law and order issues like solving crimes, preventing terrorism and detecting drugs. Strategies used include closed-circuit television, data surveillance and retention, and monitoring online activity all of who threaten our civil liberties. There is an uneasy balance between trying to help the community to be free of crime and, at the same time, impinging upon the community's freedom and privacy via surveillance methods. This issue has been highlighted by examples such as Julian Assange, the founder of WikiLeaks, and Edward Snowden, an American computer professional and former Central Intelligence Agency (CIA) employee who blew the whistle on CIA and government surveillance methods. To some they are freedom fighters and to others they are cyber-terrorists.

With the rise of cyber-crime has also come a new invasion into people's working and home lives. Criminals don't need to physically interact with their victims any longer, they can do it from a remote location without the victim even realizing they have been robbed. How free the Internet was meant to make us — how vulnerable we now are. How sweet to have the world at our fingertips — how bittersweet that the world's fingertips pry their way into our homes, wallets and workplaces.

Gun violence is another horrible blight on society, which negatively impacts how safe people feel. Gun control has been a particularly vexed issue for law enforcement agencies and governments. Gun lobbies, particularly in the United States, are large, vocal, well organized and have enormous influence over government. In the United States, the Second Amendment right to bear arms is defended with equal parts fury and reverence. However, between accidental shootings, murder and suicide, there are approximately 34,000 gun-related deaths in the United States each year,[86] far higher per head of population than virtually anywhere else. There were 372 mass shootings in the United States in 2015, killing 475 people and wounding 1870, according to the Mass Shooting Tracker.[87,88] Any attempt to limit access to guns, or certain types of guns like semi-automatic rifles, is met with the most ardent declarations of freedom and liberty as if the right to bear arms was integral to living a normal life. Evidence, however, suggests that the greater the access to guns, the greater the likelihood of gun violence. In Australia, for example, where access to guns was significantly tightened after the Port Arthur massacre, there are only 1.4 homicides by firearms per 1 million people whereas in the United States it is 29.7.[89,90] Even within the United States, gun deaths are four times higher in those states with higher gun ownership.[91,92] Is this really the product of a society protecting its liberty, or is it a society simply trapped by fear and the unfounded idea that its safety and security is assured by the number of guns held by its citizens?

Environmental crisis

Many see the environment as the major crisis facing our age. If we don't confront it soon, we may not have a viable earth to live on and, as some have said, we don't have a plan B. The environmental crisis has accelerated since we moved into the industrial age. There are some efforts to rein in the production of greenhouse gases but these are yet to bear any fruit as the globe continues to warm. The amount of rubbish finding its way into waterways, oceans and pristine environments from the Himalayas to the Antarctic is increasing apace. The amount of pesticides, chemicals, heavy metals and air pollution finding its way into the environment is unsustainable. The needed shift from unsustainable, dirty and/or dangerous forms of energy production, like coal, petroleum and nuclear, to clean and sustainable ones, like wind and solar, is meeting huge resistance from the vested interests of powerful corporations heavily invested in the status quo. Galvanizing collective action has been difficult as each individual country sees limiting its industries reliant on the consumption of fossil fuels as a potential drag on its economic development and prosperity which is politically unpopular (see 'The Tragedy of the Commons' in Chapter 4). Although greenhouse gases and global warming take a lot of our focus, deforestation, soil acidification, air pollution, water scarcity, salinification of arable land through inappropriate irrigation and farming practices, loss of biodiversity, and mass species extinctions are just a few other significant environmental challenges facing us.

The global community seems like a person who steadfastly refuses to give up smoking even in the face of a health crisis, possibly because of the discomfort and effort it would entail. Our collective addiction to our consumerist way of living is driving us, and greed and self-interest are preventing us from acting with common purpose and turning the situation around. Perhaps, addicted to laziness and the sweet pleasure of taking from the environment without restraint, we see healthy change as an impost and the status quo as freedom from responsibility. How strange. How free will we feel if we fall into the environmental trap that seems to be looming?

Global financial crisis

The global financial crisis (GFC) struck in the late 2000s. It was a massive demonstration of how brittle the world economic system really is and, some would say, how corrupt it is. Speculative and risky modes of investment, escalating levels of debt, and a lack of accountability from those profiting from it are part of the back-story to the GFC. Due to rising rates of debt, many countries hover on the edge of an economic abyss. It only takes one or two of these to fall for a chain reaction to occur, bringing down other countries with them. Despite the dilemma, there is neither the collective will nor the political strength to bring about the economic reforms needed to prevent an even bigger GFC in the future. It seems that the mentality that produced it is far too deeply entrenched in the system for effective action to take place. The behavioural enforcers perpetuating it parallel the barriers to constructive change. The required regulations against greed and injustice are too easily characterized as an unfair and unprofitable restraint on the free market for them to be adopted, and the austerity necessary to pay for previous generations living beyond their means is too easily characterized as unfair.

Terrorism

There are many places of political instability in the world today and military conflicts hit the media in more prominent ways than they used to. The most concerning issue, however, is not conflict between countries but rather conflict between cultures with the potential to involve many countries simultaneously.

Undoubtedly, the terrorism of religious and political extremists is like a malignant cancer. It is deadly, unlawful, based on perverted ideology, and seeds itself elsewhere from its place of origin. Just as the medical approach to the management of cancer reflects a war-like mentality so too does the 'war on terror'. The focus is on destroying it — slash, burn and poison. This is not only expensive and invasive but it also has a poor success rate and not infrequently kills the patient in the process. With rare exceptions, the causes of cancer, like poor mental health, unhealthy lifestyle, unhealthy environments and exposure to toxins, are generally not addressed, nor are the causes of terrorism. There doesn't seem to be enough effort to understand and address terrorism's causes while huge amounts of energy and resources are focused on railing against it. This approach is invasive, expensive, largely ineffective, causes a lot of collateral damage, and potentially alienates many honest and good-hearted people identified with the racial and religious background of the terrorists. Perhaps the conditions that lead to the cancer of terrorism like underlying racism, cultural imperialism, alienation, intolerance, injustices, disenfranchisement and social exclusion are not being addressed. If not, then will terrorism become even more aggressive (malignant) over time as cancers tend to do? It is also paradoxical that much of what seems to drive many extremists is an attempt to limit the spread of what they see as the West's extreme form of freedom and liberal ideals.

The stepwise slope

People often talk about the slippery slope into decline, but perhaps it is a stepwise slope. Many things that were once unlawful or viewed as sins are now commonplace, liberalized and even institutionalized. This process seems to go through a number of steps. For example, gambling and prostitution were once far more tightly controlled because the potential for addiction, degradation and exploitation was so significant. However, the sweet nectar of pleasure was a little too tempting so they were increasingly tolerated and a blind eye was turned to them. Then they were legalized. Then they were legitimized and soon they were increasingly commercialized. Now they are institutionalized, with many powerful lobbyists and even political parties representing these industries such that they exert significant political and economic influence. The same seems to be happening with drugs of addiction. Once something makes a contribution to government coffers, it soon gains influence and legitimacy. Once there is a legitimized industry making profits and paying taxes then governments have a conflict of interest between the interests of that industry and the wellbeing of the community they are meant to represent, who are subject to the addiction, organized crime, manipulation and abuse that commonly arises from these pursuits.

Such practices play on the lowest denominator in human nature and give that little burst of dopamine in the brain's pleasure centres that is initially so attractive, then compulsive, and then addictive. Soon reason, values and virtue are forgotten. The nectar keeps getting sweeter as the slope keeps getting more precipitous. Is this all really making us a more free society or, in the name of freedom and the pursuit of pleasure, are we merely edging towards the looming abyss of which we seem to be oblivious? Is there a point down this slope below which we should not step? If so, which step is that? Can we or should we criminalize these things?

Should we think again?

These days, we may think we are freer than in times past, pointing to the liberalization of morality, greater choice, fewer constraints on behaviour, less concern with manners and social graces and equality of the sexes. But are we happier? Perhaps not. Are we freer within ourselves? Perhaps not. Are we a more cohesive and connected community? Perhaps not. Surely the proof is in the pudding, although some might argue that we have not been baking the pudding long enough for our flourishing freedom to be properly judged. But maybe we also need to pause and consider the basic assumptions about freedom upon which we are currently relying. Let us do that now.

SOME THINGS TO REFLECT ON:

- Considering the problems society is currently dealing with, are we a freer society now than in the past?
- Do you have control over your thoughts and emotions or do you feel controlled by them?
- What compels you to do things that aren't necessarily healthy for you?
- What distinguishes a good decision from a bad one after you have made it and how can you distinguish a good from a bad decision before you make it?

SOME THINGS TO PRACTISE:

- Are you addicted to anything? If you are not sure then see what happens when you try to do without that thing.
- Learn to observe desires with less attachment to them — sometimes called 'urge surfing'.[93]
- Learn to observe your thoughts and emotions with self-compassion but without being controlled by them.

CHAPTER 4

CONTEMPORARY FREEDOM — WHERE ARE WE NOW?

We live in an age of excess and we want freedom, plenty of it, but can we have too much of a good thing? Can we take freedom too far? To explore this, we will first look at the underlying assumptions commonly held about freedom from a contemporary point of view.

How we view events is profoundly influenced by the political, cultural and ideological lenses through which we view those events. If the lens is red then we see red. If it is blue then we see blue. The problem is that, generally, we do not know, or cannot even conceive the possibility, that we are affected by bias in how we see things. We are so wedded to our biases and assumptions that we often see them as truths. If others do not think the way we do then surely it must be them that are affected by bias, not us. Whether or not it is possible to see through the clear and undistorted lens of the mind is an interesting question, but for now we will consider some of the common ruling ideologies and assumptions about freedom in the modern day, because they are determining factors as to whether some particular action, law or ideology is seen as supporting freedom or undermining it.

Creating the world in our own image

We don't see things as they are, we see them as we are.

The Talmud[1]

Many religious traditions hold that God created humankind in His own image. Whether that is true or not is hard to say, but it is certainly observable that we, as humans, like to make the world in our own image. Where we see 'other', there is the potential for threat, division and conflict, so we often want the world to be like us and to conform to our beliefs. It makes a society internally cohesive and creates common bonds, but such an approach can also have another more concerning side to it, particularly where there is a clash of cultures or ideologies.

For example, it is common to see people imposing their culture on others, for example, English colonial rule in India or the Chinese invasion of Tibet. It is common to see missionaries forcibly impose their religious beliefs, as happened during the spread of Islam in Spain in the eighth century or the subsequent Spanish Inquisition in the fifteenth century. It is also common to see the imposition of political structures on other countries, such as the spread of communism in Eastern Europe after World War II or the attempted imposition of Western-style democracy in Middle Eastern countries like Iraq, Syria and Afghanistan in the twenty-first century.

Perhaps it is also easy for a modern day 'liberation ideology' to be imposed. For example, from old forms of discrimination against women, we now have feminist ideology arising as an increasingly influential force making it hard for a woman or man to not be an avowed feminist. From the historical criminalization of homosexuality and mistreatment of homosexuals, there is now the aggressive promotion of gay-friendly ideology and practices in the community, even in conservative schools and religious groups. Now, in the name of freedom of choice, doctors with a conscientious objection to abortion are increasingly constrained by laws implicating them in the practice. Strongly held progressive ideologies don't tend to tolerate, much less welcome, conscientious objection or a diversity of views. But is this imposed kind of 'liberation' really just an ideological trap potentially as oppressive as what it replaced?

The question being raised here is not about the rightness or superiority of any particular culture, religion, political system or ideology. The issue relates to when a group of people cannot tolerate differences, or believe themselves to be right without any shadow of doubt, then a kind of fanaticism can easily arise. From that perspective, it becomes a duty to spread that particular way of thinking and living. It makes the imposition of the group's values and practices on others appear as liberating and uplifting them rather than oppressing them, despite the fact that they are no longer free to choose whether they agree with it or not. Such an approach, despite what we think, may hide behind the sweet rhetoric of 'civilizing', 'liberation', 'tolerance' or 'anti-discrimination' but it may well belie domination, intolerance, cultural arrogance, and, at times, even a wilful distortion of truth in order to support the prevailing ideological position.

The rise of democracy

There was a time when countries were ruled by a king — or occasionally a queen — and a wealthy ruling class. Such, however, is the corrupting effect of power and wealth that the working class was often neglected and abused to the point that revolutions arose, such as in England, France and the United States. These either did away with royalty altogether or saw a large part of their power handed to a democratically elected parliament. In other countries, like Australia, Canada and New Zealand, the process has been gentler perhaps because oppression from the ruling class has never been as acutely felt. In other parts of the world, such as some parts of the Middle East or Africa, democracy has had a difficult birth as it competes with oligarchies — government by a small, wealthy ruling class — and theocracies — from 'theo' meaning government of a religious ruling class.

In major revolutions, the masses fight, understandably so, to free themselves from the tyranny of a ruling class that cares more for their own interests than for the wellbeing of those they govern and from whom their wealth is derived. It is in such circumstances that the painful birth of democracy generally takes place. So entrenched is the collective faith in democracy in the Western world nowadays that it is almost inconceivable that any other form of government could be considered, let alone thought to be superior. When we compare democracy to corrupt or oppressive oligarchies, theocracies and tyrannies then the passion for it is understandable and it is easy to see why democracy has come to stand for freedom.

But the situation is full of paradoxes. For most people in the West, it is seen as a basic human right to live under a democracy, and therefore it is a duty to 'liberate' others who are not so 'fortunate' to live under one by imposing democracy on them — whether they want it or not. In a number of Asian countries, the rise of communism was seen as liberation from the tyranny of Western colonialization and capitalism, which favoured the wealthy. In the West, communism was seen as an assault on dearly held and fundamental personal and economic freedoms. Just the thought of communism finding its way into society and the political system in the United States led to the oppressive 1950s witch-hunt that was McCarthyism and a whole generation of young people being conscripted to fight against it in countries like Korea and Vietnam. Within the United States and allied countries, McCarthyism and conscripted wars in Asia were seen by some as a defence of freedom and by others as an assault upon it. Demonstrations against such wars were seen by a younger generation as defending freedom, whereas those deeply invested in a political ideology and staunch patriotism viewed them as a threat to freedom, Western values and social order.

The apparent openness of a democracy is undermined by the fact that you need a lot of money, connections and influence in order to be democratically elected. A simple, honest man or woman might be elected to the city council, but you generally need to be connected as a member of a corporate or political dynasty to be elected to the highest office. Of course, with such a need for money and influence, politicians spend much time being lobbied by people and corporations with vested interests. They then become beholden to their financial masters who then become the political masters operating behind the scenes. The fine line between 'political donations' and 'bribes' is blurry at best. Economic systems within democracies are also widening the gulf between rich and poor. Furthermore, the average person in the street is easily manipulated by the media and artful spin-doctors. Nevertheless, such things have done little to dent the unwavering faith in the rightness of democracy — the rule of the people — whether the people are free, informed, rational and unbiased or not. Although in a democracy we march to the sweet strains of freedom, we may not be as free as we assume.

The swinging pendulum

Plato's *Republic* is one of the classic texts of Western philosophy and literature. In it he describes the founding principle of democracy, which is freedom. But Plato warns that the decline of democracy contains within it the cause of tyranny, which is, like a swinging pendulum, an excess of liberty.

> **... the excessive increase of anything often causes a reaction in the opposite direction ... The excess of liberty, whether in States or individuals, seems only to pass into excess of slavery ... and so tyranny naturally arises out of democracy, and the most aggravated form of slavery out of the most extreme form of liberty.[2]**

Perhaps the increasing vitriol, extremism and polarization of political and social debate in many democracies are modern signs of the pendulum getting ready to swing. Who knows, but how can you have an excess of liberty? How can something inherently bad — slavery — come from something inherently good — liberty? How can liberty lead to tyranny? For that to make sense, we may need to consider the possibility that not everything flying under the banner of freedom really makes us freer.

East meets West

The so-called Western world — i.e. cultures arising from Anglo-European traditions and settlement — has gone through a massive process of modernization and technological advancement over many centuries now. Throughout that process many traditional values, attitudes and practices have evolved, while some have been radically changed, and some have been all but eradicated. Take, for example, the reduced influence of religious institutions, the secularization of government and the adoption of certain scientific theories over religious ones as a way of understanding the universe and our place in it. There are social conventions that have changed, such as the reduced faith in marriage or social class structures leading to the liberalization of family structures and the breaking down of class barriers. Obviously, this happens at different rates in some westernized countries compared to others, but the trend is unmistakable.

In many Eastern countries, this same process of liberalization is happening decades and even centuries later. In China, for example, a high level of conformity to social conventions and the dictates of government is still expected, although it is possibly less stringently enforced than previously. The far greater emphasis on conformity and strict law and order in countries like Singapore and China is seen as necessary for order, social cohesion and productivity, whereas in liberal Western democracies it is seen as oppressive and stifling individuality.

In some religiously conservative countries, liberalization is hardly happening at all. Many of the ideologies and assumptions adopted in the West would be considered undesirable, even seditious, in countries where there may be a very strong resistance to the adoption of Western values, which are seen not as a right but as a form of moral corruption. For example, many things taken for granted in the West are seen by many people in traditional Muslim countries, like Iran, Afghanistan, Pakistan or Saudi Arabia, as offensive. These include the secularization of government, disrespect for religion, the changing role of women, the use of substances and the liberalization of sexuality. What one group sees as freedom, another group sees as disorder and threat. For one group, the imposition of something like sharia law is seen as liberating the community from evil and for others the imposition of liberal values is seen as liberation. Of course, if someone is so completely certain that their way of thinking and living is right and just, then they may also assume that they have the right, even the duty, to impose it on others.

With the massive increase in immigration in recent decades, the clash of cultures is not just encountered when travelling overseas but within countries also. A person can immigrate to a country and still maintain the very strong conservative attitudes derived from the culture from which they emigrated. The clash of East and West is not just cultural. As many Eastern countries grow in wealth and influence, the clash is also political and economic.

From rule of conformity to rule of the individual

There was a time when conformity to social conventions, morals, duties and laws counted to a far greater extent than it does now. Curiously, despite the fact that democracy is seen as a form of government 'of the people, by the people, and for the people', in practice, it has increasingly become the government of the individual, of each man or woman for him or herself. For example, the duty the individual felt for the wider society drove tens of thousands of young people, mostly men, to sign up for military service and sacrifice their lives for 'king and country' in World War I. It would be very surprising to see such patriotic fervour again. Patriotism and self-sacrifice in war are perhaps not as strong as they used to be. During World War I, conscientious objectors were derided and it is only in recent times that they have come to be admired. There was a time when all the houses in a street would have uniformity because they conformed to the current style of architecture. Now, people increasingly want to build houses in such streetscapes that stand out and make an individual statement. If a person wishes to put a contemporary house right in the middle of a row of Victorian terrace homes then why shouldn't they? It is their land, their money and their decision. People are less inclined to conform to fashions in clothing. Why shouldn't they make a statement of individuality? If they want to wear a tie, or not wear a tie, or have short hair or long hair, or hair of one colour or another, then why shouldn't they? These days society has no right to impose its views on the individual. If an individual wants an abortion or euthanasia then who can stop them? For the most part, the only proviso on any individual choice is, 'so long as it isn't hurting anyone else'.

The point here is not so much to say that conformity is right or wrong but simply to recognize that the ruling ethical principle now governing is, by and large, autonomy (from 'auto' meaning 'self') — government 'of the self, by the self, for the self'. This will be explored in far greater detail in upcoming chapters, but autonomy is indelibly associated with modern freedom and limiting autonomy with oppression.

The tragedy of the commons

Another interesting concept highlighting tension between the individual and collective interest is 'the tragedy of the commons'. It was a term popularized by ecologist, Garrett Hardin, in 1968.[3] It refers to situations within shared-resource systems (for example, the use of fisheries, or grazing cattle on common pastureland) where individual users act according to their own self-interest and in disregard of, and contrary to, the common good of all users. Each wants more for themselves. Thus resources are depleted through their collective action (for example, overfishing the sea or overgrazing pastures).[4] This phenomenon can be observed in environmental, economic, corporate, health and political contexts and explains a lot of the reasons for the environmental and global financial crises.

Animals tend to hunt and use resources according to their needs in harmony with the constant balancing act taking place within nature, whereas humans commonly exceed their needs driven by desire and greed. Humans tend to create imbalance within the community and the ecosystem unless there is regulation informed by reason and the common good to curb that greed. The choice of the individual to further their self-interest at the expense of the common good may seem reasonable on the surface, but in this case reason is subservient to desire and greed. True reason has the whole picture in view and so would keep desire and greed in check. Greed, like a cancer, has the seeds of its own destruction sown within its nature in that, driven by its own interests, it spreads beyond its natural bounds to the point that it eventually kills the host.

From interdependence to independence

Independence has always been highly valued, but now possibly even more so than ever. Increasingly, citizens want to be independent from government, states want to be independent from federal control, children and adolescents want to be independent from their parents, women want to be independent from men, people want to live independently alone, businesses want to be independent from regulation, branches of the church want to be independent from central authority, and scientists want to be independent from traditional ethical constraints. We are at risk of losing sight of the value and necessity of interdependence. John Donne's poem, 'Devotions upon Emergent Occasions' is no less relevant now than when he wrote it.

> **No man is an island entire of itself; every man is a piece of the continent, a part of the main; if a clod be washed away by the sea, Europe is the less, as well as if a promontory were, as well as any manner of thy friends or of thine own were; any man's death diminishes me, because I am involved in mankind. And therefore never send to know for whom the bell tolls; it tolls for thee.**[5]

Forgetting the importance of interdependence potentially leaves us isolated, in conflict with others, unable to compromise, and less able to act with unified purpose.

Functional reserve: from plenty to the edge of crisis

Functional reserve is a medical term describing the excess capacity an organ has in fulfilling its biological functions within the body. So, for example, the average human could lose approximately 75 per cent of kidney function without it causing any illness or discernible symptoms. The 75 per cent functional reserve gives a lot of resilience so that small losses of function associated with intercurrent illnesses are easily accommodated and do not cause a health crisis. Nature is very generous, but past a certain point every incremental loss of function causes ever greater changes, beginning with measurable disturbances of blood chemistry, then mild symptoms, then debilitating symptoms, and then death unless the situation is rectified.

Functional reserve is also a relevant concept for the modern world we live in. In our time-poor, resource-strapped world, seeing functional reserve as waste, we have tended to cut it all out of our work and personal lives to the point that we are continually on the edge of, or totally immersed in, crisis. For example, we overfill our diaries and leave little space so that we are always rushing. We don't leave home until the last minute meaning we are constantly on the edge of being late and it only takes relatively minor holdups on the road to put us behind time. Businesses cut staff to the bone to the point that employees are constantly under pressure and it only takes a few absent workers for the system to decompensate. Airline passenger numbers and schedules are such that they are overbooked and have to rely on everything going exactly to time, and when something unexpected happens a cascade of crises impact all around the country. An employee's work schedule can be so full that time to pause and reflect is seen as wasteful resulting in their being constantly under pressure and creativity being stymied. The healthcare system commonly pushes staff–patient ratios to the point that staff burnout, patient care is compromised, and increasing errors occur.

Perhaps driven by a constant desire for more and a false sense of economy, all the functional reserve seems to have been stripped from modern life. This comes at a cost including high work stress, loss of creativity, loss of resilience, conflicted relationships, loss of enjoyment, multitasking and increased errors. It is as if we have created a mentality, a system and a way of living within which we have trapped ourselves. Maybe we don't need 75 per cent functional reserve, but it would seem that we need a little more than we currently allow. Some workplaces noted for their creativity and staff wellbeing, like Google, are going against the modern trend by providing staff mindfulness and emotional intelligence programs such as Search Inside Yourself.[6]

The normalization of deviance

If there is a normal — natural, lawful, prudent — way of living or doing something then deviating from that may not be so prudent and will come, sooner or later, with unwanted and unintended consequences. Diane Vaughan is a professor of sociology from Columbia University who explored the reasons for misconduct within large organizations. She observed the tendency to ignore protocol, warning signs and experience and called it 'the normalization of deviance'. Vaughan used it to explain the attitudes and practices underlying disasters like the explosion of the *Challenger* space shuttle in 1986[7] and the running aground of the cruise ship, *Costa Concordia* in 2012. She defines it as follows:

> **Social normalization of deviance means that people within the organization become so much accustomed to a deviant behaviour that they don't consider it as deviant, despite the fact that they far exceed their own rules for the elementary safety.[8]**

Perhaps this concept is also useful when considering a whole range of changes within society. For example, a news headline in *The Age*[9] read 'Madness? or the new normal?' It related to a 62-year-old woman who, with her 78-year-old partner, had given birth to a baby following IVF treatment. The president of the Australian Medical Association said that it was selfish and counter to the interests of the child and the wider healthcare system.[10] Not surprisingly, the specialists who work in the industry were hailing this as a breakthrough for freedom of choice, as a triumph of technology, and they predicted that in the not-too-distant future this would be normal procedure.

All sorts of things are seen as 'normal' now — single parenthood, experimenting with drugs, tattoos, body piercing, euthanasia, pornography, abortion and obesity to name a few. Is there a difference between a single person raising a child alone because their partner has died or they had to leave an abusive relationship and someone who decides to raise a child alone because it's a lifestyle choice? Are we normalizing deviance by telling children that experimenting with drugs is a normal part of growing up and merely teaching them to minimize harm and use clean needles? Are various forms of physical self-mutilation like body-piercing and tattoos now normalized? Is allowing doctors to kill their patients really helping and protecting them or is the promotion of doctor-assisted suicide and euthanasia potentially institutionalizing bad medicine? If things are being normalized that deviate from what is natural then we can be sure there will be a cost although what that cost is may take some time to reveal itself.

The rise of utilitarianism

This topic will be also explored in greater detail in the chapter on ethics, but suffice to say here that utilitarianism is a kind of democratization of ethics by asserting that people should not be governed by inflexible rules as was traditionally the case. It popularizes the notions of 'the greatest good for the greatest number', good being synonymous with happiness, and happiness being maximized by maximizing pleasure through the so-called 'hedonic calculation'.

Old ideas and customs take time to die out so, although it took quite some time between the eighteenth and twentieth centuries for utilitarianism to become the prevailing ethical creed, it was clear that it would resonate strongly with the increasing democratization of politics and society. The idea is that a person no longer needs to be encumbered by inflexible and limiting rules that restrain individual choices and preferences. With utilitarianism, there is more freedom to choose anything if one could calculate things in such a way that it appeared to satisfy the assumptions of utilitarian theory in maximizing pleasure. Even doing an obvious injustice can be justified if it looks to be for a greater good, the hedonic calculation supports it and they can satisfy themselves that relatively fewer people would be harmed — no doubt a very easy justification to make when significant personal gain is at stake. Utilitarianism, of course, unhinges the person and society from centuries of accumulated wisdom and experience and possibly leaves much room for self-deception and bias.

Actions without consequences

Nature seems to say that we can have whatever we want, but we get what comes with it, but now, it seems, most of us are determined to pursue what we desire but are far less happy to pay the price that comes with it. For example, we overindulge, but seem strangely surprised and unwilling to accept the illnesses that follow. We embrace clubs and pubs being open all night, but we seem strangely surprised and unwilling to accept the drunkenness and crime that comes with it. We embrace an economic system that allows people to make a lot of money without doing any work, but we seem strangely surprised and unwilling to accept the social injustice that follows in its wake. This suggests that we either did not foresee the consequences or pursued the course of action against our better judgement, or both.

From rule of the elders to rule of the young

Much of the breakdown of many long-standing traditions and institutions has been driven by a younger generation reacting against the unquestioning and restrictive conformity to authority and social norms seen in previous generations. A longing for freer self-expression led to a counter-cultural movement. There were rumblings in the 1950s, but it really gathered momentum in the 1960s with the age of hippies, dropping out, free love, drug use, the protest movement, changes in music, fashion and language, and many related phenomena. The younger generation was making a bold and assertive statement. Championed by film and music icons embodying rebellion and defiance, all things 'old' and 'establishment' have tended to be seen as corrupt, outdated, undesirable and oppressive. Although it would be true to say that historically youth have always had a rebellious streak, the strength and speed of this modern youth rebellion was new, singular, found its way deep into the halls of learning, and has shown no sign of abating. The age of freedom really gathered speed.

Respect for elders, listening to parents, offering one's seat on a train to an older person, or taking heed of advice from someone with a lifetime of experience are often seen as quaint but conservative aspects of a bygone era. In many Eastern countries respect for elders is still common, but now, in the West, by and large, we worship youth — young music, young fashion, young manners, young ideas and young politics. The age for voting, drinking, consenting and driving have all dropped. Respect for parental authority, and authority figures in general, is not what it used to be, and now it is more common for the elderly to show deference to the young rather than the other way around. These days even young children commonly tell their parents what they want to eat, wear, learn, own and do.

One other trend gathering momentum in our youth-worshiping culture is the dispensation of traditions, manners and social or religious conventions. These may have developed over centuries, millennia even, but within a relatively short space of time many of these are being done away with. They are often seen as pointless, dated, anachronistic or opposed to modern sensibilities. Their meaning is lost and their symbolism obscure to modern eyes. For example, the man doesn't let the woman go through the door first, bad language is no longer censored on television, getting married before having children is old-fashioned, and dressing modestly is a thing of the past. Such things are antiquated relics from a bygone era.

From the rule of reason to the rule of pleasure

When observing popular culture, it is not difficult to glean the prevailing motivation driving the thoughts and actions of the majority of people the majority of the time. Watching where the money goes is a fairly good indicator. Consumerism, luxury, indulgence, money-making, hedonism, substance abuse, gambling, sex and beauty all sell very well in the marketplace. We can see it in advertising, pop culture, music, fashion and just about anywhere we care to look. In fact, it is hard to escape it. Excess has become a kind of modern virtue, a virtue summed up by Gordon Gekko in the movie, *Wall Street*, when he famously said, 'Greed is good.' Now the prevailing view is that happiness and fulfilment are not so much strongly associated with pleasure, they are synonymous with it, and not necessarily the more elevated pleasures, but any old pleasure is as good as any other.

No doubt it is in our nature to be allured by what is pleasing, but not too long ago in historical terms the unbridled pursuit and worship of pleasure would have been looked on as in poor taste at best and, at worst, dangerous. It seems that the pendulum has swung strongly from a time when the gratuitous pursuit of pleasure was frowned upon to now when it is worshipped. But this also comes at a cost. For example, the rise in lifestyle-related illnesses has much to do with overstimulating the appetitive, pleasure-seeking aspect of human nature unhinged from reasonable or moderate limits. Having let loose the shackles from a time when the natural desire for pleasure was curtailed perhaps too much, as in Victorian times, the way has been paved for 'heaven knows, anything goes'. Now, of course, pleasure is synonymous with happiness — most people view them as being the same thing — but are they?

The worship of the body

In many countries, fewer people worship in the spiritual sense, but more are worshipping the body. Whether this is the cause or the effect of our modern lotus-eating, pleasure-seeking culture is an interesting question to ponder, but aspiring to 'the body-beautiful' is everywhere to be seen. Children, particularly young girls, are body and clothes conscious in a way not seen before, which is a key driver for low self-esteem and eating disorders. Adults are increasingly seeking plastic surgery and using Botox to appear younger than they are. A never-ending number of expensive beauty products are put onto the face or in the hair. A beautiful body will sell virtually any product you care to name. We also spend many billions of dollars, often futilely, on medical and technological approaches to trying to keep the body going and dream of the day when the body will live forever. The worship of the body seems to know no bounds.

From the rule of religion to the rule of science

Another major shift in ideology that marks the modern world, particularly in Western liberal democracies, is the decline of religion and the rise of science. If the twentieth century saw the rise of the scientific age then the twenty-first looks like its consummation. No doubt, there are many reasons for this. First, many literal and naive interpretations of religious allegory like 'new-Earth creationism' have been discredited by science. Second, many religious institutions have done their standing in the community an enormous disservice with scandals like the misappropriation of funds and sex abuse by clergy. It was not just that these things happened, but that they were covered up by those who were meant to embody the highest ethical and moral standards that really undermined the moral standing of the church. Many, feeling the effects of misplaced faith, lost interest in faith altogether and embraced science with a similar religious fervour, as many see it as objective and based on rational knowledge, not irrational faith.

With the decline of religion went faith in its teachings and the moral restraints it imposed. Humans, now apparently alone and unsupervised by an all-knowing, all-seeing God, can remake our moral code in our own image with no natural laws we need to obey. Now, freedom knows no bounds. William and Ariel Durant were American writers, historians and philosophers who wrote eleven volumes of the classic text, *The Story of Civilization*. In it, they describe the alternating ascendency of religion and science and, with them, the rise and fall of civilizations. Their point is particularly important and relevant for the modern day because although they are commenting on historical events, they might as well be commenting on contemporary Western civilization.

> **A certain tension between religion and society marks the higher stages of every civilization. Religion begins by offering magical aid to harassed and bewildered men; it culminates by giving to a people that unity of morals and belief which seems so favorable to statesmanship and art; it ends by fighting suicidally in the**

> lost cause of the past ... Priestly control of arts and letters is then felt as a galling shackle or hateful barrier, and intellectual history takes on the character of a 'conflict between science and religion'. Institutions which were at first in the hands of the clergy, like law and punishment, education and morals, marriage and divorce, tend to escape from ecclesiastical control, and become secular, perhaps profane. The intellectual classes abandon the ancient theology and — after some hesitation — the moral code allied with it; literature and philosophy become anticlerical. The movement of liberation rises to an exuberant worship of reason, and falls to a paralyzing disillusionment with every dogma and every idea. Conduct, deprived of its religious supports, deteriorates into epicurean chaos; and life itself, shorn of consoling faith, becomes a burden alike to conscious poverty and to weary wealth. In the end a society and its religion tend to fall together, like body and soul, in a harmonious death.[11]

It would seem that the potential failings of religion — stagnation, corruption, dogmatism and unquestioned faith — eventually give way to the virtues of science — new insights, knowledge and reason — until the potential failings of science — endless scepticism, irreverence and materialism — give way to the virtues of religion — hope, reverence and a deeper metaphysical understanding.

Now that religion is in decline in many Western countries, we are seeing a much more aggressive and militant form of atheism than in times past. In the not too distant future, people may not even be free to follow their religion or live according to its precepts as the new ruling secular, scientific class, emboldened by its unwavering faith in its world view and interpretation of truth, sees itself duty-bound to 'liberate' the community from the oppression of outdated, superstitious and naive religious beliefs. Unlike Einstein, who was very comfortable with a metaphysical view of the universe, the key philosophical tenet of the majority of modern scientists—indeed, the underlying paradigm — is materialism. For most scientists, science grounds us in the physical world. There is no world beyond what can be measured and experienced by the five senses. Whether that is true or not is questionable, but the belief that it is true leads to many further assumptions with major implications. Some of these will be explored in upcoming chapters.

SOME THINGS TO REFLECT ON:

- Do you live your life conscious of your interdependence on others?
- Do you make your decisions based on your core values or what you expect to personally win or lose?
- What is the effect in your life of being governed by the pursuit of pleasure when it stands in conflict with the dictates of reason?
- Is being left up to your own devices always good for you? If not, why not?

SOME THINGS TO PRACTISE:

- See what happens when you make decisions based on the pleasure principle or greed when it is in conflict with what is reasonable.
- See what happens when your decisions are consistent with the dictates of reason.
- Practise taking the needs of others into account more whether at home or work.
- Put a little more functional reserve into your life and notice the effect.

CHAPTER 5

THE PHILOSOPHY OF FREEDOM

Freedom is not a new idea. Individuals and cultures have deeply reflected upon it for millennia through philosophical discourse, contemplation and aeons of experience. It would be hard to think of a single type of mistake that has not already been made or lessons not already learned. Unfortunately, as history recedes into the rear vision mirror of life, painful lessons are forgotten, complacency sets in and mistakes have a habit of revisiting us in new and surprising ways. Notwithstanding that, religious and philosophical traditions have often been beset by superstition and false belief, passing off all accumulated wisdom as merely historical and archaic is possibly one of the first mistakes we make. So it would therefore be wise to take some time to reflect on a little of what the world's wisdom traditions have had to say about freedom.

Three people; three paths

Let's paint a mental picture. It's 6 a.m. Three men or women, with much in common, wish to be free from suffering. They all had difficult upbringings. Their lives swing between pleasure and pain. Their emotions are difficult to control and their minds give them little peace. All feel trapped, not in a war zone, but by their circumstances, fears, regrets and longings.

One morning, one of these people steals some goods, pawns them, uses the money to buy narcotics and is about to put the needle in their arm. Another is a parent with three children, busy, ambitious, with an overly full life, and is getting ready for work with an eye to wealth and promotion. The other is a spiritual aspirant who has awoken early, cleaned and worked around the retreat centre for no money and, in silence and solitude, is about to sit to meditate. Whether they are conscious of it or not, each has a philosophy about freedom and a set of assumptions that guide their life and decision-making. To each, the others' paths may look like a living hell.

We too have our own philosophy and assumptions about freedom, but not all paths lead us where we intend or assume they will. Which path is easier? Which path is surer? Which path, if any, will take us where we want to go?

What is freedom?

Freedom — of course we all know what it is. Or do we? *The Oxford Dictionary*[1] says many things about free including, 'not in bondage to or under the control of another … unrestricted, unimpeded; not restrained or fixed … released from ties or duties.' About freedom it says, 'the condition of being free or unrestricted; personal or civic liberty; the power of self-determination; independence of fate or necessity; the state of being free to act.'

That definition is simple enough in theory, but what does it actually mean in practice? What does it look like for a person to be truly free? Is it possible that we hold common misunderstandings about freedom that lead to the pursuit of a false form of freedom, a kind of fool's gold that appears free on the surface but is not really free at all? If we don't understand what true freedom is and how to pursue it on a deeper level then we may inadvertently promote, in ourselves and others, the opposite of what we intend. Like insects falling into the pitfall plants, such misunderstanding may lead us to unwittingly become trapped by hazards we did not see.

Life as a journey

The history of literature is full of stories about heroes going on long outward journeys where they face all kinds of trials before triumphantly returning home. Joseph Campbell, the twentieth-century American writer and mythologist, wrote extensively about it. Along the way, the hero uses courage and ingenuity to transcend their ordeals, discover their latent strength and inner character, and gain wisdom. The journey appears, on the surface at least, to be a venture to some far-flung country, but it is really symbolic of the journey home — home from a state of being alienated from oneself to a rediscovered state of peace, safety and unity.

> **We shall not cease from exploration, and the end of all our exploring will be to arrive where we started and know the place for the first time.**
>
> *TS Eliot*, Little Gidding[2]

John Bunyan's classic seventeenth-century Christian allegory, *The Pilgrim's Progress*, is all about the inward journey to redemption and deliverance. In it a man, Christian, sets out for the Celestial City, far away from his family and the comfortable village where he was raised, because of a deep, ominous feeling that calamity looms. He cannot convince anyone to go on this journey with him so he bravely sets out alone. There are many trials and tribulations along the way, but at one point he comes to a fork in the road. He sees what looks like an easy and attractive path along the meadow and another path that looks rugged and anything but easy or attractive. Drawn to the 'easy' path, he rationalizes to himself that it will be safe because it looks so attractive. He obviously made the wrong choice because Christian is captured by the monster, Giant Despair. Thankfully, he escaped before he was killed and continued on his way. Things are not always what they seem. What appears easy or pleasant may not be the same as what is best or wisest.

Inner and outer freedom

Freedom, in the common sense of the word, merely means freedom from external constraints, but to various wisdom traditions it is, in reality, an inner state closely associated with enlightenment. From that perspective, it doesn't much matter what is going on around a person, it is their inner state that matters. Although not necessarily obvious at first sight, these two levels of freedom — inner and outer — are different but inter-related. If we attain the former then the latter naturally follows. If, however, we sacrifice the former then, sooner or later, we also sacrifice the latter. So let us begin our philosophical search into freedom by considering two levels of freedom or liberty — one internal and the other external.

Outer freedom — liberty or licence?

There is a legitimate and noble kind of outer freedom from external and unjust constraints like tyranny, racism, and slavery. When confronted by circumstances or situations in the world that are unlawful, oppressive and harmful, the human spirit rises up to overcome them. The following quote commonly attributed to the Irish statesman Edmund Burke, exhorts us to act in the face of injustice: 'All that is necessary for the triumph of evil, is that good men do nothing.'[3] Nelson Mandela also referred to the need to act: 'Where globalization means, as it so often does, that the rich and powerful now have new means to further enrich and empower themselves at the cost of the poorer and weaker, we have a responsibility to protest in the name of universal freedom.'[4]

This is the lawful, reasonable and necessary call for us to unshackle ourselves from injustice and external oppression whenever it presents itself. But is external restraint always bad? Free of any external restraint, we can overindulge to our heart's content or do whatever we want. That we give free rein to our desires does not necessarily mean that we are free in a deeper sense of the word. In fact, we may be a slave to any stray whim or appetite and in the process be a danger to ourselves and/or others. Many a drunken hangover or fight has followed a night without restraint. Many a person suffers the pain and illness that follows eating too much and exercising too little. Many are those who have found the pain of addiction where they looked for freedom from suffering. Pain follows pleasure much like night follows day. Being free of external restraint may be more of a curse than a blessing.

Inner freedom — freedom through discipline

> **Peace comes from within. Do not seek it without.**
>
> *Buddha*[5]

Wisdom traditions look at the matter of freedom or liberation somewhat differently to the way majority of people do. They all speak at length about freedom coming not from the satisfaction of desires, but rather through freedom from desires. Hence the need for inner discipline as a path to peace and freedom. A person who wants to be free of things like desire, addiction, fear, hatred and compulsion, for example, needs self-mastery and self-discipline. That is an inner job. To be ruled by such things is real bondage.

There are many historic and contemporary examples of extraordinary people who outwardly found themselves in desperate situations, but inwardly demonstrated dignity in adversity and an unbreakable will for justice and freedom. They may have been physically in chains, but they were free within themselves — they had free minds and unbroken spirits. Interestingly, such people tended to have strong spiritual leanings although oftentimes their endeavours brought them into conflict with the oppressive religious orthodoxy of their day. Whether or not they could have done what they did in the way they did it without that spiritual orientation is an interesting question, but they undoubtedly displayed an unwavering resolve to stand for freedom, truth and justice. They could not have done that without self-mastery, without being masters of their own wants and fears.

For example, even when threatened with imprisonment and death, Plato's teacher Socrates would not cease from following his conscience and questioning his fellow citizens in his search for wisdom, virtue and justice. He was eventually executed without having his indomitable love of wisdom dimmed. Jesus Christ could not be swayed even in the face of the most extreme torture and death. The ancient Roman statesman Boethius wrote the *Consolation of Philosophy* in prison while awaiting execution. Hildegard of Bingen, the twelfth-century abbess, stood up to the church orthodoxy in search of freedom of religious worship and expression. Thomas More was incorruptible even in the face of all the power that a corrupt monarch could muster. Mahatma Gandhi endured mistreatment and imprisonment many times and yet was the archetypal champion of non-violent protest in his fight for the liberation of India. In the face of derision and aggression, Martin Luther King Jr., with dignity, love and passion, fought tirelessly for equality and freedom from racial discrimination. It eventually cost him his life. Mother Teresa tirelessly devoted herself to the service to the needy throughout her whole life. Nelson Mandela endured imprisonment without compromising his principles in order to free South Africa from the tyranny that was apartheid. Aung San Suu Kyi has fought tirelessly to free the Burmese people from the ruling military dictatorship. The Dalai Lama has been an enduring example for the peaceful fight for liberation of the Tibetan people. Malala Yousafzai stared down threats and an assassination attempt from the Taliban in order to fight for the rights of Muslim women to receive education and opportunity.

Clearly, many other examples could be given, but what is remarkable about these people is their ability to combine humility with boldness, compassion with courage, gentleness with strength, flexibility with a steely resolve, and the love of peace with effective action. That is practical wisdom. Their motivation was not for personal gain, but for the wellbeing of others. They had to be free within themselves in order to be a force for freedom in the societies in which they lived.

Freedom through non-attachment

In Africa, hunters use a simple and efficient method for catching monkeys.[6] In view of the monkey, the hunter digs a hole with a narrow opening in the side of an anthill. Inside it he places something tasty. The man then steps away and sits behind a tree. The monkey's curiosity is aroused and, when the coast is clear, it approaches the anthill, notices what is inside, and squeezes its hand through the narrow opening. In grabbing the food, the monkey makes a fist and as a result can no longer extract its hand through the hole. In its mind, it is trapped and therefore screams. The man calmly walks over and captures the monkey. If only the monkey would have let go of the tasty treats, it would have been free. This story is also a parable for how we humans become trapped by mental attachment. The monkey is us. We just won't let go, or perhaps it would be truer to say that in our distracted state we don't even realize we can let go.

We get attached to sensory pleasures, physical possessions and mental states. When we do this we no longer own the possession; we are possessed by it. The other side of the coin of attachment to the pleasant is, of course, aversion to the unpleasant. Here is a little of what a few wisdom traditions have to say about it. (Note: Please read this and the following quotes mentioning 'man' as gender inclusive, i.e. speaking equally to males and females.)

> **When a man dwells on the objects of sense, he creates an attraction for them; attraction develops into desire, and desire breeds anger. Anger induces delusion; delusion, loss of memory; through loss of memory, reason is shattered; and loss of reason leads to destruction.'**
>
> Bhagavad Gita[7]

> **Attachment leads to suffering ... To be free from suffering, free yourself from attachments.**
>
> *Buddha*[8]

> **And were we not saying long ago that the soul (psyche) when using the body as an instrument of perception, that is to say, when using the sense of sight or hearing or some other sense ... the soul too is then dragged by the body into the region of the changeable, and wanders and is confused.'**
>
> *Plato*, Phaedo[9]

It is not only physical possessions that we become attached to. We also get attached to mental objects like thoughts and ideologies, desires and emotions. For example, we say, 'to hold an opinion', or 'in the grips of fear'. We get attached to the things we identify ourselves with, like race, gender, social class, power and positions.

Once attached to the object of our desire or thought, we are no longer free, nor are we objective and impartial about it. It is a ready source of bias and self-deception. If we identify ourselves with one football team we don't tend to be very impartial or objective about umpiring decisions. When the object of our attachment is threatened, such as an opinion, then we ourselves feel threatened and can therefore become defensive or aggressive in response. If not attached, we could explore an issue more objectively and co-operatively without being caught up in our opinions. Winston Churchill's definition of a fanatic was, 'One who can't change his mind and won't change the subject,'[10] although others may have said it before him.

There are various forms of bias influencing decision-making, such as the 'sunk-cost' bias. Once we have invested a certain amount of time, resources, effort or reputation in something, we tend to keep on going because we live in the past and are unable to let go of it even when it would be prudent to do so. For example, we might continue with a bad investment decision, stay in an unhealthy relationship or try to recoup gambling losses. A country might not pull out of a bad war. There are no good wars per se but there are probably ones that should be fought — like World War II — and ones that shouldn't — like Vietnam and Iraq. The former might be an example of a necessary evil and the latter a demonstration of sunk-cost bias in that it was a bad decision at the start that only got worse over time. Another example could be a politician continuing with a bad policy having invested their reputation in it. When people are helped to be more present and let go of attachment then they are less affected by sunk-cost bias.[11]

Our modern society is engaged in polishing and decorating the cage in which man is kept imprisoned.'

Swami Nirmalananda[12]

To be non-attached means to be aware of the presence of something but, resting as the observer of it, not to be caught up with it. For example, we could be aware of an emotion like fear but not be ruled by it. We could lose a possession but be able to let it go of it without grief. If not attached to pleasure then we won't be so seduced by it. If not attached to pain then we may be far more able to endure it with equanimity. When the time comes, we could even approach death without clinging to life.

We could own very few possessions but be very attached to them or we could be very wealthy but not be attached to our money. The cost of attachment, however, is not always obvious to us, but makes itself known when the object of our attachment is threatened or lost. It is a little like walking with a leash around our neck that we don't even realize is there until we pull against it at which time its influence becomes obvious. This is the case with habits like smoking, eating chocolate or drinking coffee. If we don't have it, then the mind can't stop thinking about it. If we do have it, we are unable to put it down even if it's unhealthy or we have had enough of it.

If we are attached to our nationality, religion or gender then we might find ourselves alienated from those who are of a different nationality, religion or gender, and may even misrepresent their views or justify an injustice in the name of patriotism, religion or the battle of the sexes.

Perhaps we are a little slow to notice, let alone release, our attachments. Perhaps we will all get there in the end, no matter how slowly we learn from our experiences. As Abba Eban, the respected twentieth-century Israeli diplomat, said: 'History teaches us that men and nations behave wisely once they have exhausted all other alternatives.'[13]

Transcendence

Our revels now are ended. These our actors,
As I foretold you, were all spirits and
Are melted into air, into thin air:
And, like the baseless fabric of this vision,
The cloud-capp'd towers, the gorgeous palaces,

> **The solemn temples, the great globe itself,**
> **Ye all which it inherit, shall dissolve**
> **And, like this insubstantial pageant faded,**
> **Leave not a rack behind. We are such stuff**
> **As dreams are made on, and our little life**
> **Is rounded with a sleep.**
>
> *William Shakespeare,* The Tempest, *act 4, scene 1.*

One thing that makes attachment unwise is that everything is ultimately transient. As Shakespeare notes, not a single aspect of the universe, let alone our lives, is permanent. To be mentally attached to impermanent things is a recipe for anxiety, disappointment and grief because that thing will be lost or destroyed sooner or later. To be free of anxiety, disappointment and grief is to not be attached in the first place. The question is whether there is a level of being within us that is not transient and therefore transcends worldly existence. Transcendence is not just something for a spiritual aspirant. It sometimes happens to us spontaneously, such as when we are in 'the zone'.

> **It almost seems as though I'm able to transport myself beyond the turmoil on the court to some place of total peace and calm ... I appreciate what my opponent is doing in a detached abstract way. Like an observer in the next room ... It is a perfect combination of (intense) action taking place in an atmosphere of total tranquillity. When it happens, I want to stop the match and grab the microphone and shout that's what it's all about, because it is. It is not the big prize I'm going to win at the end of the match or anything else ... When I'm in that kind of state ... I feel that tennis is an art form that's capable of moving both the players and the audience.**
>
> *Billie-Jean King*[14]

There are two main ways we can be free of something — the outer way and the inner way. The outer way is to change the situation and the inner is to change our way of being within that situation. The outer way involves seeing a problem and being able to do something about it. If your hand is on a hotplate then it makes sense to take it off. It's pretty simple and effective, but we can't always make situations go away. If, for some reason, we cannot take our hand off the hotplate then the inner way to free ourselves of it is to transcend the pain. Consider death. Despite our best efforts to forestall it, ultimately death will come to us all. Illness, loss and failure are all inevitable at some stage. Ultimately, the only option available to us it to transcend adversity, or at least transcend our preoccupation with and fear of it.

Transcendence relates to the ability to fully participate in events while remaining totally unconcerned or impartial about their outcome. The aware, impartial self or consciousness just sits back and watches from within. That kind of liberation is independent of circumstances.

> **But when returning into herself she (the soul) reflects, then she passes into the other world, the region of purity, and eternity, and immortality, and unchangeableness, which are her kindred, and with them she ever lives, when she is by herself and is not let or hindered; then she ceases from her erring ways, and being in communion with the unchanging is unchanging. And this state of the soul is called wisdom.**
>
> *Plato*, Phaedo[15]

Ultimately, according to various wisdom traditions, if we do not know ourselves as that pure being or consciousness, which is unchanging, then we are destined to confuse ourselves with everything we are conscious of, which is constantly changing.

Self-mastery

In *The Republic*, Plato asserts that self-mastery and justice are intimately entwined. Consider this quote where he defines the just person or society as a finely tuned state of the soul with each element of the psyche in harmony with the others.

> **But in reality justice was ... concerned not with the outward man, but with the inward, which is the true self and concernment of man: for the just man ... sets in order his own inner life, and is his own master and his own law, and at peace with himself; and when he has bound together the three principles within him, which may be compared to the higher (reason), lower (appetite), and middle (emotion) notes of the scale ... and is no longer many, but has become one entirely temperate and perfectly adjusted nature, then he proceeds to act, if he has to act, whether in a matter of property, or in the treatment of the body, or in some affair of politics or private business; always thinking and calling that which preserves and co-operates with this harmonious condition, just and good action, and the knowledge which presides over it, wisdom, and that which at any time impairs this condition, he will call unjust action, and the opinion which presides over it, ignorance.'[16]**

We often think of the psyche as being one, single thing but, according to Plato, there are a number of aspects to it, each vying with the others for the throne, so to speak. In its natural state, each aspect of the psyche has its own job to do and it should not do the job of the others. What are these three principles within the soul, psyche or human nature that Plato speaks about? First, there is the higher — that with which a person is wise (the intellect or reasoning element); second, there is the middle — that with which a person is courageous (the spirited or emotive element); third, there is the lower — that with which a person has physical desires (the appetitive or pleasure-seeking element).

Appetite, emotion or reason: which part of the self should rule?

Other wisdom traditions express similar ideas to those described by Plato. For example, the following is an extract from the ancient Indian texts, *The Ten Principal Upanishads*. It relates to the conversation between Nachiketas, a young seeker after truth, and Death.

> **Death said: 'The good is one, the pleasant another; both command the soul ... Self rides in the chariot of the body, intellect (reason) is the firm-footed charioteer, discursive mind the reins. Senses are the horses, objects of desire the roads. When Self is joined to body, mind, sense, none but He (the true Self) enjoys. When a man lack steadiness, unable to control his mind, his senses are unmanageable horses. But if he control his mind, a steady man, they are manageable horses ... God made sense turn outward, man therefore looks outward, not into himself. Now and again a daring soul, desiring immortality, has looked back and found himself. The ignorant man runs after pleasure, sinks into the entanglements of death; but the wise man, seeking the undying, does not run among things that die.**[17]

Pleasure certainly feels good but, according to the wisdom traditions, it is also a sweet trap into which we commonly fall. When we pursue it as if it is synonymous with happiness we find that it keeps vanishing and we need a greater amount of it to get the same little burst of bliss as the time before. Then there is a little downer that follows the cessation of pleasure so we seek it again. On it goes in a never-ending cycle, all the while sacrificing the rule of reason as we are drawn deeper into the pitfall.

According to Plato, reason or wisdom is the highest aspect of the psyche in a well-ordered soul. Its job is to govern and regulate the others and make decisions based on what is reasonable, necessary, just, lawful and healthy. A man or woman governing themselves in such a way is wise. Keeping free from, or cutting the chains of, compulsion, addiction and unrestrained appetite is the path to freedom. It doesn't mean that the appetites are never enjoyed, but they are not overindulged. The emotive element is the middle note on the musical scale of the psyche, and it is meant to support the decisions of the reasoning element. Hence, we speak highly of a person who has the 'courage of their convictions' in that they are honourable, hold firm and are courageous in the face of fear, temptation and adversity. Clearly a person needs such conviction to be able to rise above adversity.

> **I learned that courage was not the absence of fear, but the triumph over it. The brave man is not he who does not feel afraid, but he who conquers that fear.**
>
> *Nelson Mandela*[18]

The wise person needs to tell the difference between rational and irrational fear, and know how to respond in the face of it. If we are ruled by the emotive element at the expense of reason then we may also be ruled by things like fear, anger, ambition and impulsive action. Shakespeare, whose plays are steeped in Platonic philosophy, clearly didn't think it was a desirable situation for the emotive element (blood, valour) to rule the reasoning element (judgement).

> **Blessed are those whose blood and judgement are so well commingled, that they are not a pipe for Fortune's finger to sound what stop she please. Give me that man that is not passion's slave, and I will wear him in my heart's core, ay, in my heart of heart, as I do thee.**
>
> *William Shakespeare,* Hamlet, *act 3, scene 2*

The appetitive element is the lowest note on the musical scale of the psyche. There is nothing wrong with it, in fact, there is a lot right about it because without it we wouldn't physically survive. We wouldn't eat, procreate or avoid pain if it were not for the promptings of this appetitive, pleasure-seeking, pain-avoiding aspect of our nature. The key issue is that the appetitive element is not meant to rule our decisions and actions. The reasoning element is meant to regulate the appetites, while the emotive element is meant to be courageous and firm in following the dictates of reason. Oftentimes reason dictates that it is entirely appropriate to do something pleasurable particularly if it aligns with what is also healthy. Sometimes it might dictate that it is appropriate to forgo a pleasure or do something uncomfortable but necessary even in the face of our brain's pleasure-centre protesting every step of the way.

Plato and other wisdom traditions may have been onto something if modern neuroscience is anything to go by, but for now let's deepen our understanding of how this works by considering a few examples.

We all recognize the internal battle at the meal table when one part of ourselves wants to keep eating — perhaps having a second or even third serve of dessert — but another part quietly knows we have had enough. The body may give messages that it has had enough and doesn't need more, but we may not be paying attention. Do we have the strength to stop eating or do we keep eating regardless? When the reasoning element is doing its job, then if it is reasonable to eat we eat, but, notwithstanding the occasional indulgence, we eat what is healthy and stop eating when the body has had enough.

Then there is the prodigious internal fight we often have with ourselves just to get out of bed in the morning where one part doesn't want to let go of the comfort and warmth, and another part knows that the necessities of the day await us. If it is time get out of bed and get on with the day then a wise person would do it. A person attached to indulgence sleeps in too long, is late, or perhaps doesn't even get to work at all and phones in pretending to be sick. Consider the need for exercise recognized by one aspect of our psyche and the resistance to getting out of bed coming from another aspect of the psyche. A lot hangs on which part wins that little internal struggle. From a reasonable perspective, if there is a need for exercise then it is best not to be lazy. We should bear the discomfort and do it to a level that is reasonable and appropriate.

If there is an unreasonable, unlawful or harmful appetite, for example, a temptation to use or abuse an addictive substance, then wisdom would dictate to not even go near let alone get attached to such a desire. The lifestyle illnesses and addictions confronting the modern world are largely the product of being ruled by the appetitive element with the reasonable and emotive elements not doing their jobs.

This hierarchy of the psyche is just as relevant for the whole society as it is for the individual. A society can be ruled by what is reasonable and just. Equally, it can be ruled by emotion and anger, or by whims and appetites.

It is very easy to get attached to the things we find pleasurable. Self-regulation through non-attachment, therefore, is not so much about trying to control those appetites but rather not being controlled by them. This is quite different to suppression where, because of attachment, there is a constant internal battle to control desire. Suppressing desires is like trying to keep an inflatable ball continually submerged under the water. It takes a lot of effort and it pops up sooner or later. Mental non-attachment is different. It is liberating and leaves us in peace, whereas attachment leads to a constant and exhausting internal struggle, which can range in intensity from a grumbling background unease all the way to a full-blown civil war within ourselves.

Hedonism and the decline and fall

The question arises as to whether our current trajectory as a society or civilization is towards greater freedom or one almighty fall. In Edward Gibbon's classic and authoritative book, *The Decline and Fall of the Roman Empire*, he describes the five marks of the decaying Roman culture. They bear all the hallmarks of a hedonic disposition to life. These five marks are often summarized as:

1. **Concern with displaying affluence instead of building wealth**
2. **Obsession with sex and perversions of sex**
3. **Art becomes freakish and sensationalistic instead of creative and original**
4. **Widening disparity between very rich and very poor**
5. **Increased demand to live off the state.**[19]

Undoubtedly there are many parallels today that Gibbon would recognize. Consider the modern aspirational consumer with the desire for the showy, larger house, the faster prestige car and advertising continually seducing us with words like luxury, gourmet, indulgence, wicked and exclusive.

Consider the extent to which sex is used to buy and sell everything and anything, and how pornography flourishes by peddling attitudes and practices that would not long ago have been looked on as perverse.

Consider how much modern art, music and literature is aimed at shocking, inciting or just having to be different, rather than nurturing, informing or uplifting the observer.

Consider the growing disparity between rich and poor, and how incongruous it is that in wealthy, developed countries there are increasing numbers of people without healthcare, food or shelter.

Consider that in many countries there are increasing numbers of people who live off welfare just because they can, even when they can work to support themselves.

If Gibbon's five marks of a culture in decline are anything to go by then the Western world may be reaching a tipping point, almost like we are deep inside the mouth of one massive carnivorous plant big enough to devour the whole of Western civilization. Whether the end comes in the form of a sudden, dramatic breakdown of social order on a massive scale or, due to our spendthrift appetites, slowly sliding into a murky pool of financial indebtedness to the East, only time will tell, but the signs are there if we care to look.

The ruling principle of a civilization in decline, such as ancient Rome, was hedonism. In the field of positive psychology there are two main dispositions to happiness — hedonic (pleasure-seeking) and eudaimonic (meaning). With hedonism, reason, if used at all, is merely employed to find inventive ways of furthering the search for pleasure. Unchecked, hedonism leads to injustice and greed as a person disregards law in their restless and relentless search for what pleases them, while at the same time avoiding at all costs what displeases them. But the person who prizes meaning above hedonism can forego pleasure or endure pain when it is just, meaningful and useful to do so.

If Plato walked around our streets looking at what we are motivated by today, it probably wouldn't take him too long to come to the conclusion that we are mostly ruled by the hedonic principle. He might assert that we have become too accustomed to comfort and are slaves to the appetitive element of our natures. As a consequence, we are internally preyed upon by incessant desires. Externally we are preyed upon by those who profit from and manipulate our inner vulnerability, for example, those who seduce us into debt, sell drugs, market sex or promote wasteful consumerism. Plato equated tyranny — the lowest form of government and lowest on the scale of self-mastery — with the person or society who is least internally free and most ruled by appetite and desire. But imagine if Socrates was around these days and said to us things along those lines on television or in parliament. Like Gollum in *The Lord of the Rings*, we would likely be offended, angry and lash out at him for even suggesting we curtail our precious wants. 'What a threat to our freedom,' we might say. We might even want to put him to death, which is exactly what they did in Athens in 399BCE. But does killing the messenger really clear the conscience or protect us from our own lack of insight and wisdom?

Discipline — a four-letter word or a path to mastery?

> **Your worst enemy cannot harm you as much as your own unguarded thoughts.**
>
> *Buddha*[20]

It is easy to say that self-mastery is useful, but it is quite another thing to attain it. So how do wisdom traditions suggest we attain self-mastery? In a word — discipline.

Discipline has almost become a pejorative term in recent years, almost a 'four-letter word'. The dislike and distrust of discipline may be understandable when it conjures up notions of harshness, oppression, dourness, and corporal punishment equated with some kind of Victorian-era joyless and cruel subjugation of the will. With the harsh and sometimes cruel way discipline used to be meted out in many homes, schools and orphanages, these associations have some validity. But what if we misunderstand what discipline really is — reasonable discipline, that is, and not that other kind of discipline that was cruelty covered by a veneer of virtue. What if true discipline is not an authoritarian disguise for poorly adjusted adults — mostly men — taking out their anger on the defenceless — mostly women, children and minority groups?

Discipline, correctly and wisely applied, is actually aimed at promoting, not limiting, freedom, self-mastery and self-expression. Consider the freedom of expression and beauty that Mozart displayed in his music.

> **When I am, as it were, completely myself, entirely alone, and of good cheer — say travelling in a carriage, or walking after a good meal, or during the night when I cannot sleep; it is on such occasions that my ideas flow best and most abundantly. Whence and how they come, I know not; nor can I force them. Those ideas that please me I retain in memory, and am accustomed, as I have been told, to hum them to myself. If I continue in this way, it soon occurs to me how I may turn this or that morsel to account, so as to make a good dish of it, that is to say, agreeably to the rules of counterpoint, to the peculiarities of the various instruments, etc. All this fires my soul, and provided I am not disturbed, my subject enlarges itself, becomes methodized and defined, and the whole, though it be long, stands almost complete and finished in my mind, so that I can survey it, like a fine picture, or a beautiful statue, at a glance. Nor do I hear in my imagination the parts successively, but I hear them, as it were all at once. What a delight this is, I cannot tell! All this inventing, this producing, takes place in a pleasing, lively dream. Still the actual hearing of the whole ensemble is after all the best what has thus been produced, I do not easily forget, and this perhaps the best gift I have my Divine Maker to thank for.**
>
> *A letter from Mozart to his father.*[21]

Over and above Mozart's raw ability he needed to understand and apply the laws of harmony, rhythm and metre, practise his scales, listen to and learn from previous masters, and learn from his mistakes. Consider the freedom that a champion tennis or soccer player exhibits in being able to do incredible things while lesser players look on in awe. Consider the inventiveness of a master chef or the skill and dexterity of a leading surgeon. They can all do things that we can't, and a testament to their talent is that they make it look easy, almost effortless. The paradox is that, although they might have started with some talent, their ability to harness and direct that talent is based on guidance, sacrifice, discipline and hard work. Take this quote from the champion tennis player, Roger Federer, speaking about his approach to tennis and self-mastery.

> **Until 17, 18, I was just all over the place, really, with my mind, with my emotions. Losing was like a disaster ... I was maybe an okay junior ... but I was never going to be the future world number one. I had to train really, really hard and that's the advice I can give, because if you don't work hard somebody else will. You've just got to figure it out for yourself, you've got to have the right people around you, listen to your parents, listen to your coaches, and trust them ... and also enjoy it, love it ... Chess, I used to whack the figures off the chessboard ... and all these things would drive me crazy, but not anymore. Today, I'm totally Zen.[22]**

Mastery requires the physical practice of a skill, mental discipline, and focused attention in the moment of execution. There really is no mastery of self or anything else without it. The paradox about discipline is that it works through knowing how to apply limits — learning to guide thoughts, energy and actions where they are needed and with no more or less force than is needed. It means measured use of what we have at our disposal. It takes the raw elements, works within the laws governing the task, and gives those elements shape and expression.

The product of a lack of discipline is nothing but random and discordant notes, mediocrity in tennis, inedible food or an injured patient. But discipline is not just about learning to play music or tennis, cook food or do surgery. We are all engaged in the game of life, and self-mastery in life is just as dependent on discipline — perhaps even more so — than mastering a physical skill. For example, the discipline of training attention and the mind through mindfulness meditation has helped many people to enhance their skills, perform better under pressure, and to free themselves from anxiety, anger and depression.

> **A human mind is a wandering mind, and a wandering mind is an unhappy mind. The ability to think about what is not happening is a cognitive achievement that comes at an emotional cost.**
> *Matthew Killingsworth* [23]

Training the mind requires an enormous amount of effort and patience, but it is aimed as much at freedom from the tyranny of our internal world as it is aimed at greater creativity and freedom of expression. In the middle of daily life, we really don't want to be at the whim of every stray thought or emotion that happens to be running through the mind. A monk or nun practising meditation in a sanctuary may not be doing it because it is the easiest or most pleasant thing in the world — although it may be — but because they wish to enjoy the freedom and peace that comes with a well-ordered and disciplined mind uncompelled by attachments. There is no freedom of expression and creativity without discipline, but it also requires discipline of mind to be free from anxiety, fear and compulsion. Ultimately, to be master of our own mind is, from a wisdom perspective, what true liberation is about. That is enlightenment. It is predicated on awareness. John Philpot Curran, an Irish orator, politician, lawyer and judge, gives these sage words on freedom: 'Eternal vigilance is the price of liberty.'[24]

Back to our three people

Returning to the three people at the beginning of the chapter, each wants to be free of suffering. The first may be using narcotics to numb it, the second may be distracting themselves from it by pursuing wealth and status, and the third, through inner discipline, is seeking to transcend it. Although they all seek the same thing, they approach it in entirely different ways. Each of them may view the others' paths as a living hell. We don't need to join a monastery in order to transcend, and this mental exercise is not about judging one person right and the others wrong, it merely emphasizes how we have totally different assumptions about how to pursue freedom and happiness. At an early age, we pick up unconscious assumptions from home, environment and society. Individually and collectively, whether our initial philosophy is right or wrong, it will determine whether we sip on the sweet nectar of life or follow the sweet nectar into a sticky pit.

SOME THINGS TO REFLECT ON:

- What are you attached to and what is the effect of those attachments?
- To what extent are your life and decisions governed by the hedonic and eudaimonic dispositions to happiness?
- What is the effect when the appetitive aspect of your nature rules at the expense of the dictates of reason?
- Do you live your life wanting transient things to go on forever and wishing the inevitable would never come? What effect does that have?

SOME THINGS TO PRACTISE:

- Practise letting go of something you are attached to. Notice the effect.
- Practise leaving attachment to the past behind and making decisions based on what is in front of you here and now.
- Through meditation, practise observing thoughts, emotions and sensations come and go without attachment to them.

CHAPTER 6

FREEDOM UNDER THE LAW

Like discipline, many people see the law as a restriction on personal freedom even if it is begrudgingly acknowledged as being necessary. A lecture series given by the British judge, Lord Alfred Denning, titled *Freedom Under the Law*, proposed that, contrary to popular opinion, obedience to the law goes to the very heart of freedom.[1] Obviously, in the common run of worldly life, if we disobey the law we might be put in jail or have to pay some other kind of penalty, but obedience to the law is something bigger than that. So, does the law, and our obedience to it, promote or limit our freedom? What is the difference between a good law and a bad one? Does the law define justice or can laws be unjust? What should the law of the land be based upon? Should the law ever be disobeyed? What are natural laws, and are they the basis upon which human-made laws should be made?

Is anarchy freedom?

There is a kind of freedom or liberty from external restraint that John Ruskin, the prominent nineteenth-century English art critic, philosopher and writer, wrote about in this rather colourful quote.

> **If there be any one principle more widely than any other confessed by every utterance, or more sternly than another imprinted on every atom of the visible creation, that principle is not liberty**

> **but law. The enthusiast would reply that by Liberty he meant the law of Liberty. Then why use the single and misunderstood word? If by liberty you mean chastisement of the passions, discipline of the intellect, subjection of the will; if you mean the fear of inflicting, the shame of committing a wrong; if you mean respect for all who are in authority, and consideration for all who are in dependence; veneration for the good, mercy to the evil, sympathy with the weak; if you mean watchfulness over all thoughts, temperance in all pleasures, and perseverance in all toils ... Why do you name this by the same word by which the luxurious mean license and the reckless mean change; by which the rogue means rapine, and the fool equality, by which the proud mean anarchy and the malignant mean violence?[2]**

According to Ruskin, the kind of liberty which disregards the restraints of law and reason is in stark contrast to its more just and noble expression. At a superficial glance they look the same —freedom from restraint — but they are not. In fact, they are polar opposites. There is a kind of freedom based on law and another one with disregard for it. This tension between freedom on one hand and the restraint of law on the other is a paradoxical one. Some people believe the purest form of government and freedom is to not be governed by anyone at all — by anyone other than your own self that is. This is called anarchy, from the ancient Greek 'anarchia', which combines 'a' meaning, 'not, without' with 'arkhi', meaning 'ruler, leader, authority,'[3] Essentially, it means a person or society without rulers or leaders.

Crime is a kind of anarchy or freedom from restraint unencumbered by the law. Crime, however, may not be a sign of freedom, but rather a sign of compulsion, greed or desperation often committed in non-comprehension of the results of one's actions. Crime is not a viable rule for life because, if it was, then we should all adopt it, but if we did then society would be totally dysfunctional. Virtue, on the other hand, is a sustainable rule for life. It sustains oneself and others. Paradoxically, even criminal gangs can only function effectively through honesty and virtue between the members of the gang; 'honour among thieves', as the saying goes.

Whether anarchy is a practical and effective form of government and whether it can promote freedom are interesting questions. First, given that there are no functioning anarchic states, it would be difficult to consider it an effective or stable form of government. If it were effective or stable, there would be notable and admirable examples of it in existence. Yes, there are individuals, or loosely bound small groups of individuals, who see themselves as anarchists, but they either live in the wilderness or in liberal, democratic societies that tolerate them. Although seeming to stand apart from the communities in which they live, anarchists generally enjoy many of the economic benefits and protections that come from living in societies that benefit from sound government. Canadian-born American cognitive scientist, psychologist and popular science author, Steven Pinker, had this to say about anarchy:

> **If you look in general at people who live in anarchy, they have quite high rates of death from either homicide or warfare or both. Anarchy is one of the main reasons for violence, and it may be the most important.**[4]

The brief periods of history where anarchy 'ruled' tend to be associated with the height of revolutions and the temporary breakdown of the rule of law because of the overthrow of the ruling party. Examples include the English Civil War, the French Revolution and the Russian Civil War. These events were mostly bloodthirsty and the period of anarchy did not last long. The breakdown in law led to anarchy which, like the disorder associated with disease, is a natural reaction to that breakdown. As Louis D Brandeis, an American lawyer and associate justice on the Supreme Court, notes:

> **Our government ... teaches the whole people by its example. If the government becomes the lawbreaker, it breeds contempt for law; it invites every man to become a law unto himself; it invites anarchy.**[5]

Anarchy rules until the rule of law is once again adhered to. In the abovementioned cases, law and order were soon restored before the society totally collapsed. These were hardly the highpoints in freedom and stable government to which we should aspire. The revolutions, however, may have removed something old and perhaps corrupt, thus providing the space for something new to arise in its place.

Many indigenous cultures, when viewed through the lens of colonialization, were looked upon as primitive and anarchic. That their law was orally transmitted and not written down may have created a false impression to casual onlookers that the people were savages without rule or order. In reality, these societies were not living under anarchy at all — quite the opposite. The basis for their sophisticated system of law was the law of nature, which they observed all around them and respected.

Natural law

'Natural law' refers to universal laws inherent in nature. As such it is impersonal and independent of opinion in that it acts on everything and everyone no matter what their status or opinions. It is not arbitrary. It is not transitory. It cannot be gainsaid or denied, although it can be ignored. For the purposes of the following discussion we will consider natural law on three levels:

1. **Simple physical laws.**
2. **Natural laws governing living systems.**
3. **The laws governing human psychology and society.**

Simple physical laws

The most limited but widely accepted level of natural law relates to the physical laws of the universe, such as the laws of gravity and motion defined by Isaac Newton and his successors. There are also the laws of electricity, nuclear physics, chemistry and mathematics. These laws manifest from the smallest to the largest scale. They can be tested, measured and verified scientifically and, although we still struggle to entirely and accurately define them, we accept their existence and try to master them by obeying them.

Natural laws governing living systems

Next are the slightly harder to define natural laws governing living systems relevant to health and ecology. Again, they operate in the physical realm but, compared to simple physical laws, they are far more complex, holistic and require a sophisticated level of observation and intuition to see and define them. Doctors and environmentalists seek to discover and describe such laws in order to maintain health whether of the patient or the ecosystem. For example, the four laws of ecology defined by the twentieth-century ecologist, Barry Commoner, in his book *The Closing Circle*[6] are:

1. **Everything is connected to everything else. There is one ecosphere for all living organisms and what affects one, affects all.**
2. **Everything must go somewhere. There is no 'waste' in nature and there is no 'away' to which things can be thrown.**
3. **Nature knows best. Humankind has fashioned technology to improve upon nature, but such change in a natural system is likely to be detrimental to that system.**
4. **There is no such thing as a free lunch. Exploitation of nature will inevitably involve the conversion of resources from useful to useless forms.**

These four laws of ecology are not presented here as if they are the four laws, or are the only ecological laws, or as if they couldn't be formulated and expressed in a different way. They are just an example of how such laws could be described. It is likely that indigenous cultures were far more in touch with ecological laws, which underpinned their ability to live harmoniously and sustainably within the natural environment for epochs. We couldn't say that of modern industrial societies.

Natural laws governing health also exist, but are often not acknowledged in the management of chronic illness. For example, lifestyle factors are rarely given much credence by oncologists in the management of cancer. They more commonly prefer invasive and expensive treatments with oftentimes horrible side-effects. So, for example, despite comprehensive lifestyle change and mind-body approaches being found to reverse early prostate cancer,[7,8] switch off prostate cancer genes[9] and reverse ageing on a genetic level,[10,11] it is still not part of standard management. You would think that such a revelation would be hailed as a major breakthrough, but it is largely ignored and the collective money and effort within the healthcare system is directed elsewhere at great expense to patient and system alike. Generally, in modern healthcare, first priorities, such as self-help strategies and addressing the underlying lifestyle issues contributing to chronic illnesses, are put last and last priorities, such as invasive, expensive treatments with unwanted side-effects are put first. But the laws of health and healing inevitably underlie the cause and treatment of illness. The body is always repairing itself and establishing balance or homeostasis given a chance. Without that the doctor is powerless. As Voltaire quipped, 'The art of medicine consists in amusing the patient while nature cures the disease.'[12] Nevertheless, we seem to have trapped ourselves into a healthcare mentality and economic system that often breeds problems instead of relieving them.

When something is used appropriately for what it was designed, then it works well and is less likely to break down, or at least it won't break down so soon. For example, a city car is not designed to go where a four-wheel drive will go. A coffee table is not made for standing on. Similarly, from a natural law perspective, the body and the ecosystem have their own natural functions. Within that, balance and homeostasis tend to be stable. Outside of that, dysfunction becomes increasingly likely. If something is not used in the way it is intended, like the body, then problems ensue, as was previously mentioned in relation to chronic, lifestyle-related illnesses. Too much food, too many processed and calorie-dense foods, and too little activity only leads to chronic illnesses like heart disease, diabetes and cancer, which is the cost of not following what is natural. Administering drugs to lower blood glucose rather than addressing the underlying lifestyle issues does little to extend life expectancy[13] whereas addressing lifestyle issues does make a significant contribution to better quality of life, forestalls chronic diseases and leads to significantly longer life expectancy.[14–16] Unfortunately, very few people make the effort to address the underlying issues and most hope that modern medicine will avert the natural consequences of an unregulated life.

One of the common notions associated with modern conceptions of freedom is that we can and should do something as much as we want to. Hence, the ancient Greek precept formulated as 'nothing too much' or 'moderation in all things' is not one that seems to accord with modern sensibilities. The love of excess — drinking too much, eating too much, staying up too late, being too loud — is increasingly common. Facebook pages and advertisements are full of it. It is seen as fun, happiness, self-expression and a person living freely and fully. Of course, it is mostly a façade and we get what comes with it. In the short term, there is the hangover or car accident, the stomach-ache, the sleepiness or the tinnitus. In the long term, there is the liver disease, the heart attack, the cancer, the deafness and so on. To the ancient Greeks, health, happiness and ease of living lay in finding the right limits, not in excess. It lay in knowing when to stop and it relied on discipline. Excess, like a seductive and sweet trap, is the appearance of freedom that comes with a heavy burden.

There is nothing natural about taking intravenous drugs and it has its costs such as addiction, HIV and hepatitis. Promiscuity, whether heterosexual or homosexual, comes with risks such as STDs. Too little or too much sleep is unhealthy and risks cardiovascular disease and mental health problems. Listening to music that is unnaturally loud causes hearing problems. Urban overcrowding and social disadvantage, especially in developing countries, contributes to the spread of infectious diseases such as HIV, tuberculosis and gastroenteritis. If we pursue genetic engineering then within a generation or two we will no doubt find out what comes with that. In all such cases, we are keen on pursuing what we want but we are either oblivious to, or are unwilling to accept, what comes with it. Trying to minimize harm is good, but when we try to mitigate the costs of imprudent action with harm minimization strategies, we potentially 'normalize the deviance' without ever considering whether natural laws may have been ignored in the first place. It is a little like a doctor and a patient trapped into endlessly treating or mitigating the symptoms but never addressing the underlying cause of the illness in the first place.

The laws governing human psychology and society

The third, most diverse, hardest to define, and most controversial level of natural law is the one involving human psychology and human nature. Do such natural laws exist and, if so, how should they influence human-made laws, ethics, morals and relationships within society?

If there exists a God, divine being, universal consciousness or spirit — whatever we want to call it — then should we not do its will, period? From this perspective, 'doing its will' is following the laws of human nature in as much as we are able to discern what they are. If such laws exist then freedom, as in ignoring natural law, is an illusion, is dangerous and can only lead to self-harm. If, on the other hand, there is no God, divine being, universal consciousness or spirit, and we are just living in an unconscious and blind universe, then we can largely do whatever we want, however we want. From that perspective, religious arguments for following a divine will are, at best, a meaningless and arbitrary limitation of human will and potential and, at worst, a form of social control and manipulation.

Let us consider some examples of what might be called natural laws influencing how society is shaped. The United States Declaration of Independence contains the following statement to inform all that follows after.

> **We hold these truths to be self-evident, that all men are created equal, that they are endowed by their Creator with certain unalienable Rights, that among these are Life, Liberty and the pursuit of Happiness.[17]**

Implicit in this statement is that these truths governing civilized society are indelibly imbued in human nature and are God-given. One wonders what the Declaration would have sounded like if it were written from an evolutionary perspective? Perhaps it might read more like, 'We hold these truths to be self-evident, that people are not created equal because some are better adapted than others, we arose from a primeval slime, and we are engaged in a bitter and meaningless struggle for dominance, survival and to pass on our genes however we can.' It's not quite so uplifting or poetic.

That society's institutions should be based on God-given principles is something that a significant and increasingly vocal segment of the community would not be ready to accept these days. They may recognize and support the same principles as those embodied in the Declaration of Independence, but come to them from a different line of reasoning. For example, humanism is a social movement based on an ideology emphasizing the agency of human beings and human reason. Humanist ideology has gained enormous influence in secularized societies. With the rise of humanism, or at least the popularization of beliefs and attitudes based on humanist principles, the acknowledgement of God as the source of law is not accepted. Unhooking human thinking, behaviour, morals and ethics from a higher source and putting them in the hands of human beings undoubtedly gives us a huge sense of freedom and opens up a whole new range of options for human conduct not hitherto available. The children, as it were, are fully in control of the playground without any parental supervision. Whether that is a recipe for freedom or disaster only time will tell.

Of course, whether humanism is based on a false and dangerous premise depends not on the weight of public opinion but on the existence or non-existence of God (divine being, spirit, consciousness, universal intelligence ...). If there is a God whose laws underpin the universe, and therefore must be obeyed, and over which we have no control, then ignorance or defiance is ridiculous, arrogant hubris and dangerous. The view that there is a universal spirit or consciousness behind the laws of the universe is held by many scientists, most notable among them being Albert Einstein and his contemporaries like Niels Bohr, Erwin Schrödinger and J. Robert Oppenheimer. Here is one example.

> **Everyone who is seriously involved in the pursuit of science becomes convinced that a spirit is manifest in the laws of the universe — a spirit vastly superior to that of man, and one in the face of which we with our modest powers must feel humble. In this way the pursuit of science leads to a religious feeling of a special sort, which is indeed quite different from the religiosity of someone more naive ... Scientific research is based on the assumption that all events, including the actions of mankind, are determined by the laws of nature ... However, we have to admit that our actual knowledge of these laws is only an incomplete piece of work, so that ultimately the belief in the existence of fundamental all-embracing laws also rests on a sort of faith. All the same, this faith has been largely justified by the success of science.**
>
> *Albert Einstein*[18-20]

These great scientists regularly swapped quotes from the world's wisdom traditions, with a particular fascination for Eastern spiritual classics.

Nevertheless, each side of the debate about whether a divine intelligence or being is behind the laws of the universe no doubt sees the other as both deluded and dangerous. Perhaps the only real answer to who is right will come when we see what happens if we continue to unhook social conventions, morals and ethics from natural laws. Without judging different views as right or wrong, we could look at issues from different perspectives. For example, does marriage, or at least having a long-term, stable, cohabiting relationship, accord with human nature? It isn't a law of physics, but is it a natural law nonetheless? One clue is that it seems to be almost universally adopted by various cultures throughout history. There is also consistent evidence that marriage (or a stable long-term cohabiting relationship) is associated with better mental and physical health of adults and children alike.[21,22] Having said that, through misfortune or necessity, many single parents do an extraordinarily good job of being loving and reliable raising happy children under very challenging circumstances. Furthermore, being in an abusive or unhappy marriage is clearly not good for psychological or physical health, but being abusive likely neglects another natural law of human behaviour — to treat others with compassion and kindness. From a natural law perspective, the marriage of man and woman, and the procreation and raising of children is the way nature intended it. Some animals such as humans, many primates and prairie voles, have brains that are loaded with receptors for the hormone, oxytocin — the neuropeptide of nurture and connectedness. This receptor profile primes the species for long-standing, monogamous relationships despite the competing primal urge to be attracted to other potential mates.[23–25] Biologically speaking, humans may be programmed for monogamy, so we should not be surprised that there are traditional social and moral conventions supporting it and others discouraging promiscuity. From that perspective, deviation from monogamous, heterosexual relationships is 'not the norm'. From a perspective not sympathetic to natural law, however, marriage is merely a social or religious convention that may have some practical uses, but there is nothing inherently right about it. Hence, people should be free to form, and society should support, whatever relationships they choose.

Which view is right? Will Barry Commoner's third law of ecology — nature knows best — come into play? Again, time will tell. The problem is that it is not always easy to discern, let alone have consensus on, what the natural laws governing society are and whether we may be increasing freedom or normalizing deviance heading on our current trajectory. In the end, it is not that any group in the community has a right to impose their attitudes onto others, but more a matter of discerning the laws that nature imposes on us and to either follow them or be prepared to accept what comes with not following them.

Is there freedom under natural law?

It would seem that we do or don't have freedom under natural laws, depending on how you look at it. In as much as they exist, we don't have the ability to choose whether or not to live under the influence of natural laws. We cannot, for example, say to ourselves that the law of gravity in some way abuses our right to fly and we will therefore negate it or change it. It operates whether we like it or not. We can, on the other hand, ignore it. We could step off a tall building in ignorance of gravity, due to the influence of drugs, as an act of defiance, or with a wish to harm ourselves. No matter what the motivation, natural law inevitably acts and the consequences follow. Natural laws are non-negotiable and ignorance is no excuse. Disobedience or defiance is an illusion often accompanied by rationalization, bravado or self-aggrandizement.

Although we are not free to choose whether or not natural laws will act, paradoxically, we do find freedom through obedience to them. It is by knowing and following natural law that we come to master it. To illustrate, if we understand and follow the laws of electricity, we can safely create a plethora of modern inventions and do things that were previously impossible. If we don't follow those laws, we will electrocute ourselves. At various levels, there is a constant interplay of natural laws with each other. For example, we can use the laws of aerodynamics to enable a plane to fly thus providing freedom of movement. A plane flying, of course, does not negate the law of gravity, it just means that it is interacting with other laws providing freedom to access a whole new range of possibilities.

The laws governing living systems that underpin ecology and health may be harder to define and their effects slower to appreciate, but there is not too much debate about their existence. In fact, there is an increasing appreciation that we need to define and obey them. The looming environmental crisis has largely come about through the disobedience, disregard and/or the total non-comprehension of the laws of ecology. Things such as the long-term unbridled use of fossil fuels, pollution of water and air, the indiscriminate use of toxic chemicals, and the selfish disregard for the wellbeing of other species are just a few examples from the extensive catalogue of humanity's crimes against the environment. So free we seemed in our greedy and indiscriminate use of resources, but how fettered we now are by the penalties we increasingly pay like global warming. We are starting to see the collapse of ecosystems like the Great Barrier Reef in Australia.[26] We are literally burning up the lungs of the planet with the widespread clearing of rainforests in the Amazon and Indonesia, largely for palm oil as described in the documentary *The Burning Season*.[27] All of this is being driven by the insatiable appetite of a 'free market' interested in profit and with no responsibility for its actions. This is the unregulated appetitive element of humanity displayed on a large scale.

We can ignore Commoner's first law — everything is connected to everything else — but why be surprised when the food chains collapse because we have overfished the oceans or have wiped out bees. We can ignore law two — everything has to go somewhere — and dump plastic waste in the rivers and oceans, but why be surprised when that same plastic finds its way into the food chain, kills wildlife, disrupts endocrine systems, and accumulates in massive oceanic garbage dumps. We can ignore law three — nature knows best — and think humans know best by diverting rivers and irrigating areas of land unused to large amounts of water, but why be surprised when the river system collapses and the land becomes infertile through rising salinity levels.[28] We can ignore law four — there is no such thing as a free lunch — and relentlessly burn fossil fuels only to find that they are finite and we have converted them into air pollution and greenhouse gases. Turning the environmental crisis around is going to take no small amount of time, resources and effort. Natural laws will not be denied and, sooner or later, we have to learn to acknowledge and surrender to them or suffer the consequences.

Take another example of the so-called 'mad cow disease', otherwise known as bovine spongiform encephalopathy or BSE. It was caused by some not-so-smart scientists thinking it would be a good idea to feed herbivorous cattle with the remains of other cattle (meat and bone meal). It might have seemed to make economic sense but surely it goes against the law of nature. This allowed the BSE infection to spread with massive costs and ramifications that will take decades to work their way through.

Consider the laws related to sleep. Humans are not naturally nocturnal. We are meant to be awake during the day and asleep at night. These days, in the name of freedom, we have all-night shopping, all-night dining, all-night television, all-night clubs, and all-night access to the Internet and social media. Although we seem to have the world at our fingertips 24/7, the negative health effects of chronically disrupted sleep patterns are significant. They include increased risk of hypertension, diabetes, obesity, depression, heart attack, stroke and cancer.[29,30] Shift workers are particularly at risk of poor health. To compensate there is an endless stream of caffeine to wake us up and sleeping medications to settle us down. These days, most children are left free to access electronic media as much as they wish, including in the bedroom at night. Being left free by parents to do what they want, however, comes at a cost with increased activity online at night being associated with worse sleep and poorer mental health.[31,32] And then we think that prescribing antidepressants is going to solve the problem. How can we be so smart and so stupid at the same time?

It may be a moral precept, but is it also a law of human nature to be authentic and truthful? Well, perhaps it is considering that a lie detector is merely a machine measuring the stress response. Although common, telling lies and being inauthentic is stressful and inconsistent with what feels natural and healthy. Being authentic and truthful, on the other hand, is far simpler, more relaxing and also good for relationships, which may be one of the reasons that going to confession, whether it is in a church or on a psychologist's couch, is generally associated with feeling better. That a psychopath can lie and not experience stress is more a sign of neuropathology rather than a sign that the natural law for truthfulness and authenticity don't apply.[33]

Is it also a law of human nature to be compassionate and kind to others? How could we tell? If we ignore compassion then we have to take what comes with it. As the Dalai Lama says in the book, *The Art of Happiness*:,'If you want others to be happy, practise compassion. If you want to be happy, practise compassion.'[34]

We could look at historical precedents or come up with a series of complex sociological arguments on the effect cruelty has on society, but it might be more useful to reflect on where cruelty originates from and the effect cruelty has on oneself. If we care to look, we might notice that cruelty arises from our own emotional pain and flourishes when we are not really paying attention to our actions. Like rubbing an eye with grit in it, cruelty and insensitivity provide some short-term satisfaction, but are more painful in the long-term because the problem returns worse than before. Cruelty doesn't leave us feeling relaxed and at peace. The effect of compassion, on the other hand, is quite the opposite. So, maybe compassion is a natural law governing human behaviour unless our individual nature has become so distorted by things such as an abusive upbringing, perverted ideology or negative social influences such as happened in apartheid South Africa or Nazi Germany. Despite the modern ideology of 'survival of the fittest' being a justification for why humans can and should be predatory and brutish with each other, maybe compassion and co-operation are actually far more integral to our survival. Maybe the golden rule of loving or treating your neighbour as yourself is not aspirational but merely a statement of fact. In this interconnected world, our neighbour is an extension of ourselves. We are all one.

Consider laws governing the mind. Is it good to leave the mind free to go wherever it has a whim to go, or is it a natural law of the human mind to be mindful? Well, considering that, among other things, being unmindful as in distracted, inattentive and disengaged — otherwise known as default mode — is associated with higher rates of depression and anxiety,[35,36] poor immunity,[37] ADHD, lack of empathy,[38] errors, declining memory, and more rapid ageing of the brain[39] and genes,[40] one would have to say that there is nothing particularly natural about living a distracted life, unless by 'natural' we mean it has become 'second nature' as in 'habitual'. Mindfulness, although not common these days, has the opposite of the abovementioned effects, so perhaps there is something intrinsically right and natural about it. Mindfulness, however, is a mental discipline and we need that discipline in order to be free of the problems that otherwise come with distraction. That is, freedom comes through mental discipline and obeying the law.

If there are laws of human nature and we ignore them then, like jumping off that tall building, we might enjoy a temporary illusion of freedom on the way down, but the effects will be both inevitable and painful. To know what such laws are and to act consistently with them requires awareness and that we use conscience (from 'con' to connect or join, and 'science' Latin for knowledge). Conscience is connecting with our inner knowledge, but if we ignore there is discord and disease within and without.

Equality versus sameness

One thing commonly equated with freedom these days is equality. There are many examples of injustice and inequality, like racism, which have been corrected, at least to some extent. But is it a natural law that all people are equal? Yes and no, depending on what you are referring to and how you define equality. Equality and sameness are two different things. On one level, we are all different and not the same, but on a deeper more essential level we are all equal. We potentially run into problems if we confuse those two things. There is inherent danger in wrongly ascribing equality to things that are not equal and inequality to things that are equal.

To illustrate, people have different physical attributes, abilities, life situations and characters, so in that sense we are all individual and not equal. But on the level of an inherent right to exist, to respect, to be judged on merit, to be protected under the law or to opportunity, then all people are equal despite differences. Skin colour, for example, might be relevant in terms of who is physically better suited to living in a sunny, equatorial environment, but it wouldn't be relevant in deciding who is more worthwhile, intelligent or meritorious. The former is just a biological fact and the latter is racism.

Economically speaking, it may be consistent with natural law that people should be financially rewarded on the basis of merit and effort, but in a capitalist society there is the risk of greed leaving some people unjustly disenfranchised. The law of compassion would say that everyone in need, regardless of their capacity, should also be cared for in a civilized society. On the other hand, a communist system treating everyone as equal potentially ignores individual merit and hard work thus breeding apathy and resentment.

> **The inherent vice of capitalism is the unequal sharing of the blessings. The inherent blessing of socialism is the equal sharing of misery.**
>
> *Winston Churchill*[41]

Equality of the sexes

What about the natural relationship between men and women and the equality of the sexes? Is gender, as some would suggest, just socially engineered or conditioned and we are free to decide gender roles any way we like, despite the fact that no other species on the planet does things that way? Some might contend that other animals are prisoners of their biology but humans don't have to be. Indeed, we can resist our biology, but should we? Is there something inherently natural, different and complementary about men and women that should be both celebrated and encouraged in society? Yes, men and women are, or should be, equal in the sense of status and respect, but does that mean they are the same? Male and female biology is different, their brains have differences, and their anatomy is different. Even their stress responses are different with men being more primed for 'fight or flight' and women more for nurturing through the 'tend and befriend' response.[42] Although those differences predispose each gender to have different strengths, capacities and dispositions, and to excel in different roles, this is not to say that a man can't nurture or a woman can't provide for the family or fight. Men, by and large, are physically stronger and have more aggression, largely because of testosterone, and are therefore better adapted to a protector role. That doesn't mean that women can't play the protector role. Equally, women, by and large, have a greater capacity to nurture, largely because of oxytocin and oestrogen, but that doesn't mean that men can't also nurture. There are undoubtedly times when women may need to be aggressive and men may need to nurture. Some women are stronger than some men, and some men are more nurturing than some women, but does that mean that we, as a society, can and should ignore our biology seeing it as irrelevant, arbitrary or a limitation on our freedom? Is the current trend of seeing gender as a matter of individual choice not promoting freedom but merely imposing an ideologically driven agenda on society? If so, what will the cost be? It is hard to say because that sociological experiment has never been done before, but within the next generation or two we will probably find out.

It is as if the pendulum has swung from women at one time having too little choice and being defined by a stereotype, to a situation now where we almost deny gender altogether. Has society been freed from one set of oppressive social conventions to now be constrained socially, legally and politically to a new ideology that denies biology? Is the desire of many women for independence and not wanting men to be protectors an ideological trap that leaves men confused and women vulnerable? Is it better to create an ideological war between the sexes or do we need co-operation and complementarity? It would be hard to conceive that those natural gender differences did not have a rhyme and reason to be there, but acknowledging those differences flies in the face of modern gender equality ideology stating that gender differences are merely socially imposed. In that view even our DNA is irrelevant, but how free from our biology are we really? It is interesting to note that many advocates for gender equality are very selective in the way it is done. For example, in sport there are loud cries for equal recognition and prize money for male and female athletes, but the same advocates stop short of wanting real equality because if men and women openly competed against each other in most sports then women wouldn't even qualify for the main draw of tournaments, or make it onto the Olympic team, let alone making it to the finals. Men and women are equal in some ways, but they are not the same and perhaps those differences need to be recognized and fostered.

Does the fact that men and women can play any role mean that they should? Does the fact that men and women are naturally suited for particular roles mean that they must only be restricted to those roles? Perhaps there was a time when those roles were too strictly adhered to, but can we go too far in rejecting them? Should we embrace gender differences rather than reject them? Can differences be embraced and yet still retain the flexibility for individual men and women to use and express their individual strengths?

Crimes against ourselves

There are laws against committing crimes against others, but do we have freedom to do anything we like to ourselves even if that action leads to harm? How much can and should we be a law unto ourselves? Well, that could be considered on a number of levels based mainly on the extent of the resulting harm and our level of competence, our capacity to make a rational choice. For example, we don't give children freedom to choose whether to go to school or not because they wouldn't go if it were left up to them, and schooling is seen by society as inherently good despite most children seeing it otherwise. Children are not deemed competent to make decisions on such important matters, so they are sent to school whether they like it or not. There are also laws against minors smoking because they are not deemed mature enough to make that decision. Smoking is addictive, costly and harms health, so increasingly there are laws regulating advertising, especially to minors. There are laws about where you can smoke, as well as financial disincentives like taxing cigarettes and higher life insurance premiums. What initially appears to be the free choice — to smoke —soon becomes a compulsion to continue smoking through addiction. What initially appears to be a limitation on freedom — regulation and disincentives — helps people to remain free of the trap of addiction and the harm they inflict on themselves by taking it up.

Suicide and self-harm

Do we ever really make a free, rational choice to harm ourselves? Is not the choice to take up something harmful like smoking just the result of things like peer pressure, conforming to cultural norms and being deceived by marketing? Surely it goes against our nature to harm ourselves. There are laws against suicide, although they are currently being watered down in many places with some libertarians claiming a person, even with depression, should be allowed to make their own decision about suicide and be assisted by a doctor. But is a depressed person, even though they can speak about it in a clinical and calculating way, really making a free choice to harm themselves? Is the decision really being driven by courage and reason, or by exasperation and hopelessness? Is suicide really liberation? Who really knows what happens after death? And what should be the response of a compassionate community in the face of a desire for self-harm? Is it more compassionate to go with their decision or to support and value their ongoing life? Despite it being characterized as an individual's right to choose, does suicide not also affect others in a very significant way? If we collectively come to a conclusion that a person has a right to suicide, especially to the point that it is normalized as a legitimate way of dealing with misery, then we may find ourselves at the bottom of a very slippery slope in the not too distant future considering the rising rates of depression and self-harm, especially among young people. Is this really a sign of a more liberated society or a society without the wisdom to prevent the problem nor the strength and insight to deal with it?

Organized crime

One of the greatest blights on society is organized crime. Once entrenched, it is very hard to remove as the corruption quietly makes its way into all walks of society. What greater tyranny could there be than a society being ruled by organized crime? The domain of most organized crime rings are things such as drugs, gambling and the sex industry. It preys on the vulnerability of individuals so possibly organized crime begins with the crimes we commit against ourselves. Our vulnerability always seems to be related to us not regulating wisely that little region of the brain that seeks the dopamine sugar-hit of pleasure, which slowly edges us ever closer to the tipping point. The stepwise descent for society seems to begin with us turning a blind eye to such things. Then we tolerate them and accept them as a part of normal life. Then they are not policed. Then regulations limiting their availability are watered down. Then they are legalized. Then they are taxed, and once taxed then they are legitimized. Once legitimized, then they are lobbied for and soon have a seat at the decision-making table of government. The appearance of legitimacy hides the crimes we commit against ourselves and the organized crime groups that make profit from such practices. Soon we are immersed in it and rationalize it is a fact of life. But if we weren't vulnerable in the first place then there wouldn't be a market for organized crime.

Human-made law

Natural laws may be impersonal and universal but human-made laws are particular to the place, society and time. What should be the relationship of human-made law to natural law? If there are no natural laws or objective standards, then it may be reasonable to assert that justice is whatever the law says it is. Or should our laws, as Sir William Blackstone wrote in his classic text, *Commentaries on the Laws of England*, be indelibly entwined with natural law?

> **Law, in its most general and comprehensive sense, signifies a rule of action; and is applied indiscriminately to all kinds of action, whether animate or inanimate, rational or irrational. Thus we say, the laws of motion, of gravitation, of optics, or mechanics, as well as the laws of nature and of nations. And it is that rule of action, which is prescribed by some superior, and which the inferior is bound to obey. Thus when the Supreme Being formed the universe, and created matter out of nothing, He impressed certain principles upon that matter, from which it can never**

> **depart, and without which it would cease to be ... But laws, in their more confined sense, and in which it is our present business to consider them, denote the rules, not of action in general, but of human action or conduct: that is, the precepts by which man, the noblest of all sublunary beings, a creature endowed with both reason and free will, is commanded to make use of those faculties in the general regulation of his behaviour[43,44]**

Whether or not we believe in a Creator may not make a difference as far as Blackstone is concerned. To him the laws of nature are evident however they came into being. Consciousness can observe them, reason can define them, and our will can decide whether or not to obey them. If we acknowledge natural laws then it follows that the laws the community makes through the parliament and judiciary should be consistent with them. There are many examples of human-made laws, which echo the natural laws upon which they are based, such as laws against harming others, stealing, bearing false-witness and breaking contracts. There may also be human-made laws that may not be consistent with natural laws. If so, then that is futile, pretentious and dangerous. For example, in the United States, complex laws in the corporate world significantly contributed to economic injustices as outlined in the documentary *The Corporation.*[45] Such convoluted laws obscure natural justice and contributed to an environment in which the GFC could flourish. Oftentimes laws are introduced for good reason, such as the Fourteenth Amendment to the United States Constitution in 1886, one aspect of which viewed corporations as 'persons' having the same rights as human beings. When personal responsibility was unhooked from corporate responsibility, individuals within corporations were less accountable for their actions and decisions, and were protected from litigation. The fact that corporations could readily act without conscience created the corporate environment that brought the GFC about. It is not difficult to see that when legal systems become increasingly complex and convoluted increasing legal loopholes appear, through which many a guilty party has slipped. Natural justice is denied to the communities and workers who have to bear the brunt of the things like the GFC. Many parts of the world like Australia remained relatively free of the impact of the GFC, but they tend to be countries with higher levels of banking regulation and safeguards. The freest and least regulated markets were hit the hardest. Can the sweet nectar of too much economic freedom lead us into an economic trap? Was it really that surprising, or was it inevitable but the timing was unknown?

> **You know, people talk about this being an uncertain time. You know, all time is uncertain. I mean, it was uncertain back in — in 2007, we just didn't know it was uncertain. It was uncertain on September 10th, 2001. It was uncertain on October 18th, 1987, you just didn't know it.**
>
> *Warren Buffett, American business magnate, investor and philanthropist*[46]

What will happen if we don't learn the lessons learned from our recent experiences? Natural laws, being what they are, cannot be unjust. They just are. Only human-made laws can be unjust, but by what measure? If we collectively decide not to follow natural laws, or decide that they are dumb and that humans are smarter than nature, or if we deny that they exist at all, then no doubt we will see where that goes.

Scientific hubris and short-term economic interests often conflict with common sense and the precautionary principle, which leads to the hasty adoption of technologies like genetic engineering in agriculture and medicine. Some experiments include mixing genetic material from different species, which would never normally happen in nature. If we do not have the clarity or collective will to restrict such practices then nature will no doubt give us cause to do it, but by then the genetic genie may be well and truly out of the bottle. Will we open up new genetic windows for hitherto unheard of viruses to jump species? Will we create undesired and unpredictable mutations? Will we ever be able to remove these from the genome again? Genetic variants once released into the environment are very difficult, if not impossible, to recall.

It could be said that it is a natural law of human conduct to be governed by reason, not appetite or pleasure, and if we make decisions that go against reason then other laws come into play. Human-made law is there to curb the tendency of humans to act irrationally or harmfully. The guiding principle of the law is not what the person desires but what is reasonable and just. Desire and reason are two different things. They can accord with each other but often they do not. Perhaps now laws pander too much to human desires rather than reason, like liberalizing illicit drug laws or indefinitely extending opening hours for pubs and clubs. The effects may take some time to be fully appreciated but will surely come if such laws are unwise. Desire can, and commonly does, lead to misery, whereas reason is the principle upon which free societies and individuals make decisions and act. Surely it is up to those who are deemed most learned and just in society to determine and interpret the human-made laws that the rest of us must follow. If the people making those laws are far from the most learned and just then surely that does not auger well. The question therefore has to be asked, how did they get into that position of authority in the first place? Who elected them? That leads us to an investigation into democracy, our next port of call.

SOME THINGS TO REFLECT ON:

- What are your views on natural laws?
- How do those views influence your decisions and actions?
- Are there any things you would think or do differently if you were more conscious of the role of natural laws?

SOME THINGS TO PRACTISE:

- Use your physical, mental and emotional state as a barometer of when your thoughts and actions may be in accord with your nature or against it.
- Aim to live daily life with a greater sense of balance and moderation.
- Look at some contemporary issues from a perspective of natural law and from a perspective without natural law. What are the implications for each view?

CHAPTER 7

LIBERTÉ, EGALITÉ ET FRATERNITÉ — THE POLITICS OF FREEDOM

The well-known philosopher Alfred North Whitehead wrote 'The safest general characterization of the European philosophical tradition is that it consists of a series of footnotes to Plato.'[1] Plato had much to say about freedom and sound government, so in this chapter our pursuit of freedom will expand on Plato's conception of the psyche and the forms of government based upon it. It would be easy to dismiss his views as an historical anachronism except for the fact that his description of human nature has far too many parallels in modern psychology and neuroscience to be ignored. These will be explored in the next chapter.

Pallas and the Centaur

Plato's language is strong in places and his message will no doubt offend modern sensibilities especially when he gives his unflattering description of democracy, but in as much as we are able, we should discern the underlying message rather than dismissing it without reflection. Plato describes the underlying philosophy and motivation of what governs us as individuals and then the corresponding form of government. This was symbolized in a painting by one of the Renaissance's most famous artists, Sandro Botticelli. One of his most iconic paintings, *Pallas and the Centaur*, represents a beautiful and graceful woman, Pallas Athena, holding a staff. She is the goddess of wisdom, justice and all things civilized, and has an expansive view as her backdrop. Beside her is a centaur, half horse and half man. He is carrying arrows and has solid rock as his backdrop. Centaurs are noted for their animal-like, savage and appetitive nature. Pallas looks to be subduing the centaur by grabbing the hair on top of his head. In this painting, Botticelli represents key themes from Plato's philosophy of the human psyche and the implications for natural and healthy government. Pallas Athena, as the goddess of wisdom, represents the highest aspect. The centaur represents the middle and lower aspects. Botticelli depicts their proper relationship according to Plato with Pallas subduing or taming the potentially savage and avaricious centaur. In modern psychology we use the word 'regulate' — as in emotional regulation or appetite regulation — to depict the ability of a person to rightly manage the various competing aspects of their nature.

Plato's five forms of government

Largely through his book *The Republic*, Plato describes three aspects to the human psyche vying with each other for governance whether of the individual or of the society. The highest aspect is wisdom or reason, the middle aspect is the emotive element, and the lower aspect is appetitive. Plato aligned these different aspects of the psyche with various forms of government. Democracy, largely ruled by the appetitive element, was not, according to Plato and his teacher Socrates, the highest of the five forms of government he described. In fact, it was second from last. The five forms of government described by Plato are:

1. **Aristocracy — from the Greek 'aristo', meaning government of 'the best' in virtue and wisdom (ruled by reason).**
2. **Timocracy — from 'timē' meaning the government of 'honour' (ruled by the emotive aspect).**

3. **Oligarchy — from 'oligoi' meaning 'few', the government of the small, wealthiest class (ruled by a moderate expression of the appetitive element).**
4. **Democracy — from 'demos' meaning government of 'the people' (ruled by an immoderate appetitive element).**
5. **Tyranny — government of the tyrant with 'tyrannos' meaning master (lawless, ruthless and self-serving).**

In Chapter 5 there was a brief discussion of the three aspects of the human psyche as described by Plato. He deduced their presence and characteristics by observing himself and also how people lived and thought collectively as a state (society). For him, the state and its various forms of government were just human nature writ large, and government was a reflection of these three aspects. It is important to remember that all these aspects are present in us all, male and female alike, and in every society. It is just the mix of them that varies.

The natural progression through these forms of government begins with a humble, self-governing community as the most innocent form where people have simple tastes and rule themselves naturally and moderately. It is like a golden age of innocence. The plot, however, thickens with the rise of greed and people desiring to own other people's land and possessions. Then the community needs to organize, enlarge and defend itself. It is not long before the state is formed and it needs a government higher than self-government. The purest and highest form of government, aristocracy, thus comes into being. All is well for some time, but eventually things run down in a descending order over time through timocracy, oligarchy and democracy before the final decline into the lowest form of government, tyranny.

Aristocracy

According to Plato, an aristocracy is the government of the wisest, most reasonable and just people in the state. Aristocracy, as we have come to know the term these days, means royalty, that is the government of the wealthiest, but in Plato's hierarchy this is an oligarchy, not an aristocracy.

The hallmark of a wise man or woman is that they are ruled by the highest aspect of the soul, the reasonable element, with which they are wise. As such, they are not easily swayed by greed, pleasure or pain when they run counter to the dictates of reason. Therefore, the wise man or woman is the hardest to corrupt and, being rare, they are also the smallest class in a society. Their wisdom and virtue are not an appearance only, for their conduct has long been fostered in their education, tried in the fire of temptation and adversity, and their selfless motivation proved. The hallmarks of true wisdom include virtues like justice, moderation, courage, humility, self-sacrifice and compassion. One other key point is that the wise live a simple, humble lifestyle and are not ambitious for power, wealth or position. They only accept office as a duty and to protect the community from being governed by lesser rulers but do not crave personal reward and recognition.

The government that is led by the wisest in the community is aristocratic and it will not be easily swayed by greed, pleasure or pain when it is counter to what is just, reasonable and right. The aristocratic individual and state are unified, healthy, just and free, and remain free as long as this natural order is followed. The emotive and appetitive elements are present but are not indulged any more or less than is healthy and necessary. Each aspect of the soul is in its proper place and playing its proper part. The highest aspect of the soul, reason, is only present in human beings. Animals, even the higher ones, by and large, only display the two lower elements as represented by the centaur.

Many commentators on Plato such as Karl Popper[2] criticize his conception of aristocracy as the highest form of government because they assume that if government is put in the hands of a small ruling class then it is by nature a totalitarian dictatorship resulting in comparisons with the tyranny of Nazi Germany. This is a misrepresentation of what Plato advocated. Plato's aristocracy and tyranny are ruled by totally different people and totally different aspects of human nature. The issue is not whether the government is in the hands of a small ruling class but rather whether it is ruled by reason and wisdom. If it is ruled by wisdom then it is an aristocracy. If the government is ruled by self-serving greed and hatred then it is a tyranny made all the worse by the veneer of wisdom and benevolence that such a tyrannical ruler often adorns themselves in. Many a greedy and ambitious potential ruler has, like a wolf in sheep's clothing, donned the appearance of being benevolent and wise and so fooled a population that are not really awake. Their sweet-sounding rhetoric has drawn many an unquestioning society into a deep and bitter trap.

Timocracy

Over time, the highest ruling principle becomes mixed and eventually the middle aspect of the soul, the emotive element, rises up and vies for authority with the reasoning element. This emotive element is that with which we are courageous and high spirited. True courage is where we know the potential for danger but stand firm regardless. False valour is where we rashly proceed headlong into danger without comprehension. Humans display this emotive quality as do animals especially the fiercer varieties. It is the element with which we go to battle, seek honour and stand firm in the face of adversity. Someone who has the 'courage of their convictions' has the strength to do what they need to do when they need to do it. A government governed by the timocratic principle would be austere, indomitable and strong militarily where honour and valour are highly revered. In Socrates' time, Sparta was an example of such a government. Such a society or individual can be aggressive and war-like when the emotive element is not being regulated by reason. The rightful job of the emotive element is to support the wise decisions made by reason. Like a faithful guard dog, it is there to obey and protect its master. But when the emotive element waxes too strongly at the expense of the moderating or regulating effect of reason it has the potential to turn to anger, ambition and even violence at which time, like a dog that has turned on its master, it is dangerous for the person themselves as well as those around them.

Oligarchy

The next and lowest aspect governing the soul is the appetitive element which, over time, vies for governance with the emotive element. It is materially acquisitive and values pleasure, money and possessions. According to Plato, it was the largest or most vocal part of the soul and represents the largest class in a community. A person with an oligarchic nature aspires to make money and acquire possessions. Merchants, bankers and the like would be examples of people with a strong oligarchic or acquisitive disposition. Because of their desire to make, maintain and extend their wealth, such people are not spendthrift, at least not initially. They invest well and use intelligence to guide business decisions. Desire governs and reason is there to do its bidding, not the other way round as is the case in an aristocracy.

An oligarchic government and society are of a similar nature. They are ruled by the few wealthiest people in the society. Such a society worships wealth and seeks to accumulate more. What we call aristocracies from centuries ago — a wealthy, landed ruling class or royalty bent on extending wealth — are examples of oligarchies. The strong desire of a country like the United States to work hard and acquire wealth since its foundation would exemplify a strong oligarchic nature. Intelligence and emotional strength are there, but they are also largely serving the furtherance of economic prosperity.

Over time, such is its nature, this acquisitive, appetitive element waxes more and more strongly. The ruling class becomes complacent, greedy, corrupt, desirous of luxury, and less concerned with the wellbeing of the working people upon whom their wealth is built. This reaches a point where the working class will not bear the burden any longer and they rise up against the wealthy ruling class. The French Revolution is a classic example of such an event. It is out of such fertile ground that democracy arises — *'liberté, egalité et fraternité'* — liberty, equality and brotherhood.

Democracy

Democracy, having thrown off the shackles of the oppressive oligarchic masters, bursts with apparent freedom. Here the ruling element of the soul is the appetitive element but it is less and less moderated by reason or virtue. Any desire is now as good as any other. By and large, happiness is interpreted as pleasure. Freedom, whether of the community or individual, is interpreted as having free rein to satisfy the strongest or most vocal desire of the moment. In fact, moderation and virtue are seen as rather prudish and frowned upon in a democracy the more it becomes dominated by desire. As Plato writes in *The Republic:*

> **If any one says to him (the democratic person) that some pleasures are the satisfactions of good and noble desires, and others of evil desires, and that he ought to use and honour some and chastise and master the others, whenever this is repeated to him he shakes his head and says that they are all alike, and that one is as good as another ... He lives from day to day indulging the appetite of the hour; and sometimes he is lapped in drink and strains of the flute; then he becomes a water-drinker, and tries to get thin; then he takes a turn at gymnastics; sometimes idling and neglecting everything, then once more living the life of a philosopher; often he is busy with politics, and starts to his feet and says and does whatever comes into his head; and, if he is emulous of any one who is a warrior, off he is in that direction, or of men of business, once more in that. His life has neither law nor order; and this distracted existence he terms joy and bliss and freedom; and so he goes on.** [3]

The main measuring stick of what is right or wrong in a democracy is what the majority of people desire most ardently, whether or not it is wise, natural or right. Because the desires are so many and diverse, it is hard for a democracy to act with common purpose due to opposing motivations and interests pulling in competing directions.

With desire ruling, and with reason and virtue bowing to their ruler, overindulgence and overspending become common and debt grows. Because happiness is not the same as pleasure, but people pursue it as if it were, increasing numbers of people ultimately find the opposite of the happiness and wellbeing they seek. The person driven by desire without the moderating effect of reason is at risk of being taken advantage of by unscrupulous people wishing to profit from their vulnerability. They are lured into excessive debt, waste their wealth on meaningless indulgences, and are vulnerable to gambling and addiction all in the name of freedom. Soon that unfettered freedom becomes a kind of inner slavery. Chaos, misery and disorder soon foment within individuals and society.

This is the fertile ground from which the tyrant appears. Part of this process is the breakdown of natural order and roles, and the rise of equality among equals and unequals alike; parents and their children; the wise and the unwise; men and women; teachers and students; humans and animals.

> **Father grows accustomed to descend to the level of his sons and to fear them, and the son is on a level with his father, he having no respect or reverence for either of his parents; and this is his freedom, and metic (wise person) is equal with the citizen and the citizen with the metic, and the stranger is quite as good as either ... And these are not the only evils, there are several lesser ones. In such a state of society the master (teacher) fears and flatters his scholars (students), and the scholars despise their masters and tutors; young and old are all alike; and the young man is on a level with the old, and is ready to compete with him in word or deed; and old men condescend to the young and are full of pleasantry and gaiety; they are loath to be thought morose and authoritative, and therefore they adopt the manners of the young ... Nor must I forget to tell of the liberty and equality of the two sexes in relation to each other ... And I must add ... how much greater is the liberty which the animals who are under the dominion of man have in a democracy than in any other State. ... And all things are just ready to burst with liberty.** [4]

Plato could almost be describing the modern day. So accustomed to unfettered liberty do the citizens become that any restriction to it is seen as a threat and vigorously, if not violently, attacked. The originally prudent appetitive rule of the oligarchy over time becomes the undiscerning appetitive rule of the democracy.

> See how sensitive the citizens become; they chafe impatiently at the least touch of authority and at length ... they cease to care even for the laws, written or unwritten; they will have no one over them ... Such, my friend is the fair and glorious beginning out of which springs tyranny ... The ruin of oligarchy is the ruin of democracy; the same disease magnified and intensified by liberty overmasters democracy, the truth being that the excessive increase of anything often causes a reaction in the opposite direction ... The excess of liberty, whether in States or individuals, seems only to pass into excess of slavery ... and so tyranny naturally arises out of democracy, and the most aggravated form of slavery out of the most extreme form of liberty.[5]

Like a pendulum that swings too far towards a false form of freedom, it eventually swings to the opposite extreme. The decline of the German democracy in the 1930s into the madness and tyranny that was Nazism may well be an example of this decline. Considering the current political instability and polarization of political and social discourse of so many democracies around the world, considering social problems, addiction and escalating debt, we may increasingly see the rise of other 'strong leaders' in the not too distant future. We should all watch with interest because this may be the sign of things to come.

Tyranny

If oligarchy symbolizes the landing of the insect on the lip of the pitfall plant, and democracy represents the unwary insect going deeper inside the chamber following the sweet nectar, then tyranny represents the inevitable fall into the trap. From the disorder and imbalance of a democracy in decline comes pain and suffering on many levels. People look for a strong leader, a protector, someone who can deliver them from the gathering but self-made miseries. If care is not taken, the people can readily elect someone who appears to be wise or have their interests at heart but really only has personal ambitions for power and dominance.

> **The people have always some champion whom they set over them and nurse into greatness ... This and no other is the root from which a tyrant springs; when he first appears above ground he is a protector.**[6]

Thus arises the tyrant and with him (or her) the state of slavery and servitude. The tyrant is a slave to their own desires and anger, and the people are slaves to the tyrant. The tyrant is in many ways a reflection of, or gives expression to, the dominant mentality of the people. From the perspective of wisdom, desire is blind. If the people were governed by other principles then they would see through any potential tyrant and not elect them to power. But the people are blind and see what they want to see, or what they are fooled into believing.

The society becomes even more miserable under the tyrant but over time, for a variety of reasons, it becomes increasingly difficult to remove the tyrant from power. The tyrant diverts the people's gaze from looking within and finds enemies outside the society to blame for the society's internal problems. The tyrant rules alongside people who pander to their wishes. He or she also recruits an extensive bodyguard for personal protection. Over time, there is no crime that the tyrant will not turn to in order to maintain power and satisfy their hatred and greed.

> **As the saying is, the people who would escape the smoke which is the slavery of freemen, has fallen into the fire which is the tyranny of slaves. Thus liberty, getting out of all order and reason, passes into the harshest and bitterest form of slavery.**[7]

Interestingly, despite the superficial appearance of freedom, according to Plato, the tyrant is the most wretched and miserable of people, and the society living under a tyranny is the most wretched and miserable of societies. Each are ruled by the lowest aspects of human nature, and neither has any true freedom at all. They are trapped but did not see the trap coming until it was too late.

> **The best and justest is also the happiest, and that this is he who is the most royal man and king over himself; and that the worst and most unjust man is also the most miserable, and that this is he who being the greatest tyrant of himself is also the greatest tyrant of his State.[8]**

Is the decline of democracy inevitable?

To Plato, like birth and death, this decline of the state is a natural, cyclical process. Things are born, then run down and have to be rebuilt again. No doubt, in the fullness of history, there are small cycles within larger ones. Within a society predominantly governed by one aspect of human nature there may be individuals who are governed by other aspects. You could have a wise person living in a tyrannical society, but the chances are they would be imprisoned or put to death. You could have a greedy person living within a society of the wise.

The remedy to society's ills, according to Plato, is wisdom. The lover of wisdom is the true philosopher, although Plato might compare much modern academic philosophy to sophistry, or just the love of thinking too much, not wisdom. His belief, however, that people should rule their lives by wisdom gives rise to this famous quote.

> **Until philosophers are kings, or the kings and princes of this world have the spirit and power of philosophy, and political greatness and wisdom meet in one, and those commoner natures who pursue either to the exclusion of the other are**

> **compelled to stand aside, cities will never have rest from their evils — no, nor the human race, as I believe — and then only will this our State have a possibility of life and behold the light of day.**[9]

Parallels with modern democracy

What parallels are there between contemporary times and Plato's description of democracy as described in *The Republic*? Plato has an uncanny way of describing political events that have contemporary parallels, like an astute political observer commenting on recent history. For example, his description of the shift from oligarchy to democracy parallels the great revolutions in Britain, the United States and France of the seventeenth to nineteenth centuries. Then there is his description of tyranny, which bears an uncanny resemblance to the descent into brutality and madness that we associate with Hitler's Nazi Germany. He rose to power as a 'protector'.

Democracy no doubt looks like the best form of government to modern eyes because it is only compared to degraded oligarchies or tyrannies, both of which look a lot worse than democracy lacking, as they are, in freedom and fairness.

Governments of the wise, no doubt, are few and far between although it would be true to say that occasionally wise and virtuous people such as Mahatma Gandhi, Nelson Mandela or Aung San Suu Kyi have come to power through a democratic process. There must have been just enough wisdom among the people at that time to recognize and elect such leaders, although there were clearly lower aspects of human nature at play in those countries because of the injustices that ruled there. These leaders had much to contend with including imprisonment, attempted assassination, resistance, prejudice and injustice. Such wise leaders prefer non-violence, uplift and inspire, appeal to reason, model a noble sense of self, and seek unity. A tyrant in waiting, however, will win the people by appealing to aggression, disillusionment and a lower sense of self, and they soon breed division.

Plato foreshadows the waxing nature of freedom and equality in modern democracies. Examples include the democratization of wisdom as public opinion rules whether or not it leads to wise actions. Opinion polls constantly measure which way the wind of public opinion is blowing. There is the breakdown of respect for authority figures including parents, elders and teachers. There is mounting personal and national debt around the world with corruption in banking and financial institutions becoming harder to check. We have political leaders and spin-doctors who do not lead on principle but are the mercurial followers and manipulators of public opinion. We have lobbyists who surreptitiously wield huge amounts of power by influencing political decisions for their vested interests. The modern interpretation of artistic freedom and free speech leads to some rather dubious outcomes. Just about everything that flies under the banner of freedom is viewed as worthy, and anything that flies under the banner of restraint is seen as oppressive. Lastly, we have many and varied 'liberation' movements as democracy dispenses equality without acknowledging or respecting the natural differences that fit people and animals for different roles according to their natural dispositions and abilities.

Running in parallel with the abovementioned issues, and perhaps because of them, many things naturally follow. Plato probably wouldn't be surprised to see the increasing use and normalization of drugs, rising rates of promiscuity, laws facilitating suicide, self-harm and self-mutilation, the rise of aggressive and offensive forms of music and literature, the rise of unhealthy lifestyle, the corruption of religious institutions, the abuse of children, not censoring that which degrades people, and increasing corruption within business and government. Although the term was not used in his day, he would probably see these as the 'normalization of deviance' and as indications of democracy in decline. He may well warn that things will get far worse unless an opposite impulse is provided. Without that then misery, disorder and tyranny are not too far away. The wheels may not have fallen off the 'streetcar named society' just yet, but we are certainly loosening the wheel nuts at a rate of knots.

Whether Plato is just a product of his historical period or whether he is both relevant and prophetic can be debated, but if what he says is right then we will be in for a very bumpy ride in the not too distant future unless we start thinking and doing things very differently. Whether he is a prophet or a historical anachronism only time will tell, but it is likely that if someone such as Plato or Socrates entered the public limelight now in a modern democracy, saying what they said back then, they would be quickly executed or at least have their reputations quickly assassinated, and in a very public way. The oftentimes reactive, vociferous and unreasonable beast that is social media would probably have a field day.

Life in the cave

Plato's famous allegory of the underground cave or den at the beginning of book VII of *The Republic* is where he describes the enslavement and subsequent liberation of the soul. This allegory also finds expression in modern-day movie classics like *The Matrix* trilogy.[10,11] We live in a dark cave chained like prisoners so that we only see the wall of the cave in front of us. There is a fire burning behind the prisoners and objects passing back and forth in front of the fire, but we only observe shadows of the objects endlessly passing in front of us on the wall of the cave. Beyond that, there is an opening to the outside world but to us the expansive, sunlit spiritual world outside the cave doesn't exist. In the cave what we take to be real is merely an illusion, a shadow world. The shadow world is the world of materialism and, to the prisoners, deeper levels of existence do not exist. Such a metaphor has been widely used in classical philosophy and literature, not just by Plato. For example, from the Sufi tradition:

> **For in and out, above, about, below,**
> **'Tis nothing but a Magic Shadow-show,**
> **Play'd in a Box whose Candle is the Sun,**
> **Round which we Phantom Figures come and go.**
>
> *The Rubaiyat of Omar Khayyám*[12]

Rarely, someone in the cave throws off their chains and climbs out of the shadowy world of materialism, up a steep and rugged intellectual (spiritual) ascent. Eventually, they emerge into the light-filled world of truth which equates with 'the good', God or consciousness and is symbolized by the sun. It takes a time for the eyes of the prisoner to adjust to the light of the upper world. Similarly, on descending back into the dark cave to help liberate other prisoners, the eyes are then unaccustomed to the darkness. The liberated soul talks to the prisoners about the world outside the cave but to them it is a non-existent world. The wider perspective of a world outside the den would not be understood by the prisoners who have never experienced it. Their response is not insightful or kind, and they are just as likely to put to death the one leading others to liberty, as the Athenians did with Socrates.

> **This entire allegory you may now append to the previous argument; the prison-house is the world of sight, the light of the fire is the sun, and you will not misapprehend me if you interpret the journey upwards to be the ascent of the soul into the intellectual world according to my poor belief, which, at your desire, I have expressed whether rightly or wrongly God knows. But, whether true or false, my opinion is that in the world of knowledge the idea of good appears last of all, and is seen only with an effort; and, when seen, is also inferred to be the universal author of all things beautiful and right, parent of light and of the lord of light in this visible world, and the immediate source of reason and truth in the intellectual; and that this is the power upon which he who would act rationally, either in public or private life must have his eye fixed.**[13]

It is likely that Plato had his teacher, Socrates, in mind when he wrote this allegory, not only for the fact that he saw him as a liberated soul who could liberate others, but also because he was put to death for doing just that. Plato wrote about his conception of the human psyche or soul nearly 2500 years ago, but there are many interesting parallels not just with modern politics but also with modern neuroscience, and it is to that we will now turn our attention.

SOME THINGS TO REFLECT ON:

- What aspect of your nature tends to rule your decisions and actions — the appetitive, the emotive or the wiser (reasonable) aspect?
- What is the effect of you being ruled by one or other aspect of your nature?
- Are those aspects of your nature generally in harmony or in conflict with each other?
- How can you bring those aspects of your nature into greater harmony?
- Is your view of yourself and the world essentially materialistic or is there something beyond the physical?

SOME THINGS TO PRACTISE:

- Practise following the dictates of reason when it arises and see what comes of it.
- Cultivate non-attachment to emotional reactions and appetites to enhance the ability to regulate rather than suppress them.
- Observe the predominant ruling motivations in the world around you and consider where they will lead if they continue to become accentuated.

CHAPTER 8

THE SCIENCE OF FREEDOM

One thing marking the modern age from previous historical periods is the rise of science and technology. Indeed, through science and technology many things are possible now that would have been viewed as miracles just a few generations ago. But so worshipful of science has society become these days that it has almost become a new religion in itself. It has its prophets, prophesies, high priests, monasteries of higher learning, miracles, ancient relics, shrines and places of worship. Then there is the blind faith entertained by many scientists that science will one day solve all the world's problems (omnipotence), and explain everything (omniscience). That faith would be rather endearing if it were not so scary.

Setting that aside, let's explore a few examples where there is great synergy between wisdom traditions and science.

Science is one form of knowledge

Science comes from the Latin word 'scientia' meaning knowledge. There are many different kinds of knowledge. For example, there is knowledge as a piece of information, like knowing a telephone number or what is the approximate population of a country. Then there is the knowledge about the physical world and its laws, which is what science aims at elucidating and technology aims at mastering. Then there is knowledge as wisdom. A person could know a lot about science and technology but not be wise, compassionate, just or ethical, but a person could not be called wise without these qualities.

Etymologically, wisdom is traced back through words like 'wis', 'wit' and 'weid',[1] but originally comes from the Sanskrit word 'vid',[2] which is related to words like 'veda', and means spiritual knowledge. Wisdom has an enduring quality about it in that it doesn't change because it is knowledge about things that don't change. It is metaphysical in that it looks beyond the surface to see what lies behind the physical world and its phenomena. Mostly science doesn't do that as most scientists take a materialist view of the universe. Wisdom is universal and holistic and can be derived from intuition as well as empirical experience. Truly great scientists, like Einstein, were also intuitive.

> **Albert Einstein called the intuitive or metaphoric mind a sacred gift. He added that the rational mind was a faithful servant. It is paradoxical that in the context of modern life we have begun to worship the servant and defile the divine.[3]**
>
> *Bob Samples, from* Metaphoric Mind: A celebration of creative consciousness

> **I believe in intuition and inspiration. Imagination is more important than knowledge. For knowledge is limited, whereas imagination embraces the entire world, stimulating progress, giving birth to evolution. It is, strictly speaking, a real factor in scientific research.[4]**
>
> *Albert Einstein,* On Cosmic Religion and Other Opinions and Aphorisms

Science, in the hands of a humble genius like an Einstein, is informed by benevolence and a deep respect for nature. To him, it was a form of worship of the spiritual and a source of awe, inspiration and wisdom. In the hands of a lesser scientific mind of dubious motivation, limited insight, disdain for nature and puffed-up arrogance, science can be dangerous. It has the potential to put the means of mass destruction — for example, a thermonuclear warhead, agents of chemical or biological warfare — into the hands of people who consciously mean to harm others or who commit harm inadvertently. It also allows people to cross boundaries, in the name of scientific freedom, that nature would normally not cross, like mixing the DNA from different species. Science and technology, like a gun, are neither good nor bad in themselves, but are good or bad depending on the motivation and insight of the people wielding them. What will be the motivation behind much science if it unhooks itself from long tried and tested ethical and moral codes?

Wisdom and science, when done well, give insights into what lies beneath the surface and both express those insights through their practical application. This chapter will explore some useful insights from science that may inform our understanding of freedom as well as raise questions of concern.

The neuroscience of wellbeing

In the last chapter we explored a little of what Plato had to say about the make-up of the human psyche and its implications for government, whether of the individual or the society. He must have been a very astute observer of human nature because millennia later modern neuroscience has come to very similar conclusions as Plato, although now there is more detail and the names for what he described are different.

In broad terms, there are three main regions of the human brain vying for authority. They bear an uncanny resemblance to Plato's higher (reasoning), middle (emotive) and lower (appetitive) levels of the psyche. They have their own distinct roles although they all interact with each other. From a neuroscience perspective, these three regions are the:

- **prefrontal cortex — relating to higher (executive) functions**
- **limbic system — relating to emotions**
- **mesolimbic reward system — relating to appetites and instincts.**

The most reasonable, sociable, happy, harmonious, healthy and functioning human being has these three regions well integrated with each other. Their natural order is the executive functioning centre regulating, not suppressing, the expression of the other two centres. Executive functions include working memory (the ability to hold and process information), decision-making, self-awareness (the ability to observe one's mind, body and behaviours), self-regulation (the ability to regulate rather than be ruled by emotions), impulse control and appetite regulation. This, on a neurological level, is self-mastery.

The executive functioning area of the brain is far more highly developed in humans than other species, and it is the last area of the brain to fully develop. This happens from late adolescence to early adulthood and occurs more slowly in males than females, which explains a lot about young males, impulsivity and bad behaviour. Upbringing and environment have a major impact on the development of this vitally important area of the brain. For example, the brains of adolescents brought up in hostile and unsupportive environments, especially males, are predisposed to anti-social behaviours in later life because of overstimulation of the brain's stress centre (the amygdala — part of the limbic system important for the stress response) and underdevelopment of the prefrontal cortex.[5] Such people are primed for learning, social, behavioural, physical and mental health problems. An adolescent with excess aggression, particularly a male, has a significantly larger and more reactive amygdala and a less developed prefrontal cortex than those who do not have issues with aggression.[6–8] A child may have had a chaotic upbringing but, unless they learn strategies for self-awareness and self-regulation in adolescence or early adulthood, they will likely find themselves trapped by their own compulsions and emotional reactions later in life, with negative consequences for themselves and those around them. The extent to which this absolves an individual of responsibility for their crimes is vigorously debated. Are we trapped by our neurology, in which case we are not responsible, or are we meant to be masters of our neurology?

Neuroplasticity — as we think, so we become

Our understanding of the brain has gone through a major revolution in the last two decades. It was long taught that, once wired in childhood, the brain did not change apart from losing brain cells as we age. That view sees us as prisoners of our neurology. Now we know that the brain wires and rewires itself right throughout life so we have more scope for change than previously realized. Every time we think, do, say or respond to something, we activate the corresponding neural pathways encouraging them to make further connections and to stimulate new brain cell growth (neurogenesis). Circuits that are not being used get pruned back. This is called neuroplasticity and it can work for or against us. When we cultivate useful thoughts, attitudes and behaviours then they get easier to think and do. The same thing happens with unhelpful thoughts and behaviours. The longer they are engrained then the harder they are to change. We become constrained by those patterns until they become habits or 'second-nature'. One environment in the home, peer-group or school will bring out one aspect of a child's behaviour whereas another environment will bring out other aspects.

Here are some examples of neuroplasticity at work. If we practise compassion through compassion training it gets easier to be compassionate.[9] Borderline personality disorder is generally thought to be unamenable to change, but just three weeks of loving-kindness and compassion meditation increased acceptance of the present-moment experience and led to significant improvements in the severity of borderline symptoms, self-criticism, mindfulness, acceptance and self-kindness.[10] In another study,[11] an intensive multifaceted mindfulness-based intervention for young adults led to substantial and enduring improvements across multiple cognitive and neuroimaging measures, like substantial improvements in physical health, working memory, performance, mood, self-esteem, self-efficacy, mindfulness and life satisfaction. Improvements in mindfulness were associated with changes in the insula, an area of the brain that is very important for regulating appetite, habit and addiction. Improvements were also observed in the executive control network. Furthermore, the precuneus is a brain region that becomes active when experiencing consciousness, wakefulness and self-awareness. It is important for attention, memory retrieval, working memory, conscious perception and visuospatial processing. It is impaired by distraction (default mental activity) and is larger in happy people.[12] Just a six-week mindfulness program was enough to significantly increase the amount of grey matter within the precuneus.[13]

The issue in relation to freedom is that we have more choice and potential to change the way the brain is wired than we realize, but the longer a pattern has gone on and the older we are then the greater the effort and perseverance required to rewire those circuits. The brain wired itself to a significant extent in childhood according to our environment, upbringing and genetic make-up. So to foster freedom within ourselves we need to consciously choose the environments we put ourselves into, the thoughts and attitudes we wish to live by and to practise disciplines like mindfulness. We also foster it in others, especially the next generation, through upbringing and education. Mind you, this is not a new idea.

> **Mind is the Master power that moulds and makes,**
> **And Man is Mind, and evermore he takes**
> **The tool of Thought, and, shaping what he wills,**
> **Brings forth a thousand joys, a thousand ills: —**
> **He thinks in secret, and it comes to pass:**
> **Environment is but his looking-glass.**
>
> *James Allen*[14]

Health and illness

The implications for our ability to self-regulate emotions and appetites are enormous as far as health and wellbeing are concerned. It goes to the heart of lifestyle-related diseases and addictions, which are so much a part of modern life. If ruled by unhealthy emotions and appetites in opposition to the promptings of our executive functioning then physical and mental disharmony, disease and disorder follow as a natural consequence, sooner or later depending on our genetic constitution. The apparent freedom associated with a lack of restraint comes at a heavy cost, one that few are prepared to pay willingly. On the other hand, the apparent restriction of freedom associated with reasonable, healthy restraint or moderation comes with an unexpected bonus, one for which we are increasingly thankful as life goes on.

The development of self-restraint starts early in life. There was a famous series of experiments performed on young children. Scientists put a marshmallow in front of children and then said that they would be leaving the room for a while. The scientist explains that while they are away the child could eat the marshmallow if they want to, but if they have not eaten the marshmallow by the time the scientist returns the child can have another one as well.[15] The scientists found that some children could restrain themselves but others, though they tried, couldn't. What is interesting is that when they followed these children up as young adults they found that those who could restrain themselves as children performed far better on college entrance scores,[16] overall educational attainment,[17] body mass index (BMI),[18] and other capacities like the ability to cope with frustration and stress.[19] In other experiments, a preschool child's attention span-persistence (the ability to stay with a task or form of play for a long period) is strongly associated with later school achievement and college completion.[20] Children who were rated higher on attention span-persistence at age four had nearly 50 per cent greater odds of completing college by age 25. Such is the importance of simple developmental disciplines like self-restraint and maintaining attention. But these days, in the name of freedom and self-expression, it is more common to see a lack of self-restraint and shortening attention spans.

Paradoxically, the short-term happiness that comes with no restraint leads to a long-term burden, and the short-term unhappiness that comes with restraint leads to a long-term wellbeing as illustrated by one population study[21] on people aged 35–65 years. It looked at the eight-year reduction in the relative risk of developing major chronic diseases like cardiovascular disease, diabetes and cancer associated with four healthy lifestyle factors. These were never smoking, having a BMI of less than 30, having 3.5 hours per week or more of physical activity, and healthy dietary principles (regular intake of fruits, vegetables and wholegrain bread, and low meat consumption). The risk for developing a chronic disease decreased as the number of healthy factors increased. If a person had all four factors at baseline they had an overall 78 per cent lower risk of illness (diabetes, 93 per cent lower risk; myocardial infarction, 81 per cent; stroke, 50 per cent; cancer, 36 per cent) than participants without a healthy factor. Another study followed men[22] aged 45–59 years over a 30-year period and identified five healthy behaviours as being integral to having the best chance of leading a disease-free lifestyle:

1. **Not smoking or being ex-smokers.**
2. **BMI: 18 to 25 kg/m^2.**
3. **Diet that includes three or more portions of fruit and/or vegetables a day together with fewer than 30 per cent of calories from fat.**
4. **Physical activity, including 'vigorous' exercise described as a regular habit.**
5. **Three or fewer standard alcoholic drinks per day.**

Men who followed four or five of these healthy behaviours had half the risk for diabetes and vascular disease and a delay in vascular disease events up to twelve years. They also had a one-third reduced risk of any cancer, a 60 per cent reduction in dying from any cause and a two-thirds lower risk of dementia.

Lifestyle-related problems are only going to get worse if we keep on our current unhealthy trajectory as illustrated by our increasing waistlines. Across the world, the prevalence of obesity has increased in men from 3.2 per cent in 1975 to 10.8 per cent in 2014, and from 6.4 per cent to 14.9 per cent in women,[23] but in some countries like those in Polynesia more than half the population are obese. The cost, socially, economically and medically, will be felt for generations to come.

Restraint versus regulation

Our inability to reasonably restrain ourselves comes at an increasingly heavy cost as time goes on. Reasonable restraint, however, should not be confused with a life of deprivation. It is not about suppression but is more about knowing when to stop and being able to stop rather than being compelled by unhealthy impulses and habit.

The problem with restraint — as in suppression — is that it is not so easy. Commonly there is a gap between what we know is good for us and what we do. We commonly know something is good for us but we don't do it, or know something is not good for us but we keep doing it anyway. The issue is not just about individual willpower. Bridging that gap between knowledge and action needs to take into account our psychology and social and home environments as well as our neurology and genetics. Considering obesity, if our upbringing regularly exposed us to overly sweet foods and we live in an environment where the desire for those foods is constantly being stimulated, it can create an addiction very similar to that seen in substance abuse.[24] The brain's dopamine-based reward circuits keep craving the sweet reward and the genes that regulate our brain and metabolism switch themselves towards reinforcing that behaviour. Oblivious to what is happening within and around us, we become a genetic, psychological and environmental prisoner to something that is doing us damage. The book *Sweet Poison: Why sugar makes us fat* by David Gillespie[25] goes into this issue in much detail. How sweet the taste, how bitter the trap.

The environment we live in has a strong but subtle influence. It is much harder for an individual to act reasonably and moderately if they are in a social and/or home environment that is constantly pulling them back to old, unhealthy behaviours. People of lower socioeconomic status are targeted by gambling, fast food and alcohol outlets far more than those from higher socioeconomic status, explaining in significant part the inequities in health status between the wealthy and less wealthy members of the community.[26,27] Unregulated advertising and commercial environments leave many of the most vulnerable people in the community even more at risk. Reasonable regulation of advertising and exposure is not about limiting freedom but promoting it by helping people to be free of the manipulation and addiction that comes with a lack of self and community regulation.

Being ADEPT at changing unhealthy habits

Within our own minds we are often at war with ourselves, dragged from one unhealthy desire to another. Enabling strategies empower us to act upon conscience, healthy advice and knowledge, and help to bridge gap between knowledge and action. Enabling strategies can include clarifying motivation, mindfulness skills, stress management, self-awareness, self-efficacy, and fostering the internal locus of control (autonomy). Changing unhealthy habits is not so easy. If we want to be 'adept' at making healthy change in our life then it requires the things summarized in the following acronym, which was developed to help people deal with unhelpful habits.

- **Attention: when not paying attention, we act habitually on automatic pilot. We have to pay attention in order to act in non-habitual ways.**
- **Decision: unless we are motivated to make a clear decision to do things differently, then we just keep reverting to the old behaviour. It has to be our decision, not someone else's.**
- **Effort: it is easy to do things the habitual way and it takes effort to do things the non-habitual way. Unless we are prepared to put in effort we will not change.**
- **Perseverance: we have to persevere again and again until our brain establishes new pathways to support the new behaviour.**
- **Tolerance: changing behaviour is not comfortable. We have to be prepared to tolerate the discomfort that comes with doing something new. As the brain rewires the new behaviour soon becomes more comfortable.**[28]

Epigenetics and freedom from genetic determinism

Like the brain, we also used to think of our genetic make-up in a deterministic way. The view was that our genes are what they are and we are either dealt a good hand at birth or we're not. Now we understand that, although our genes don't change by and large from what we inherited at conception, they do change in terms of their expression. We have been dealt and genetic hand but we have a choice in how we play that hand.[29] Science has now moved beyond genetics and into the age of 'epigenetics'.

A complex chemical network around our chromosomes is in constant interplay between genes, mind, body and environment. This chemical network changes various genetic levers and switches, activating some genes and silencing others. So, although we may have a genetic disposition for a particular illness, that disposition may or may not play out depending on our lifestyle, the way we think and our environment. We have more scope to modify the way our genes express themselves than we have hitherto realized. If we are unconscious of this process and choose poorly then we will likely find ourselves the victims of our genetic risks.

Transgenerational genetics

Once a gene changes its expression then those changes can pass themselves down from generation to generation in what is called the transgenerational effect. To illustrate, data previously gathered from people born in Overkalix, a remote town in northern Sweden, by Lars Bygren in 1890, 1905 and 1920 was re-examined some years later. Byrgen had originally explored whether a grandparent's nutrition when they were children affected their grandchildren's growth and life expectancy two generations later.[30] He looked at the family's access to food during the grandparents' slow growth period and determined whether years of plentiful food had a different effect to years of low food availability. Interestingly, Byrgen found a higher risk of early death and shorter life expectancy in the grandchildren if there was an abundance of food when the paternal grandfather was a 9- to 12-year-old boy. Much of the early death was attributable to metabolic and lifestyle-related diseases like diabetes and heart disease but death from all causes was increased as well. If, on the other hand, food was scarce during a father's slow growth period, then fewer sons died early. This is sometimes called caloric restriction, which has been known for some time to be associated with longer life expectancy,[31–33] but it is important to note that programming genes in response to environment and lifestyle passes down generations.

Another study by Marcus Pembrey called the Avon Longitudinal Study[34] gathered evidence from British children born to approximately 14,000 mothers in the early 1990s. They found that lifestyle factors like smoking had an effect across generations. Of the more than 5000 fathers in the study who either smoked or had been smokers, some had started smoking during the slow growth period before puberty (9 to 12 years of age). The sons of these men were significantly more likely to be overweight (a sign of metabolic problems) at the start of their own slow growth period.

We don't have much choice over many things like what our grandparents did when they were children, but we should be aware that the choices we make now for ourselves not only affect ourselves for better or for worse, but will also impact generations yet to come. Our excesses become a kind of trap for future generations.

Addiction

Addiction is the antithesis of freedom and is a complex problem with many causes and contributing factors. Like the sweet taste at the entrance of the pitfall plant, addictive substances promise much enjoyment but deliver something entirely different. A major problem that comes both with mental illness and the hedonic view of happiness is the co-morbidity of drug and alcohol addiction. The neurotransmitter dopamine is central to the activity of the brain's mesolimbic reward system. This system is very important for our ability to experience pleasure but has implications for addiction. When the brain's pleasure and reward centres are over-stimulated then they keep asking for a greater level of stimulation to get the same effect. Very soon comes a level of tolerance and then a neurological entrapment that is very hard to reverse. Soon the person cannot control the behaviour.

For a person with a genetic predisposition to addiction, exposure to environmental insults produces changes in gene expression and behaviour.[35] These effects can also be passed on to future generations.[36] Stress, especially early in upbringing, affects the brain's dopamine pathways for life with implications for a future of impaired executive functioning, impulsivity, reactivity and risk of addiction.[37] Once the genetic levers and switches for addiction within the brain are thrown they can be very difficult, but not impossible, to switch off again. Increased dopamine release during 'relaxation response' is associated with the experience of reduced reactivity and impulsivity, implying that things like the regular mental discipline of meditation practice can assist in reversing the negative impact of psychological stress to help overcome addiction.[38] This has been confirmed in various studies on substance abuse[39,40] and gambling.[41] Choosing an environment and company where a person is not exposed or encouraged to use the addictive substance is also important, as are community policies that help people not to be exposed to addictive substances in the first place.

Ageing and lifestyle

Ageing and death, despite scientists' best efforts, are not optional. We will never be, nor should we want to be, free of that fact of life. What is optional, however, is how fast we age, how long we are likely to live and how well we live. For example, people who regularly exercise prior to and after retirement are nearly eight times less likely to get a chronic disease before their mid-seventies compared to those who are sedentary.[42] Those with five or more lifestyle risk factors (sedentary, diabetes, poor diet …) are nearly eight times more likely to get dementia than those with a healthy lifestyle.[43]

There are important genetic determinants of ageing, risk of chronic illness and life expectancy. Telomeres are little caps on the end of our chromosomes that keep the chromosome's DNA from unravelling in a similar way to how the plastic aglets on the end of shoelaces stop them from unravelling. Telomeres are at their longest and healthiest at birth, but throughout life they progressively shorten and fray. The shorter the telomere length, the older we are biologically and the greater the risk of chronic illnesses associated with ageing like cancer, heart disease and dementia.

Chronologically we could be 50 years old but have the DNA of a 40-year-old or a 60-year-old depending on how we have lived. Some of the things that shorten telomeres and accelerate ageing even before we are born include significant maternal stress during pregnancy.[44] Higher emotional and physiological reactivity to stress is associated with already short telomere length even in five-year-olds.[45] Thus, helping children to learn to regulate their emotional response to stress early in life may be a very important investment in their long-term health and ageing. In adults too, more physiological stress and poor coping means more rapid ageing of at least a decade by late thirties.[46,47]

Short telomeres are an important reason that people with chronic depression have an increased risk of age-related illness.[48] Pessimism is associated with a decade of accelerated ageing by middle age, an increased risk for chronic disease, early mortality and more inflammation.[49] Men with a disposition to high levels of hostility and anger age faster than men with a lesser tendency to hostility.[50] Poor sleep,[51] internalizing racial discrimination[52] and prolonged workplace stress all speed up ageing.[53] Women who work full-time for a longer period of their life[54] and people who don't have a spiritual or religious dimension to their life age faster.[55] Being sedentary is not good from an ageing perspective[56] whereas physical exercise protects our chromosomes from the negative impact of emotional stress.[57] Accelerated ageing is also associated with smoking, eating processed meat, inflammation and having a high BMI.[58] Some nutritional factors associated with slower ageing are the Mediterranean diet, a healthy level of vitamin D, folate, omega-3 fatty acids, fibre, vitamin C and vitamin E.[59–64] Exposure to various chemicals and pollutants at home and work is associated with rapid ageing, including traffic-related air pollution, pesticides, lead, exposure in car mechanical workshops and hazardous waste exposure.[65]

Mindfulness training not only reduces stress but also slows and even stops telomere shortening.[66] When you combine mindfulness with a comprehensive healthy lifestyle program, as was done in one study on men with early prostate cancer, then telomeres got longer over a five-year period, which is effectively a reversal of the ageing process.[67] These men also reversed the progression of their prostate cancer,[68] switched off prostate cancer genes,[69] and switched on genetic repair.[70] As expected, the lifestyle group struggled initially to make these healthy changes but once they were established their quality of life improved significantly. It seems that if we want to be happy and free of disease then we need self-mastery and to follow the laws of nature. We are not free to choose whether the laws of health exist, but just whether we choose to follow them or not.

Information technology (IT)

The dawn of the IT era brought with it the promise of greater freedom than any previous generation had ever known. We have unlimited electronic access to information and people in a way that would not have been imaginable even one generation ago. The downside to this story of greater freedom includes addiction to mobile devices and social media, and negative effects on education and emotional intelligence (see Chapter 11).

Like anything else, it is not that the technology is bad in itself, or that we should go back to an age before it was available, but what we do need are limits on the quantity and quality of what we are exposed to, and for parents and schools to have clear guidelines on how to limit it.

To turn on the IT is one thing, but knowing what to tune into and when to turn it off is something else. If we don't use IT discerningly there will be a far more profound disconnection from the people and world we actually live in while living in a virtual world that barely exists.

Virtual reality (VR) is one form of technology for which advocates have promised much but we really have no idea what its long-term effects will be. Do we really know what the effect of VR will be on a developing brain? What is the effect of a diminishing ability to distinguish between the real world and a virtual world where someone has what they want instantly but where there is no responsibility? What effect will it have on happiness, resilience, empathy, authentic social engagement and a person's expectations of what reality can and should deliver? Nothing good one suspects, but that probably won't deter vulnerable people from being allured by the sweetness of a beautiful dreamworld. The people profiting from selling that dreamworld to a generation thirsting for satisfaction while living a deeply dissatisfying life without meaning probably won't be too concerned. The tyranny depicted in the movie *The Matrix* may be closer than we think.

SOME THINGS TO REFLECT ON:

- Is the scientific description of the three aspects of the human psyche more or less influential for you than the philosophical one? Why, why not?
- What are the implications for neuroplasticity for the thoughts, attitudes and actions you wish to cultivate?
- Do you ever consider future generations in the lifestyle decisions and actions you make in your life? Should you?
- Are you in control of the IT in your life, or does it control you?

SOME THINGS TO PRACTISE:

- Choose an unhealthy habit and apply to it the ADEPT model for three weeks.
- Unplug from social media for a week and see what happens.
- Rationally limit the amount and nature of your IT use for a week and observe the effects.

CHAPTER 9

THE PSYCHOLOGY OF FREEDOM

True freedom is primarily a state of mind, not a physical condition, therefore the study of the mind is central to our inquiry into freedom. Although philosophers and theologians have had much to say about the nature of the mind over millennia, the discipline of psychology as we know it is relatively new. In this chapter, we will confine our inquiry to the views of a few notable psychologists on the subject of freedom.

What is psychology and how do we study it?

An '-ology' is a branch of study. Anthropology is the study of people and societies. Ecology is the study of the natural environment. Oncology is the study of cancer. Well, psychology, simply put, is the study of the mind. Simple? Maybe. Maybe not.

Just the fact that we can study the mind presents us with a conundrum because it implies there is something in us, other than the mind, doing the studying. What can that be? Well, in order to study and understand a society, the anthropologist sits back and unobtrusively observes people as they go about their normal lives, taking care not to interfere with what they are observing. Similarly, to study and understand the mind means to sit back and observe the mind. We see how it works by watching what is does. We can observe or infer about someone else's mind by watching their actions and speaking with them about their thoughts and emotions. The essential factor is the observer, the consciousness, which is doing the watching. If we ignore the observing self, as psychology has done until recently, then we may have been looking at the mind from the wrong perspective, like trying to understand the mind by thinking about it rather than observing it. It is not until relatively recently in psychological circles that the mind has been studied from this contemplative perspective. Now there are groups like the Mind and Life Institute that are taking contemplative neuroscience and psychology to a whole new level and it is revolutionizing our understanding of the mind.[1] So, what do some of the big names in psychology have to say about freedom?

William James

William James (1842–1910) was a physician, psychologist and philosopher — and possibly the most influential one America has ever produced. His most influential work, *The Principles of Psychology*, was the foundation for modern psychology and described many important principles we now take for granted.

Three key themes of James' work relate to attention, determinism and spirituality. First, in relation to attention, he identified its importance long before the modern interest in contemplative neuroscience gathered momentum. To James, awareness was a prerequisite for understanding oneself and leading a healthy life emotionally and socially.

James' attitude to determinism was what he called 'soft determinism'. He abhorred the limited and fatalistic thinking that subsequently became common in neuroscience and genetics, and believed we have the scope to freely choose our actions, attitudes and way of being in the world.

> **Old-fashioned determinism was what we may call hard determinism. It did not shrink from such words as fatality, bondage of the will, necessitation, and the like. Nowadays, we have a soft determinism which abhors harsh words, and, repudiating fatality,**

> **necessity, and even predetermination, says that its real name is freedom; for freedom is only necessity understood, and bondage to the highest is identical with true freedom.**[2]

There may be strong influences on our thoughts, emotions and behaviours derived from our biology and external forces beyond our control, but that doesn't define us. The ultimate freedom ties in with what he calls 'bondage to the highest', or spirituality. James wrote an influential book on the subject called *The Varieties of Religious Experience*. The ultimate freedom, according to James, is knowing God or 'the highest' and following its will. This he equates with necessity, but how can necessity, which we equate with constraint, lead to true freedom? It largely lies in the view that we have the freedom to choose to obey necessity or to rail against it. If, however, that necessity exerts itself through the laws of nature then to follow it leads to mastery and freedom whereas ignoring or railing against it is an exercise in futility and self-harm.

Sigmund Freud

Sigmund Freud (1856–1939) is possibly the most famous of all psychiatrists. His popularization of psychoanalysis provided our image of the archetypal psychiatrist with the couch, chair, beard, writing pad and long silences. Freud took a fairly gloomy and misanthropic view of human beings possibly because he formed his theories almost exclusively on the basis of a relatively small number of the most miserable and neurotic of people.

> **I have found little that is 'good' about human beings on the whole. In my experience most of them are trash, no matter whether they publicly subscribe to this or that ethical doctrine or to none at all. That is something that you cannot say aloud, or perhaps even think.**[3]

Freud's influential focus on psychopathology may be the chief reason that, for the following century, psychology almost exclusively focused on abnormality and mental illness and never took an interest in positive psychology and wellbeing. Freud never aimed very high as far as therapeutic outcomes were concerned, famously saying that the task of psychoanalysis was to 'transform neurotic misery into common unhappiness'.[4] He was also openly hostile to religion, dismissive of religious experience and not much of an observer or man of science.[5]

As far as freedom is concerned, he was largely a hard determinist of the view that our actions and decisions are essentially predetermined by unconscious processes and, because we are unaware of them, we don't get to choose them nor are they under our control. In this view, free will is an illusion. This quote, attributed to Freud, succinctly sums up his view on determinism.[6]

> **The deep seated belief in the psychic freedom and choice is absolutely not scientific and should give a way to the assertions of determinism, which controls mental life.[7]**

Thus, to Freud, we are prisoners of our biology, our upbringing and, above all, our unconscious urges and conflicts, most of which were selfish and sexual in nature. Rather than wanting freedom, Freud's view was that freedom is shunned by the great majority of people because it comes with something most people want to avoid — responsibility. 'Most people do not really want freedom, because freedom involves responsibility, and most people are frightened of responsibility.'

Mind you, there is an inherent contradiction in saying that we choose or do not choose to embrace freedom because it is counter to the primary tenet of hard determinism — we don't get to choose. But, if Freud is right, then we might as well stop discussing freedom or pursuing it because it is just an illusion.

Carl Jung

Carl Jung (1875–1961) was a Swiss psychologist who, in the early days, was a close associate of Freud. Subsequently, Jung went in a very different direction to Freud, particularly in relation to his views on the unconscious, religion and free will. Jung was a deeply spiritual man, in part inspired by his familiarity with the world's great mythologies and wisdom traditions, but also because of his deeply introspective and contemplative leanings.

To Jung, we are all connected, not just because of our physical proximity to each other in society, but also through a collective unconscious. This is like a universal mind and consciousness which, for the most part, we hardly know exists as we go about our distracted day-to-day existence. The personal transformation from an isolated individual to a free, universal, enlightened being Jung likens to a kind of spiritual alchemy.

> **The alchemists saw it in the transformation of the chemical substance. So if one of them sought transformation, he discovered it outside in matter ... But some were clever enough to know, 'It is my own transformation — not a personal transformation, but the transformation of what is mortal in me into what is immortal. It shakes off the mortal husk that I am and awakens to a life of its own.[8]**

Self-reflection was something that Jung wholeheartedly embraced but Freud vigorously avoided. For Jung, personal growth was about awakening to self-knowledge and self-awareness.[9] The difference between the unconscious and conscious mind is like comparing a room with the light on to one with the light off. What is there is there, but in one state we can't see it and in the other we can. Many of us, it seems, are afraid of turning on the light, or perhaps we do not even know that there is a light switch in the first place.

> **There is no coming to consciousness without pain. People will do anything, no matter how absurd, in order to avoid facing their own Soul. One does not become enlightened by imagining figures of light, but by making the darkness conscious.[10]**

This, for Jung, was the path of liberation and it changes how we engage with the world. Freedom is inseparable from morality and morality is inseparable from our level of awareness.

> **Without freedom there can be no morality.**[11]

> **Our moral freedom reaches as far as our consciousness, and thus our liberation from compulsion and captivity.**[12]

Jung believed in free will and viewed hard determinism as merely a mode of thought preoccupied and confined by causality. If we don't connect with the core of our being and realize that it is continuous with universal being then we will be ruled by instinct, cause and effect as described by Freud. This stamps Jung as being quite distinct from Freud and the nihilism associated with many proponents of existentialism.

> **Freedom could be put in doubt only because of the one-sided and uncritical overvaluation of causality, which has been elevated into an axiom although, strictly speaking, it is nothing but a mode of thought.**[13]

We have to be self-aware in order to be conscious of, and discerning about, our choices. He calls 'instinctuality' being driven by our instincts and appetites which, being the lowest and most unreflective and habit-driven aspect of ourselves, does not rely on self-awareness, reason or discernment.[14]

BF Skinner

Burrhus Frederic, or BF, Skinner (1904–1990) was an American psychologist who taught at Harvard University. He was largely responsible for popularizing behaviourism and the experimental approach to understanding human behaviour. Laboratory-based experiments are useful, but they are inherently artificial and limited by the things you can, or choose to, measure and control. Skinner's view of behaviourism is strongly deterministic and materialistic, not metaphysical. He saw free will, emotion and motivation as illusory covers for the real causes of human behaviour — the effect of environment and conditioning on our biology.

> What is felt or introspectively observed is not some nonphysical world of consciousness, mind, or mental life but the observer's own body. This does not mean ... that introspection is a kind of psychological research, nor does it mean ... that what are felt or introspectively observed are the causes of the behavior. An organism behaves as it does because of its current structure, but most of this is out of reach of introspection. At the moment we must content ourselves ... with a person's genetic and environment histories. What are introspectively observed are certain collateral products of those histories ... In this way we repair the major damage wrought by mentalism. When what a person does [is] attributed to what is going on inside him, investigation is brought to an end. Why explain the explanation? For twenty-five hundred years people have been preoccupied with feelings and mental life, but only recently has any interest been shown in a more precise analysis of the role of the environment.[15]

Thus, Skinner's view was that you could condition or train human beings, like animals, to think or do what you want. You can reinforce some behaviours and punish others, and this conditions the brain and biology to be the way it is. In Skinner's theory the person who commits a crime has no real choice because they are propelled to it by environmental circumstances and personal history, making breaking the law, for some people, natural and inevitable.[16] For others, being law-abiding is just as natural because of their environment and upbringing.

> Two features of autonomous man are particularly troublesome. In the traditional view, a person is free. He is autonomous in the

> **sense that his behavior is uncaused. He can therefore be held responsible for what he does and justly punished if he offends. That view, together with its associated practices, must be re-examined when a scientific analysis reveals unsuspected controlling relations between behaviour and environment.[17]**

The legal and moral implications of the determinist, behaviourist view would be enormous if it were to be widely adopted, and indeed, this view is increasingly influential with courts taking into account a person's upbringing and environment in mitigating their culpability for a crime.

Environment clearly has significant influence on us and the sciences of neuroplasticity and epigenetics give further credence to that view, but is there a risk in taking one factor to be all there is? What works against us can also work for us. Although environment and conditioning do play a major role in determining our makeup and behaviour, are we inevitably prisoners of them? If we are, then how is it that people have thrown off the shackles of their upbringing and social conditioning in situations such as apartheid or a poor upbringing? How is it that we can choose to change our brain and genetic expression if biology and environment is all?

Viktor Frankl

Viktor Frankl (1905–1997) was an Austrian psychiatrist whose views were deeply influenced not by laboratory experiments like Skinner but by real-life experiences in Nazi concentration camps. There he had little or no control over his circumstances, but what he discovered from that adversity was a deep sense of self-reliance, insight and meaning confounding our usual assumptions about how a person should think and feel in such a situation.

> **A thought transfixed me: for the first time in my life I saw the truth as it is set into song by so many poets, proclaimed as the final wisdom by so many thinkers. The truth — that love is the ultimate and the highest goal to which Man can aspire. Then I grasped the meaning of the greatest secret that human poetry**

> and human thought and belief have to impart: The salvation of Man is through love and in love. I understood how a man who has nothing left in this world still may know bliss, be it only for a brief moment, in the contemplation of his beloved. In a position of utter desolation, when Man cannot express himself in positive action, when his only achievement may consist in enduring his sufferings in the right way — an honorable way — in such a position Man can, through loving contemplation of the image he carries of his beloved, achieve fulfilment.[18]

Such insights profoundly changed the way Frankl experienced his ordeal and environment. It was not that the conditions of the camp changed or that the guards were suddenly pleasant and caring, but that, paradoxically, he found freedom from the misery by transcending it, by finding meaning within it, and by embracing the opposite to the hatred and bitterness which would have been expected. As he wrote:

> Life is never made unbearable by circumstances, but only by lack of meaning and purpose.[19]

> When we are no longer able to change a situation, we are challenged to change ourselves.[20]

Echoing the ancient philosopher Epictetus — who said, 'Man is not disturbed by events but by the view he takes of them' — freedom, to Frankl, was not an external affair, but an internal one, based on choosing the attitude to any event. This is radically non-determinist. From a behaviourist perspective, humans are sophisticated animals but humanity can be free from circumstances whereas an animal cannot. Frankl, when being asked to comment on Skinner's view, said:

> Man does not cease to be an animal, but at the same time He is infinitely more than an animal ... Everything can be taken from a

> **man but one thing: the last of the human freedoms — to choose one's attitude in any given set of circumstances, to choose one's own way.[21]**

An important part of the ability to choose and transcend is, again, self-awareness, which Frankl likens to a space between stimulus and response. This strongly echoes the emphasis on awareness previously exhorted by various wisdom traditions and in mindfulness-based approaches.

> **Between stimulus and response, there is a space. In that space is our power to choose our response. In our response lies our growth and our freedom.[22]**

Martin Seligman

Marin Seligman (1942–) is an American psychologist very active in turning around psychology's fascination with negative psychology and encouraging it to explore the realm of positive psychology. Seligman's early animal research led him to discover what he called 'learned helplessness'.[23] This arises when you consistently create inescapable aversive or painful situations for an animal from which it can't escape. Soon it will cease trying to escape, even when the potential for escape is reintroduced. Seligman drew parallels with people living with depression who, being unable to stop having the thoughts and feelings they passionately did not want to experience, learned a kind of helplessness and resignation.

Seligman wanted to look at psychology differently. Rather than just mitigating the symptoms of psychological distress or masking them with drugs, he wanted to see what were the positive resources a person had within themselves. The discipline of positive psychology is interested in what makes people happy and well, what helps them to thrive and find meaning, and what builds strong relationships with others. It looks at things like character, strength and virtues.

> **So Positive Psychology takes seriously the bright hope that if you find yourself stuck in the parking lot of life, with few and only ephemeral pleasures, with minimal gratifications, and without meaning, there is a road out. This road takes you through the countryside of pleasure and gratification, up into the high country of strength and virtue, and finally to the peaks of lasting fulfilment: meaning and purpose.**[24]

The conclusions he and co-researchers have come to echo what many wisdom traditions exhorted for millennia. Seligman and his team explored the virtues and strengths promoted by wisdom traditions of East and West and came to six broad categories of character strengths: wisdom/knowledge, courage, humanity, justice, temperance and transcendence. Within these categories there are also a number of particular character strengths.

Positive psychology is in part deterministic in that happiness is in part determined by genetics and environment, but it also acknowledges the importance of freewill, for it is within our ability to choose what we cultivate in our character and resources within any given set of circumstances. Pessimism leads in one direction and optimism in another

> **Habits of pessimism lead to depression, wither achievement and undermine physical health. The good news is that pessimism can be unlearned, and that with its removal depression, underachievement and poor health can be alleviated.**[25]

Seligman's views on choosing the beliefs we focus on in times of adversity are strongly aligned with Frankl's and have profound consequences for physical and mental health. Depending on what we choose we will come out better for the adversity or scarred by it.

> **It's a matter of ABC: When we encounter ADVERSITY, we react by thinking about it. Our thoughts rapidly congeal into BELIEFS. These beliefs may become so habitual we don't even realize we have**

them unless we stop to focus on them. And they don't just sit there idly; they have CONSEQUENCES.[26]

Key characteristics associated with 'negative psychology' include isolation, individualism, a lack of limits, self-centredness and hedonism. Individualism and a passion for immediate gratification are associated with the hedonic attitude to happiness, whereas meaning and engagement are associated with the eudaimonic approach to happiness. Individualism and hedonism are two characteristics of the so-called 'me-generation' whereas our ability to find meaning in times of adversity is a major mediator of resilience. Happiness based on hedonism is the most fragile and easily threatened.

In a society in which individualism is becoming rampant, people more and more believe that they are the center of the world. Such a belief system makes individual failure almost inconsolable.[27]

People whose disposition to happiness is primarily eudaimonic tend to be far happier and more resilient to stress and disappointment. Forgoing pleasures and enduring hardships is far easier when it is for a meaningful cause and the view is kept large.

Another key idea challenged in positive psychology is that freedom is simply the absence of limits, a view that society generally, and many parents in particular, seem to have adopted. Whether this is because an absence of limits and discipline is actually believed to be beneficial, or whether it is because most adults no longer have the strength to stand firm in the face of increasingly vociferous children and adolescents driven by impatience and an unwavering sense of entitlement is hard to say. But, paradoxically, according to research on positive psychology, setting consistent and reasonable limits is associated with happier and more resilient children.

The clearer the rules and the limits enforced by parents, the higher the child's self-esteem. The more freedom the child had, the lower his self-esteem.[28]

One potential escape from our own misery and negativity has to do with how we relate to others. Compassion and kindness are not only beneficial for the recipient but are most powerful for the doer.[29] Giving to others buffers against stress and is associated with lower mortality.[30] If kindness to others has the unexpected effect of improving our own wellbeing, then it naturally follows that acts of cruelty are not only an expression of our own inner misery but are also a potent means for deepening it. Put another way, acting on our bitterness and hostility only reinforces the bars to the prison cell within which we imprison ourselves.

Jon Kabat-Zinn

Jon Kabat-Zinn (1944–) is not a psychologist but, through his long-standing passion for teaching and researching mindfulness, he has had a profound effect on the modern understanding and practice of psychology. He was a molecular biologist trained at MIT in the United States, but as a student developed a deep interest in Buddhism and mindfulness meditation. He took what he learned into the community to help people in need. In the late 1970s, he founded the Stress Reduction Clinic at the University of Massachusetts Medical Centre in Worcester, and developed what he called mindfulness-based stress reduction (MBSR). Mindfulness is an approach that is based on a wisdom tradition, although a person does not need to necessarily adopt that tradition in order to derive benefit from the practice of mindfulness.

Kabat-Zinn published some early studies on reducing stress and chronic pain that attracted significant attention, including from a group of psychologists and researchers, John Teasdale, Zindel Siegel and Mark Williams. They were looking for new strategies to help people deal with the escalating rates of chronic, relapsing depression. From MBSR they developed mindfulness-based cognitive therapy (MBCT) and found extremely promising results which have been subsequently and consistently confirmed in many studies since.[31,32]

Mindfulness-based approaches are revolutionizing psychotherapy. In mindfulness, the first and most central point is cultivating awareness.

Without awareness, we are essentially an automaton, without understanding and with no conscious will of our own: a state called 'automatic pilot'. In such a state, the hard determinism of Freud and Skinner might be a fair description of the human condition.

> **But when we start to focus in on what our own mind is up to, for instance, it is not unusual to quickly go unconscious again, to fall back into an automatic-pilot mode of unawareness. These lapses in awareness are frequently caused by an eddy of dissatisfaction with what we are seeing or feeling in that moment, out of which springs a desire for something to be different, for things to change.**[33]

Dissatisfaction, regret, addiction and fear essentially come from ignoring the present and living in the imaginary future or relived past. In our restless, unmindful search for happiness we constantly look for things outside ourselves. What we find in the shifting sands of our experiences is impermanence and constantly missing the bedrock of our being.

> **All the suffering, stress, and addiction comes from not realizing you already are what you are looking for.**[34]

It is all too easy to become a prisoner of the mind if we forget the underlying awareness. We tend to identify ourselves with passing thoughts and feelings and take them as facts. Liberation from suffering and distress, therefore, lies in our ability to rest in simple, non-judgemental and compassionate awareness and not to be moved by transient experiences by not mentally attaching to them.

> **Awareness is not the same as thought. It lies beyond thinking, although it makes no use of thinking, honouring its value and its power. Awareness is more like a vessel which can hold and contain our thinking, helping us to see and know our thought as thought rather than getting caught up in them as reality.**[35]

Relative to the awareness, transient thoughts, feelings and sensations are insubstantial because they so readily come and go.

> **It is remarkable how liberating it feels to be able to see that your thoughts are just thoughts and that they are not 'you' or 'reality.' For instance, if you have the thought that you have to get a certain number of things done today and you don't recognize it as a thought, but act as if it's the 'the truth,' then you have created a reality in that moment in which you really believe that those things must all be done today.**[36]

If we cultivate awareness and non-attachment to the mind and its contents, then we have the opportunity to live more fully and authentically and without the same level of hindrance from our compulsions, desires and addictions.[37] From this self-awareness all things flow.

> **Mindfulness is about being fully awake in our lives. It is about perceiving the exquisite vividness of each moment. We also gain immediate access to our own powerful inner resources for insight, transformation, and healing.**[38,39]

Thus, mindfulness has much more in common with the views of James, Jung, Frankl and Seligman than it does with the views of Freud and Skinner in that the former emphasize awareness and the latter automatic pilot.

The tendency to live without awareness is not a modern phenomenon. Awareness is the single most important theme described by the psychologists who recognize the potential for liberation, self-determination and self-knowledge. Conventional approaches to psychotherapy and psychiatry have traditionally not spoken about flourishing, freedom or liberation, but merely the amelioration of the symptoms of emotional distress. The modern uptake of meditation, and mindfulness in particular, is revolutionizing the way we understand the mind because it gives psychologist and client alike the chance to stand back from it, observe it and understand one's relationship to it. This puts distance between oneself and the mind, providing the potential for freedom.

It only takes a moment to stand back from it and watch it without involvement to realize that we are not our thoughts — we are the observer of them. It is a revelation when it first happens even though the habitual thoughts soon return. When we practise more consistently then we experience an enduring level of freedom from states like depression, anxiety, addiction, attention deficit disorder and pain.[40–43] The thoughts, feelings and sensations may continue to arise, but we are less and less moved by them as they come and go.

This doesn't discount the fact that there are chemical changes in the brain associated with states like depression, that we can inherit a genetic disposition to mental health problems, and that we may have a less than optimal upbringing or environment. We can take control of many but not all of those factors but it seems that we don't have to be prisoners of our upbringing, biology or environment. Determinism is a way of thinking, not a biological fact.

Personality

Personality is an interesting word. From the ancient Greek, it is based on the word 'persona' (mask, character played by an actor).[44] Thus, an actor in the amphitheatre would put on a mask communicating a particular type of character to the audience whether angry, happy, sad or comical. The actor clearly was not the mask or the character they played, but merely assumed the mask and character to play the part.

Personality can be classified in many different ways. For example, the 'Big Five' personality traits are openness to experience, conscientiousness, extroversion, agreeableness, and neuroticism (emotionality). There are the Myers Briggs[45] classification and personality types A, B, C and D[46] among others. No matter how we classify it, personality traits have long been seen as fixed, with genetics and environment equally important in determining which traits dominate.[47] But we tend to be defined and confined by the dispositions in our personality if we keep on thinking and doing whatever we have always thought and done. Then personality becomes more and more deeply ingrained throughout life. Through upbringing, habit, practice and conditioning, and the consequent epigenetic and neuroplastic changes, we get trapped by our personality. Hence, the flexibility of our responses restrict over time until we find ourselves a prisoner of personality traits like anger, neuroticism, paranoia, introversion or extroversion. In most extreme forms, there are what are called 'personality disorders' where a particular trait dominates a person's thoughts, feelings, behaviour and interactions in a negative and oftentimes destructive way. Approaches like dialectical behaviour therapy (DBT) provide the potential to help people transcend or mitigate many of the most unhelpful aspects of personality disorders, such as reduced psychiatric and clinical symptoms, less emotional reactivity and less impulsivity.[48] Increasingly reports are being published of people no longer satisfying the diagnostic criteria for personality disorder after such treatment, a finding that is supported by corresponding neural changes.[49] Studies on borderline personality disorder show major reductions in symptoms and anger.[50] This work requires insight and motivation on behalf of the client, skill and training on behalf of the practitioner, and patience and compassion on behalf of both.

The mental trap

The way into mental traps often begins with things that at the outset seem sweet enough. Take rumination — it promises resolution or insight but generally delivers deeply etched ruts in our thinking from which it is increasingly difficult to steer the mind. Then there is worry — so tempting and so able to masquerade as something useful like planning, preparation or as an insurance policy against negative events. Or anger — that bittersweet form of rumination in which we seem to be punishing the object of our anger but in reality we merely punish ourselves. And then there is fantasy — a very sweet and seductive world indeed where the happiness is as substantial and satisfying as drinking a mirage and the residual effect is an unrequited thirst and an ever-increasing dissatisfaction with the life we are actually living.

Things like self-awareness, self-actualization, non-attachment and acknowledging a deeper, observing self are ways to avoid or to extricate ourselves from the mental traps we unwittingly stumble into. The bottom line is we do not have to be trapped by the mind. If we train and use it well, the mind resembles a faithful servant rather than a tyrannical master.

SOME THINGS TO REFLECT ON:

- What is your view of determinism and what are the implications of that view for your life?
- Do you make efforts to cultivate greater awareness and non-attachment in your life?
- Do you feel trapped by your mind or are you the master of your mind?
- How will you go about increasing self-mastery in your life?

SOME THINGS TO PRACTISE:

- Practise mindfulness both formally and informally whether you learn it in a course, through books or the use of online resources.
- Assess[51] and then practise cultivating your signature strengths.[52]

CHAPTER 10

THE ETHICS OF FREEDOM

To Socrates, ethics was a pretty simple affair based on the question, 'What should I do?' From that simple question things get pretty complicated pretty quickly. How do we decide what we should do? What are the criteria? Is being ethical just doing and saying what the majority of people do and say? Is it just a matter of individual choice? Is ethics based on natural laws, virtues and/or objective principles? How will we know if we make the right decision? Why be ethical in the first place?

In this chapter, we will explore some prevailing ideas underpinning contemporary ethics and focus particular attention on the extent to which these may promote or undermine freedom. This is important because if we do not consider these issues carefully we may find ourselves vilifying the just, justifying the unjust, and trapping ourselves with laws and customs that are unethical and denigrating. We will begin by exploring some of the widely used terms and concepts in ethics.

Deontology and utilitarianism

Until recently, the ruling paradigm in ethics was deontology, which defined things as right or wrong depending on whether or not they were faithful to widely accepted absolute rules like, 'thou shalt not kill', or 'thou shalt not steal'. On the surface, such rules were relatively easy to follow and interpret, and did not dispose themselves to deep philosophical reflection. Such rules were generally seen as God-given natural laws. That deontology is most commonly associated with religion has done it no credit lately considering how many well-publicized abuses have been done in the name of religion. That is not an argument against deontology per se, but against hypocrisy and deception within religious institutions.

From a deontological perspective, the inherent rightness or wrongness of an act is in the act itself, i.e. what motivated it and whether it accorded with rules based on natural law. Important though they may be, consequences are secondary and a natural corollary of just or unjust acts. They will be bad for a bad or unjust action because the fruit of the act is in its seed — its motivation and inherent rightness. A good act will lead to good fruit or consequences.

A commonly raised objection to deontology is that, although rules might be a good guide in most cases, surely there are situations when a person might need to break them, for example, to kill in self-defence or steal in order to feed a starving child. Therefore, although they may be good guides, there is no such thing as a universal truth, law or rule that should be followed in all cases, and as such they are an unreasonable and unjust limitation on behaviour. Therefore nuanced approaches were offered — utilitarianism was one such alternative.

Utilitarianism was originally described by the English philosophers Jeremy Bentham and John Stuart Mill in the eighteenth and nineteenth centuries. The basic tenets of utilitarianism are:

1. **the consequences of an act, not its inherent rightness, determines whether or not it is good (consequentialism)**
2. **the consequences are good if the act does the greatest good for the greatest number**
3. **the greatest good is to make the most people happy**
4. **the greatest happiness comes about by maximizing pleasure and minimizing pain.**

Of course, utilitarianism is wrong if the tenets upon which it is based are wrong. For the creators of utilitarianism, there was a preference for higher intellectual and aesthetic pleasures over lower ones, like mere physical gratification, although that distinction is no longer emphasized by the majority of modern day advocates of utilitarianism. According to utilitarianism, in order to work out what we should do in a given situation, we have to calculate all the possible consequences in terms of pleasure for all options and for all parties so as to maximize the outcome, sometimes called the hedonic calculation or calculus.

Utilitarianism proposed a profound shift in thinking to what had gone before. It is a kind of democratization and freeing up of ethics — the greatest good is whatever most people want. But what if some of the underlying premises are wrong? For example, happiness and pleasure may not be the same thing. A person can think something will make them happy when it won't. A short-term pleasure, even a very strong one (an illicit drug), can lead to unhappiness in the long-term (addiction). A short-term discomfort, even a very strong one (going to drug rehabilitation), can lead to happiness in the long-term (freedom from addiction). Pleasure and pain are very seductive but deceptive indicators of good and bad, right and wrong, whereas reason is not. Is not happiness therefore dependent on reason and not pleasure? Where will utilitarianism lead us if it is unhinged from the higher intellectual and aesthetic pleasures or respect for natural law?

Can rules be inviolable and flexible at the same time?

Deontology is often seen as being an unnecessary restriction on freedom, but the characterization of deontological rules as being rigid may be inaccurate. Can a rule be both absolute and flexible at the same time? For example, 'thou shalt not kill' may require interpretation. As an analogy, we have an immune system that is never meant to kill its owner, but it does kill 'foreign invaders' like bacteria and cancer cells that threaten its owner. The immune system kills not for the sake of killing but in order to save life in self-defence. Pathologically, sometimes the immune system turns on its owner as in autoimmune conditions even to the point of death, but there is never a case where autoimmunity is healthy or adaptive. It goes against the laws of health. Analogously, it is never right to kill another person unjustly, that is, if they are not threatening innocent life, but killing may be justified in self-defence or war. If a person is threatening life then the taking of life is in order to preserve life — 'thou shalt not kill'. From that perspective, it is never right to take the life of a foetus unless there is no alternative to abortion in order to save the life of the woman.

Consider an example of ethical behaviour that illustrates the difference between the dogmatic and superficial adherence to deontological rules versus interpreting an applying laws wisely. It relates to the Biblical story of a woman caught in the act of adultery who was brought to Jesus by the Pharisees.[1] They stated that the law of Moses was such that the woman should be stoned for her crime and asked Jesus what his view was. Clearly, as rigid deontologists, they wanted to kill two birds with one stone — trap Jesus and stone the woman. Jesus drew on the ground for a few moments, then stood saying to the assembled crowd, 'Let he who is without sin should cast the first stone.' The Pharisees and crowd were stopped in their tracks. In shame, they lost their sense of righteous indignation and shuffled off one by one, each knowing that they would be hypocritical if they cast the first stone. When the crowd had dispersed Jesus said to the woman, 'Go and sin no more'.

To respond in such a simple, direct and decisive way, to turn away an angry crowd, not with physical force but by gentle wisdom and teach a lesson in mercy and humility at the same time, is nothing short of brilliant. You would have to be very courageous, clear-headed and wise to do something like that. It illustrates not rigidly following dogma and rules but adapting law to the time, place and circumstances. It was not that the woman's conduct was excused as being innocent, or that being unfaithful to your partner doesn't matter, but just that the law of mercy and forgiveness can have a far greater effect of uplifting someone than meting out an angry punishment. Although the rules are enduring, their application will be rigid and superficial in the hands of someone of lesser wisdom, and adaptable and deep in the hands of someone of higher wisdom. One can only imagine what Jesus would have done if his measuring stick was the greatest happiness of the greatest number — the woman would have been stoned in no time at all.

Thus, if utilitarianism is based on false premises, and if rules, rightly understood, can be both absolute and flexible at the same time, then the apparent freedom that comes with dispensing with rules and applying utilitarian calculations and justifications may lead to some unjust and unethical outcomes. If the rules of ethics are based on natural laws then, like the laws of the physical world, they interplay and interact with each other but can never be denied.

Autonomy — the rule of the self

The number one ruling principle in ethics and society today is autonomy — the rule of the self. In medicine, for example, by and large patients used to unquestioningly do what doctors told them to, such was patients' trust in the doctors' knowledge and integrity. That's called paternalism — the doctor being like the powerful parental figure and the patient being like the vulnerable child in need. There are many instances, however, of doctors harming patients or totally disregarding their wishes, which have resulted in patients increasingly wanting to make their own decisions. Respecting a competent person's right to choose for themselves is autonomy, and it was initially used to justify — and rightly so — a competent person's right to make an informed decision on whether or not to have a particular treatment based on the information provided by the doctor.

In no small part because of some notable abuses of power by men, and in the institutions of medicine, government, law enforcement, education and the church, the community is far less likely to trust authority figures today than in times past. In fact, such is the way the narrative has been shaped and the pervasive level of cynicism in the community today, abuse of power is seen by many as being synonymous with maleness and the abovementioned institutions, which probably does an injustice to the great majority of people serving in positions of authority. The great many doctors, politicians, police, lawyers, teachers and clergy who do their work with integrity and a sense of service are overshadowed by the few who give their professions a bad name. The risk, however, that people sip on the sweet nectar of independence and no longer trust or respect the institutions that underpin society may lead to a slow but sure slide into something even less desirable.

The rule of the self has gathered enormous momentum as the pendulum has swung from one extreme to the other. Today, anything goes. Now, autonomy is used to justify many things that would have been frowned upon previously. Two or three generations ago things like premarital sex, living together, having children out of wedlock, divorce and abortion would have been seen as socially and ethically undesirable. Now they are commonplace. They have become normalized and people are criticized for suggesting it should be otherwise. Other more recent changes include gay marriage and adoption, and how we define gender. Whether such things have a detrimental effect on marriage, family, child-rearing or society can be debated, but there is little doubt that a person's freedom to choose is now the main arbiter between what is right or wrong.

The point here is not to argue for or against any particular position in relation to these matters, but as sweet sounding as the freedom rhetoric may be, where does an unfettered adoption of freedom in the name of autonomy eventually take us; to greater freedom or into a sticky trap from which it may be difficult to extricate ourselves? Where does the distinction lie between what should be illegal, tolerated, promoted or imposed? From the original movement to promote individual freedom in someone's private life, are we reaching a tipping point where the freedom to bring up children or educate them in the way schools or parents see fit is being increasingly limited by imposing a modern liberal ideology upon them? Is that really freedom of choice? It raises the question as to whether the 'liberal agenda' was ever about freedom in the first place or whether it was more about promoting and then imposing a particular worldview. Where the line should be drawn we do not know, but to characterize what is currently happening as a victory for human rights is perhaps a little premature. A safer characterization might be that we are currently engaged in large-scale sociological experiments, the long-term results of which are yet unknown. No doubt we will find out in due course, but it may not be the first time that a sociological experiment has gone badly wrong because it went beyond reasonable limits. In so many ways, these days society is moving into unchartered waters. Whether we are sailing towards bright new vistas of hope and freedom or whether we are sailing onto rocks, time will tell. What's next?

Which part of the self should rule?

Perhaps a simple point is being missed in the autonomy debate. If autonomy as self-rule is good, which part of the self should rule? Will the unrelenting pursuit of an indiscriminate kind of autonomy actually lead to the opposite of freedom as we become trapped by our own ignorance, compulsions, fears, perversions, selfishness and slavish mentality? No, it won't, if one assumes that in the 'rule of the self' it doesn't matter which part of the self rules. Yes, it will, if one assumes that in the 'rule of the self' there is a higher aspect of the self that is meant to rule and lower aspects that are meant to obey. The reasoning principle of the psyche leads to one form of ethics by regulating pleasure, and the pleasure principle leads to another form of ethics by subverting reason.

As explored in previous chapters, there are different aspects to what we call the self. The higher self could be seen as pure reason, conscience or executive functioning, and the other aspects are the emotive and appetitive or pleasure-seeking elements. A commonly used justification for a radically libertarian view is that, 'a person should be able to do whatever they want so long as they don't harm someone else'. But regardless of the damage done or not done to someone else, when we act in an ignorant way do we not damage and degrade ourselves? When we act in a noble or just way then, no matter what our outward situation or whether someone else sees it, do we not ennoble ourselves? When a society accepts rank ignorance in the name of freedom then does it not damage and degrade itself despite complex intellectual justifications? When vile and unconscionable practices are tolerated by faulty and superficial reasoning, cannot anything be justified through the same reasoning?

Of course, to advocate for something ridiculous, first you need to argue inconvenient things like love, virtue, conscience, natural law or long-held community standards out of the picture. Perhaps this can only happen in a period of history dominated by a view of science that looks on humanity and the universe in a superficial and materialistic way. Consider this quote from Francis Collins, one of the heads of the Human Genome Project. 'We will not understand important things like "love" by knowing the DNA sequence of homo sapiens ... If humanity begins to view itself as a machine, programmed by this DNA sequence, we've lost something really important.'[2]

Malignant ideologies can and will be accepted by a significant proportion of the community for various reasons. First, like the Pied Piper leading unsuspecting innocents to oblivion with a sweet-sounding tune, sophistry can be advocated in an eloquent, calculating and superficially appealing way to people who have too little wit or too much apathy to argue against it. Put the sweet strains of freedom into the tune and it seems to get people marching in no time at all. Second, some advocates whip up emotions like greed, fear or hatred to such an extent that many people lose touch with reason and are easily manipulated. Third, some advocates artfully distract people from what is actually happening so that they do not see it, like pickpockets distracting someone with a bauble or a ruse while taking their wallet. Consider how many laws liberalizing gambling or the free market have left poor people poorer. Consider how many artful rhetoricians have pointed to the evil outside their borders in order to distract from the evils within the borders.

Paternalism

The opposite principle to autonomy, in ethical terms, is paternalism. It is generally seen as a pejorative term these days and means to be like a father. It is synonymous with authority, like a doctor instructing a patient what to do or a government directing the citizens. There is 'strong paternalism' such as when an unconscious patient has their decisions made by the doctor in a medical emergency or a government implementing marshal law during a crisis. 'Weak paternalism' could be when the doctor or government merely explains and recommends a treatment or policy but stops short of imposing it.

The thing about paternalism is that it is generally seen in a one-dimensional way but, correctly applied, paternalism is not about having and maintaining authority over someone else. It is actually about using authority when needed, but it is also about promoting the independence of those under authority. A 'good' parent doesn't bring up a child to be dependent on them for their whole life. They make decisions for the child while the child lacks understanding to make their own decisions but, over time, as is safe and appropriate, more decisions are put in the hands of the child until eventually the child is independent. Similarly, the 'good' paternal doctor doesn't want their patients to be dependent on them. They want their patients to be informed, empowered and enabled, looking after their own health, and only seeking the doctor's assistance when necessary. Similarly, the 'good' paternal government promotes and supports the independence, ingenuity and self-reliance of the citizens. To do this, it needs to create the necessary opportunities, environment and resources for the citizens. In a compassionate society, those who can't look after themselves need support and a welfare safety net, although too much welfare, especially for those who can look after themselves, creates an environment where people become dependent, lazy and/or entitled. As Shakespeare wrote:

> **Neither a borrower nor a lender be;**
> **For loan oft loses both itself and friend,**
> **And borrowing dulls the edge of husbandry.**
>
> *Shakespeare, Hamlet, act 1, scene 3, lines 75–77*

A more enlightened view of paternalism is entirely complementary with a more enlightened view of autonomy, but when each is viewed in a superficial way then they inevitably compete and conflict with each other.

An inappropriate use of paternalism will create an environment when people react negatively and thirst for ever-greater autonomy. On the other hand, the wide scale rejection of reasonable authority in the presence of inflated desire and an absence of self-mastery leaves a vulnerable society in serious danger of self-harm. The problem is, as seems to be the case these days, that an increasing number of people reject and mistrust authority altogether and think that ever-increasing autonomy is always right, and so, with bright hopes, good intentions and eloquent advocates presiding, we may nevertheless be drinking too deeply on the sweet nectar of freedom as we edge ever closer to an inevitable downfall.

Human rights and human duties

Another powerful driver of modern ethics and social policy is human rights. There are many examples around the world of people having their just rights to basic things, like food, education, shelter, healthcare, safety, and freedom of speech and association abused. Understandably, there are many instances of the inspiring struggle to restore those rights. To deny such rights is unjust — it's just not right. But, just as in the case of autonomy, we need to look beyond the surface of human rights lest we advocate for things for which there is no right at all. According to the *Oxford Dictionary*,[3] a right is, 'Just, required by morality or duty, proper, true, correct. What is just or fair treatment of a person'. Rights are just one side of the coin. Duty is the other. A duty is, 'Moral or legal obligation; binding force of what is right'. It is related to the word due as in, 'person's right; what is owed'.

Rights don't exist in a vacuum. A right does not exist without a corresponding duty. Much advocacy for rights revolves around the things that people expect to be provided with, but ignores the fact that a right to anything is only meaningful in relation to the complementary duty required of others to provide that right. They break down when we don't honour our duties to others, that is, when we don't give others their dues. The ignorance of duty comes first before the loss of rights. If, for example, we claim to have a right to basic healthcare then that implies that someone else has a duty to provide it, like government, community, doctors and allied healthcare workers. If we have a right not to be discriminated against on the basis of race, then others have a duty to treat us equitably and with respect. We cannot do the duty of another, we can only do our own. Others' actions are their responsibility.

Duty only applies to the conduct of people in a society. Animals or inanimate objects don't have duties because they don't have the required reasoning capacity and freedom of will. A case can be made that a right is only right if it accords with what is naturally due. If it doesn't then how could a right be claimed to it? Nature lends a deaf ear to our appeals for human rights. If, for example, we were in a jungle by ourselves, we can't really scream out to the jungle and say, 'I have a right to food — give it to me,' or say to a tiger about to eat us, 'I have a right to safety — leave me alone.' The monkeys would probably look down at us and say, 'Climb a tree you fool! You'll find food here and be safe from the tiger.'

Consider an example — in society we have a right to food because we need it to remain healthy, but do we have a right to overeat or eat unhealthy food? If a parent was to give a child its due, then surely they would give the child whole, healthy food and only as much as the child needed. To do anything else would be ignoring the duty of a parent and abusing the rights of the child. The child's ardent and persistent requests for excessive or unhealthy food is not an expression of the child's freedom or its rights. It may be more rightly described as the appetitive element of its nature unregulated by reason, and an expression of its addiction to what its palate has become accustomed to. The parent is meant to provide reason to for the child's wellbeing. Mind you, the world of corporate food production and unregulated food advertising make the parents' job very challenging. But does an adult have the right to eat excessive or unhealthy food? Does society have a duty to put policies in place to limit or discourage such consumption? Possibly. In some parts of the world, like the United Kingdom, 'sugar taxes' are being used to reduce the consumption of sweetened beverages as a part of the fight against obesity and related metabolic illnesses. There is good evidence to support such a move.[4] Some might see this as an abuse of people's rights and freedom by penalizing their food choices, and others might see it as the promotion of human rights and freedom by reducing our collective addiction to sugar. Despite all that might be done by external agencies, if a person still chooses to overeat then it should probably not be called a right, in fact, it might more rightly be called a dereliction of one's duty to oneself.

Virtue ethics

Virtue ethics can be defined as 'an approach to ethics that emphasizes an individual's character as the key element of ethical thinking, rather than rules about the acts themselves (deontology) or their consequences (consequentialism).'[5] Virtue is a word that went out of favour for quite a while, although it is making something of a comeback in educational, corporate and ethical environments possibly because vice has become so fashionable.

There are many virtues. The four main ones that Plato described were justice, courage, temperance (or moderation) and wisdom. These are also called the 'cardinal virtues', cardinal coming from the Latin word for 'hinge'; i.e. human conduct and society hinge on them. The following discussion will be restricted to whether the pursuit of vice — the opposite of virtue — is another seductive trap.

The first question is whether vice is a false form of freedom. To be left to do anything we desire, no matter how unjust, appears to be the ultimate kind of freedom, but it is really just leaving certain aspects of human nature unchecked, which may not be a good thing.

Vices such as the 'seven deadly sins' have such juicy names. Take, for example, the vice 'greed'. It is like a thirsty person drinking seawater. It increases the more it is pursued and never gives satisfaction, rest or peace. It leads to imprisonment mentally, metaphorically and literally. It deprives others of their rights and breeds injustice. If those around us are greedy then they deprive us of our rights. The vice 'gluttony' is unrestrained eating. It leaves us with obesity, immobility and illness; anything but freedom. The vice 'sloth' is associated with laziness and not feeling compelled to do anything. It only leaves disinterest, wastefulness, dependency and illness in its wake — hardly a path to fulfilment. The vice 'lust' might appear to be a sure path to happiness through pleasure, but the resulting happiness is fleeting. Pleasure-seeking soon becomes a compulsion and only leaves us with unrest, broken egos, distrustful relationships and painful STDs. 'Pride' is a kind of unrestrained self-esteem that unhooks itself from reality and belies a fragile ego forever seeking recognition and living in fear of being discovered. 'Envy' relates to a desire to have what someone else has, which only leaves us with dissatisfaction and inadequacy. 'Wrath' is unrestrained anger unhinging from reason and, like a person rubbing their eye with some grit in it, it only exacerbates the problem. Sooner or later it leads to the destruction of self and other. The origin of anger, according to the *Bhagavad Gita*, is materialism and desire.

> **When a man dwells on the objects of sense, he creates an attraction for them; attraction develops into desire, and desire breeds anger. Anger induces delusion; delusion, loss of memory; through loss of memory, reason is shattered; and loss of reason leads to destruction. But the self-controlled soul, who moves amongst sense-objects, free from either attachment or repulsion, he wins eternal peace.**[6]

No doubt a lot of the anger we see in the modern world and in public discourse belies much attachment and loss of reason. Is this a signpost on the way to somewhere we really don't want to go?

True virtue is not prudish or superficial. It is authentic and although it involves restraint it is incorrectly seen by many as a restriction on freedom. It restrains what is less desirable within us — desire — by what is more desirable — reason — and is the natural expression of a harmonious, well-ordered psyche. Although virtue may look unpalatable, the outcome is far better and freer than vice. It leaves us not just free from illness of the body and conflict with others, but free within ourselves, the kind of freedom that comes with a clear conscience and the mind and heart at rest.

Matters of life and death

There is probably no other domain of ethics more important and none that tests ethical principles in the crucible as much as life-and-death issues like abortion and euthanasia. But before we consider them, it would be useful to consider how the way we define ourselves has radically changed in recent years.

Personhood

> **I am fond of pigs. Dogs look up to us. Cats look down on us. Pigs treat us as equals.**
>
> *Winston Churchill*[7]

These days one of the main means to 'liberate' animals has been the blurring of the natural demarcation between species. What does animal liberation really mean? If you tell a pig that they are liberated, what does that mean to the pig? It doesn't mean they have a choice to stop being a pig, that they can vote in the next election or that they will take up an interest in philosophy. An animal doesn't have a choice to behave or think in any way other than the one it has been biologically programmed for. It would seem that only human beings have the capacity to do that. Animal liberation is really only a meaningful concept for people, not animals. That humans, by virtue of intelligence, have dominion over other species on the planet is simply a statement of fact, but it comes with responsibility and duty that can be discharged wisely and compassionately or irresponsibly and cruelly. If 'animal liberation' means appealing for the just and compassionate treatment of animals by humans then it is undoubtedly a very good thing. If, on the other hand, it means elevating animals and lowering humans to an equal status that is not natural to them, then it is potentially delusory and dangerous. The way this has been done in secular academic philosophy is by inventing something called 'personhood'.

Defining a person as a human being used to be pretty simple, but it is a little more complex now. Elevating animals to 'personhood' status, as the contemporary philosopher Michael Tooley does in his book and seminal article titled *Abortion and Infanticide*[8,9] and Peter Singer does in his book *Should the Baby Live*, does not make an animal other than what it is. Potentially, what it does do is lower the status of humans to a level with or below that of animals. This opens the door to justifying killing the disabled, abortion on demand, infanticide and foetal experimentation among other things, which is what ethicists such as Tooley and Singer do. Whether such a philosophical manoeuvre is intended to protect animals, or whether it is really a means of denigrating humans seen as worthless or inconvenient, is interesting to ponder.

At first glance the 'personhood' argument looks rational, benign and benevolent and roughly goes as follows. A 'person' is not a human being with a human genome. To be a person any creature merely has to display certain attributes like having an individual or separate sense of self, having a mental picture of a future full of plans and expectations, having desires and aspirations, making a contribution to society, and having a basic intellectual capacity. A foetus or infant, so the argument goes, does not display these attributes whereas a dog, monkey or pig might so these animals have a greater claim to being persons than the human foetus or infant. They are therefore more morally relevant. That the foetus or infant has the potential for these capacities is irrelevant according to the argument. From the personhood perspective it is speciesism (as in racism, sexism etc.) to discriminate between humans and other animals.

The sting in the tail of the personhood argument, and perhaps the real reason it was put forward in the first place, is in order to 'free us up', to condone things that would have been previously hamstrung by ethical constraints like abortion, infanticide and euthanasia. It is interesting, however, that, according to this argument, even though a human baby is totally defenceless and innocent, rather than that being the overwhelming case for protecting it, it is what makes it expendable. But surely the law of nature is such that a species is meant to foster and protect their young, not harm them. If you got between a tigress and her newborn cub, and told the tigress that your right to life was greater than the cub's, the tiger wouldn't be particularly sympathetic.

But how strong and unambiguous is this definition of personhood? For example, do we cease to be a morally relevant person while asleep because we are not doing something productive or displaying intellect? Do we, as a human adult, cease to be a person when completely awake in the present moment with no mental projections about the future or preoccupations about the past? Although Einstein described individuality as an optical delusion of our consciousness in which we imprison ourselves,[10] do we cease to be a person if we transcend our separate, individual sense of self and expand to a universal sense of self? Do we cease to be a person when the mind is peaceful, clear, lucid and free of agitation? Is it our wanting that makes us morally relevant or our being? Do we cease to be a person when desireless and completely content? If so, then the wisest and most enlightened in our community are not morally relevant persons at all and, as a result, we can do anything we like to them without disturbing our consciences.

Maybe the other possibility is that the abovementioned definition of personhood — full of desires, living in the future and past, separate self, etc. — is the definition that the ego would give for what it means to be a person. The same things the wisdom traditions see as causing the fall of humanity the personhood-oriented ethicist sees as putting us on a pedestal. From a wisdom tradition perspective, the ego, being illusory, delusionary, self-centred and self-absorbed as it is, when creating an ethical code will use any intellectual device and philosophical manoeuvre it can in order to remove barriers to exerting its will. A community, increasingly driven by a similar mentality, will willingly embrace an ethical code based on such flimsy justifications. What the personhood argument interprets as the coming of moral relevance — an infant exerting desires and individuality, and unhooking from the immediacy of the present moment — the wisdom argument interprets as humanity's fall from innocence. What the personhood argument interprets as freedom from archaic ethical taboos, the wisdom argument interprets as a slide into barbarity rationalized by sweet-sounding justifications all the while stumbling into a very sticky ethical, social, medical and legal mess.

Abortion

Unfortunately, despite modern contraception, unwanted pregnancy is still very much a fact of life with at least half of pregnancies being unplanned and over 40 per cent of these ending in abortion meaning approximately one quarter of pregnancies end in termination in most developed countries.[11] Until relatively recent times, abortion was illegal as it was seen as taking innocent human life. Women, finding themselves in the undesirable situation of having an unwanted pregnancy, demanded reproductive choices not just in terms of preventing pregnancy through contraception, but also by being able to terminate unwanted pregnancy. This was 'pro-choice' — this was freedom. Clearly, a pregnant woman's physical, psychological and social wellbeing is paramount, but does abortion necessarily protect this? The great change in abortion law was justified on the basis that to continue with an unwanted pregnancy is detrimental to a woman's mental health to the point that her life is in danger through self-harm. This assumption, however, might not be correct. According to large evidence-based reviews, following termination of pregnancy there is significant risk of post-traumatic stress.[12] Following abortion there is an 81 per cent increased risk of mental health problems, and if a woman terminates an unwanted pregnancy rather than carrying it to term then she is 55 per cent more likely to experience mental health problems.[13] It has also been associated with an increased risk of anxiety, alcohol and substance abuse.[14] Some argue that women who have unwanted pregnancies had higher rates of prior mental health problems anyway.[15] Post-termination of an unwanted pregnancy, a woman is at significantly greater risk of suicide, but is at significantly lower risk if pregnant or if she has a young child.[16] Surprisingly, this is despite the fact that unwanted pregnancy and childbirth are risk factors for depression. Finnish population studies have found that post-childbirth there is roughly half the risk of suicide in the following year whereas post-termination of pregnancy it is triple the national average, i.e. termination of pregnancy is associated with a sixfold greater risk for suicide than having a child.[17] In later studies, the risk of suicide post-termination were still over double the national average.[18] Possible explanations include either abortion is a risk-factor for suicide, or that personal, social and economic factors that predispose towards suicide are more common among women who have unwanted pregnancies, or a combination of both.

If a woman has prior mental health problems, then a termination of pregnancy may compound them, whereas having a dependent child may be protective against suicide, which is not to say that parenthood, especially unwanted parenthood, doesn't come with considerable challenges like disruption to career or study, financial costs and stress. Women who have an abortion will understandably feel deeply conflicted by tension between their natural biological instincts of protecting the young and their social, career, financial and personal aspirations. But the detrimental effects of abortion may be significant[19] and have perhaps been under-recognized, meaning that the ethical justifications for it on the basis of the woman's emotional wellbeing may not be as solid as many assume they are. It is possible to put a case that rather than abortion freeing society of the problem of unwanted pregnancy and progressing human rights it may have created greater health problems and ignored the duty of care to the foetus and the woman. It may have contributed to more deaths than it has prevented. Perhaps greater support for women (and their partners) who find themselves in a difficult situation is a better solution than merely trying to eliminate it?

Pro-choice or no-choice?

The slogan we most associate with the coming of abortion is 'pro-choice'. Initially, as set out in the landmark US legal case, Roe v. Wade and supported by the 14th Amendment[20] — which protects the right to privacy against state action— abortion was only meant to be legal in the most extreme circumstances, such as where the woman's life was in significant danger and, even then, only after extensive counselling and deliberation. But soon, in practice, abortion was on demand and no stringent tests were applied or counselling provided other than perhaps medical information about the procedure. Now, interestingly, the pro-choice movement seems to be less and less about being pro-choice. The woman seeking abortion is seen as autonomous and with rights but now, it seems, that the doctor has little autonomy or ability to choose for themselves whether or not to be implicated with it. Increasingly, ethicists are arguing that it is untenable that a doctor could maintain a position of conscientious objection[21] and such has been the intensive lobbying of governments and lawmakers that the law is increasingly compelling doctors to comply, conscientious objection or not.[22]

It seems that now only some people's choices are respected and not others. It is not that a doctor with a conscientious objection necessarily wants to impose their views on others, they just did their training and hung up their shingle with a view to preserving life and treating illness, which is the natural duty of a doctor. From that perspective, seeing the foetus as a human life, the doctor may not feel that they can participate in terminating that life, even when a woman in the unfortunate situation of having an unwanted pregnancy comes through the door. The doctor is no longer free to hold the view that a foetus is a human life because if they did then it would be completely incongruous to participate in any abortions except perhaps to save the woman's life — but even that is aimed at saving, not taking, life. From the perspective that a foetus is irrelevant then abortion doesn't matter, but from the perspective that it is relevant, abortion is taking a human life — period. Was the idea behind abortion really ever 'pro-choice' or was pro-choice the ideological Trojan horse draped in banners of freedom, but secretly carrying a 'no-choice' agenda.

Contraception

Prevention, of course, is always better than cure. If we go back a step, the arrival of contraception was meant to be a wonderfully liberating thing. From the 1960s onwards, the sweet nectar of the sexual revolution had arrived and unwanted pregnancy was meant to be a thing of the past. Unfortunately, it seems that the opposite has happened. As mentioned, at least half of all pregnancies in many developed countries are unintended, but among adolescents and women over 40 years old it is over 75 per cent[23] with the rate of unwanted pregnancy particularly going up in young and poor women.[24] Unwanted pregnancy related to rape accounts for approximately 1 per cent of the nearly 3 million unwanted pregnancies in the United States annually[25,26] and is therefore an uncommon, although pressing, justification for abortion. In another 1 per cent of cases, the abortion is for a potentially life-threatening medical condition, so in the other 98 per cent of cases it is related to social, economic and psychological issues.[27]

The problem with unwanted pregnancy is not about the potential protective effect of contraception but the actual protective effect, which is not so good because it is not taken reliably especially by young women. From a natural law perspective, if we ignore a basic natural law that sex is pleasurable because it is primarily meant for reproduction then we get into some complicated territory and potentially sticky traps. We can have what we want — sexual liberation — but we get what comes with it — unwanted pregnancy and associated psychological, social and health-related problems.

What's in a word?

If the philosophical line of reasoning deems someone or something to be morally irrelevant, like a foetus, then it is not protected by human rights and as a consequence a range of actions become valid, which would otherwise have been considered wrong, like abortion or foetal experimentation. You have to deny the moral relevance of the foetus in order to turn what would be otherwise wrong into a right. If one holds the view that the foetus is a morally relevant entity — i.e. human life — then abortion is wrong, except perhaps if it was a medical life-saving procedure for the mother. If the foetus is not morally relevant — i.e. not a human life — then the embryo is just a collection of cells. Heralding the changing social, ethical and legal landscape, the status of the foetus was systematically changed in the middle of the twentieth century. The original Hippocratic oath, for example, was clear, simple and unambiguous in relation to euthanasia and abortion.

> **I will give no deadly medicine to anyone if asked, nor suggest any such counsel; and in like manner I will not give to a woman a pessary to produce abortion.[28]**

Codes of ethics were re-examined and re-worded but the new terminology left much open to interpretation. For example, the World Medical Association Declaration of Geneva in 1948 reworded the Hippocratic oath.

> **I will maintain the utmost respect for human life from the time of its conception.**[29]

From 'conception' is unambiguous but 'utmost respect' is less so. It certainly means that life will be taken into account but it does not necessarily mean, as the Hippocratic oath originally did, that the doctor will under no circumstances take life. Then the declaration was again subtly reworded in Venice in 1983, but this rewording was far more significant.

> **I will maintain the utmost respect for human life from its beginning.**[30]

The cat was now out of the bag. What does 'from its beginning' mean? Some say conception, some say quickening, some say when the foetus is viable at around 25 weeks and, as previously mentioned, some notable ethicists even go so far as to state that an infant has little just claim to a right to life until possibly one year of age. In the words of Peter Singer:

> **Whichever way we decide this difficult factual question, infants will be deemed not to have a right to life at birth, nor for some time afterwards ... We must recall, however, that when we kill a newborn infant there is no person whose life has begun.**[31]

As the definition of when life begins became increasingly grey so too did the rights of the child. Where this will ultimately lead we do not know for we are in uncharted territory.

Euthanasia

A generation ago, euthanasia and assisted suicide would have been frowned upon but now, in the name of autonomy, the moral and legal barriers to them are being eroded. The reduced moral standing of the church has no doubt had much to do with this, and it has been successfully characterized by advocates of liberal agendas as the enemy of autonomy and free choice.

Currently, there is a strong and persistent push in most developed countries to introduce laws legalizing euthanasia. It is seen as humane, progressive, kind and putting power back into the hands of people to freely choose when and how they want to die. In this case, it is not so much driven by the pursuit of pleasure but more about the avoidance of pain. On the face of it, this is a very attractive and persuasive argument, but here too there may be a few traps we may be unwittingly about to step into.

It does seem strange that at a time when most countries have removed the ability for judges to sentence to death even the most hardened and violent criminals, we seem ready to blithely put the power to take innocent life into the hands of doctors with little or no accountability or oversight. How amazing that is. How strange and conflicted that a doctor is trying to save life one moment and then takes it the next.

A predominantly secular society with a materialist outlook will quickly dispense with spiritual and religious considerations by denying that there is something more transcendent to us than the body. Nor will it be concerned about any potential transmigrational issues after death associated with euthanasia and suicide. The common mantra these days is that we were not given a body; we own it and can do with it what we choose. But how did we get into the body we are in? Did our parents make the body or did they just make love and the rest happens mysteriously? If they didn't make it then who or what did? Chance?

Putting all those spiritual questions aside, and turning to more pragmatic concerns, the figures on euthanasia in countries where it is allowed belie a concerning picture that has been widely discussed since the Netherlands introduced the world's first laws decriminalizing it in the early 1990s. A paper by Brian Pollard, a palliative care physician, draws attention to the following figures taken from original surveys of Dutch doctors.

> By adopting the narrow definition of euthanasia as 'active termination of life upon the patient's request', the Dutch reported (in 1991) there were 2,300 instances of euthanasia in the year of the survey, or 1.8 per cent of all deaths. When, however, to these are added instances of killing patients without request and intentionally shortening the lives of both conscious and unconscious patients, the figures are dramatically altered. They now become: 2300 instances of euthanasia on request; 400 of assisted suicide; 1000 of life-ending actions without specific request; 8750 patients in whom life-sustaining treatment was withdrawn or withheld without request, 'partly with the purpose' (4750) or 'with the explicit purpose' (4000) of shortening life; 8100 cases of morphine overdose partly with the purpose' (6750) or 'with the explicit purpose' (1350) of shortening life; 5800 cases of withdrawing or withholding treatment on explicit request, 'partly with the purpose' (4292) or with the 'explicit purpose' (1508) of shortening life.[32–36]

The doctrine of double-effect or double-meaning?

The most common way of doctors causing the death of their patients is by giving high doses of morphine in order to 'alleviate their suffering' but, as the 'doctrine of double effect' decrees, the patient also dies in the process. Practices such as giving high doses of morphine to hasten death do not need to be recorded as euthanasia and they therefore evade scrutiny, but an important point needs to be made regarding this. Prescribing morphine therapeutically is like trying to kick a goal between two goal posts in football. Too far to the left or the right and you don't kick a goal. Kicking wide to the left is like administering too little morphine to have the desired pain-relieving effect. Kicking wide to the right is administering so much morphine that the patient is rendered unconscious, unable to maintain breathing and dies. In between the posts you have a conscious patient in little or no pain unless, of course, the real pain is emotional and/or spiritual/existential, in which case the treatment is not morphine but is emotional and/or spiritual/existential support. Setting that aside, any trained palliative doctor knows how to kick that therapeutic goal, that is, to titrate the dose of narcotics and administer them effectively. To not kick such a goal is either incompetent medicine, lazy or a convenient cover for the hidden primary objective of ending the patient's life in the first place. This is euthanasia by stealth and accounts for the great majority of such deaths. Imagine if a surgeon came to the ward in the morning and asked the resident doctor how the patients fared overnight and the resident said that they were all kept pain free, which is the main thing, but that meant half of the patients died from too much morphine. You would have to question the motivation or the ability of the resident.

A 'good death' or bad care?

The widespread use of euthanasia potentially undermines the training, resources, energy and motivation needed for competent palliative care and the support of patients. Increasingly we are likely to see the last option — euthanasia — being used as the first option, especially in cash and resource-strapped healthcare systems being manned by oftentimes overworked, burned out staff without the time or energy to care humanely.

In Holland and Belgium, where the practice is most tolerated, the number of deaths attributable to euthanasia has tripled over the last decade. Now, using the narrowest definition of euthanasia that ignores the many dying through morphine overdose, 4.6 per cent of people in Belgium die from assisted suicide.[37] Originally, it was only meant to be done in the most extreme cases of suffering where a person was near to death. In practice, however, it is a different story. Like abortion, the 'strict guidelines' are being watered down or not enforced to such an extent that a person doesn't need to be near death any more — they just need to be suffering. Furthermore, the definition of suffering is being watered down and increasingly the method of dealing with suffering in a society governed by pleasure and pain is to cut it out rather than face it or transcend it. In the Netherlands, there are now dozens of cases each year where people as young as in their thirties are euthanized for mental health problems like depression,[38] and an increasing number are euthanized just because they are 'tired of living' and most of these are lonely.[39] What is happening to the care ethic in our community? Is this another example of the 'normalization of deviance'?

In the grips of fear

People with a radical pro-autonomy position on euthanasia argue that being tired of living or the anticipation of ageing or dependency are valid reasons for such a request. Indeed, fear of suffering or incapacity is a more common reason for requesting euthanasia than actual suffering.[40,41] So now, can we add the fear of ageing to the list of valid causes to request death? When is a fear of ageing or incapacity adequate enough reason to have euthanasia? Eighty? Seventy? Sixty? Fifty? It will be hard to know where to draw the line, but many older people already feel like a burden so will widespread euthanasia create an environment where they feel obliged to request death? Is fear really a sound foundation upon which to base laws, practices and policies?

Further, society creating laws based on some individuals' so-called freedom has implications for the environment of care that all people in society find themselves in. It potentially undermines the care and support given to others particularly the elderly, chronically ill and disabled.

Certainly, it is not easy to confront discomfort and death — they come with life. Is it how we meet them that really determines whether it is a good life or a good death, not merely ending the life in the quickest and most convenient way possible? We do not admire a sporting team who, losing badly late in a game, quits the playing field before the siren sounds. We admire and are inspired by the team that plays with courage and wholehearted effort right to the end. What we may be currently faced by are euthanasia laws not based on courage but playing into and being driven by fear and avoidance. Potentially, we are not supporting quality care but undermining it. Despite the rhetoric, the push for euthanasia may not rest on criteria and safeguards that are well defined but are nebulous, ever broadening and which cannot be adequately monitored let alone policed. Even the original Remmelink Report[42] from Holland in 1991 noted that the majority of the thousands of annual deaths at the hands of doctors were involuntary, yet none are ever prosecuted for not following the 'strict guidelines'. By embracing euthanasia, we may unintentionally be doing the opposite of promoting freedom for the sick and dying and their families. If so, the medical and medico-legal complications will be enormous.

Equally, family members and health practitioners who have a fear of death, or cannot let go, can multiply suffering by persisting too long with painful, invasive and futile treatments that do not allow a person to properly and peacefully prepare for death. Knowing when and how to let go would be a pretty useful skill in the final stages of life. If we don't go down the path of euthanasia then that leaves us with the other option — to enjoy the good times in life when we can, to learn courage, resilience and patience in the hard times, and ultimately to transcend adversity. Perhaps through death we have the potential to find that which is deepest within us in those times of adversity, and perhaps that is the only authentic path to freedom we have when death knocks at our door. If we never stay the course we may never discover that which is deepest within us.

SOME THINGS TO REFLECT ON:

- Which part of the self do your decisions tend to be ruled by?
- Do you care as much about duties as you do about rights?
- What virtue do you need to cultivate more of in your life?
- What will make your life a life well lived such that one day you could be content?

SOME THINGS TO PRACTISE:

- Notice what happens when you follow conscience as it presents itself in the present moment.
- Notice what happens when you follow your desires for things in the future at the expense of conscience.
- Let your actions be based on virtue as it presents itself rather than desire and observe the effect.

CHAPTER 11

CHILD REARING AND EDUCATION

Clearly, there is a necessary balance between providing freedom and encouragement for children to express themselves, versus their need for discipline and to know where the limits are. Like a potter throwing a pot, two hands are needed — the inner one for expansion (love) and the outer one to set the limits (discipline). If either is 'heavy-handed' or missing — i.e. all love that never sets a limit or all discipline that is oppressive and constricting — the result will not be successful nor will the child be truly happy. In this chapter, we will explore some of the contemporary issues confronting parents and children to understand not only where we stand now but where coming generations may be heading. Although many issues are perennial there are others that are quite new.

Children and self-restraint

There is a German advertisement that shows a father at a supermarket with his young son.[1] They pass the lolly section and the son instinctively grabs a packet of sweets and puts them in the shopping trolley. The father patiently takes them out and puts them back on the shelf. The boy, with a defiant look on his face, puts them back in the trolley. The father, trying to keep calm, puts them back on the shelf again. The son calculatingly decides that a tantrum is the only way to bend his father to his will. He lets loose while other shoppers look on in varying states of disbelief, irritation and pity. The final caption is, 'Use condoms'.

There are not too many parents who cannot relate to the conflicted emotions of dismay, love, anger and total non-comprehension arising in the face of an emotional onslaught by a child too young to be reasonable but old enough to know how to get its way.

Teaching by modelling

The apparent competition between child and parent is a learning opportunity in disguise. The parent is supposed to have a sufficient level of executive functioning that they can model for the child how a reasonable, moderate, patient, loving, equanimous, courageous, just, magnanimous, prudent and wise person would act in any given set of circumstances. That's a pretty tall order. The child embodies the less reasonable aspects of human nature — appetite and emotion. Unfortunately, as adults, we are all a work in progress and we often model the opposite of what we intend, and then that is what we teach the child.

From a young age, children very quickly take on the attitudes and behaviours of their parents and other important adults in their lives whether they are transmitted consciously or unconsciously. As a case in point, a study of first- and second-grade children looked at how parents' anxiety about maths related to their children's maths anxiety and maths achievement.[2] Parents who were more maths-anxious tended to have children who learned significantly less maths over the school year and had more maths anxiety by the school year's end, but — and this is the key point — only if maths-anxious parents regularly helped their children with their maths homework. If maths-anxious parents didn't generally help with maths homework then the children's maths achievement and attitudes were fine. The maths-anxious parents thought they were teaching their children maths when they were actually teaching them how to be anxious about maths.

Children learn quickly and once the behaviour or attitude has been learned it is unconsciously reinforced and habituated by practice. Once it has been reinforced for long enough it begins to be an indelible part of their character unless a major effort and a supportive environment to change the situation are provided some time later. Therefore we need to be very aware of the attitudes and behaviours we model for children lest we want them to be prisoners of unhelpful habits and attitudes like their parents and teachers are.

The challenges of parenting in the modern world

In days gone by, home and parenting arrangements were generally a lot simpler. The father mostly worked, the wife mostly stayed at home looking after the children, and the children went to school. Then these roles became blurred as women were increasingly freed from the expectations of being housewives, which was less than fulfilling for many of them. But modern parenting and family life is certainly not a bed of roses.

The modern woman

The modern, liberated woman is meant to have it all — family, work, social life, health and all the rest. Starting the family is deferred for career until there is a race against the biological clock, then the race from the maternity ward back to work, the race from work to childcare, the race home for a little distracted, multi-tasking time with the children, the race for promotion, then the race home to the drinks cabinet, then stagger to the pantry for some chocolate, and then to bed for a sleepless night, then the alarm clock starts the race back to work in the morning, and then eventually the race to the doctor for antidepressants, sedatives or blood-pressure medications. Is this really what it means to have it all? Maybe there is the rare woman who lives the 'ideal life' but there are far more who struggle to attain this ideal. Family life seems to have little or no functional reserve these days. The reality is not quite as sweet or liberating as the rhetoric.

The modern man

For many men these days, there is the confusion of being caught between the traditional and, some would say, biological roles of breadwinner and head of the household versus the expectations of modern-day husbands and fathers of being sensitive new-age men who are just as likely to stay at home or raise the children as the wife. Men tend to identify themselves far more with work and the provider role than women hence unemployment and retirement have a far more negative impact on a man's mental health than a woman's.[3]

The modern family

The old model of man and wife being one seems to have long gone. For an increasing number of households these days, the traditional model of marriage or even living and raising children in a stable co-habiting relationship is becoming less common. Evidence clearly shows that marriage, even if it is only moderately happy, has a positive effect on people's mental and physical health, although that effect is more pronounced for men than women.[4] Clearly, a very unhappy or abusive marriage has a detrimental effect on mental and physical health, especially for women.[5,6] In most countries, the criteria for divorce were loosened some time back, which corresponded with divorce rates going up and more children being raised by single and step-parents. Although many do an incredibly good job under trying circumstances, this is not the preferred option for many reasons.

Although more women working after World War II provided freedom outside the home and a greater net family income, the original luxury of two incomes has been steadily eroded by inflation such that now the average family can only survive with two incomes.[7] What seemed to be a step into liberation outside of the home is now a necessity. With both parents generally under the pump in today's fast-paced world, many parents are too busy to properly engage with their children when they eventually get home from work. Parents often rely on various forms of screen time to keep the children quiet, and there are increasing numbers of families where both parents work not because it provides fulfilment but because they have to make ends meet.

Simple things can make a big difference in family life. For example, now busy and distracted families rarely have meals together, but research has shown that is probably the most important time of the day for families to connect. According to a massive study in the United States, adolescents from families who regularly have the evening meal together were far less likely to get into trouble like substance abuse, crime, violence, mental illness and suicide.[8] The same study also found that the most protective factors were adolescents having a sense of connectedness at home and/or school, the parents having higher expectations for their child's conduct and taking an interest in what they are doing, and the child having a spiritual dimension to their lives. Also important were not having easy access to alcohol, drugs or weapons in the home, and not having too much discretionary income.

Information technology (IT) is a great potential servant but is an increasingly tyrannical master in many homes these days. It has made it easier for work to creep into the home and into parts of our lives where it has no right to be, like family time, sleep, the meal table, holidays and weekends. Work–life balance has become a thing of the past for many. Has this led to happier, freer households? Maybe for some, but perhaps not for most.

Protecting children from harm

How does a parent protect a child these days? How do you protect children from online bullying or developing low self-esteem from the way they engage with social media? How does a parent unplug their children from an artificial world and engage them with the actual world? How do you rein in things when they are being driven by an ideology that keeps asserting an alluring freedom agenda? How do we help adults, let alone children, to develop a clearer understanding of the world as it is when their idea of reality is increasingly drawn from the unreality of 'reality' television?

Whether it is porn, substances, gambling or addiction to IT, it would seem that the little dopamine reward centre in the human brain is being primed from an early age. Maybe the problem needs to get a lot worse before we will question our assumptions about what freedom really means.

Maybe the pain associated with our current trajectory will have to reach a point of desperation before we wake up to what is going on and rein it in.

Pornography and sexting

How does a modern parent keep their child safe when so many potentially harmful things are put readily within reach, for example, accessing increasingly explicit pornography and other degrading or violent material on the Internet? Younger and younger children are accessing such material and in doing so normalizing extraordinarily abnormal behaviour and attitudes. Addiction, poor mental health, dysfunctional relationships and exploitation are some of the common side-effects,[9] but what are the long-term effects on the development of children's brains and relationships when the larger part of a whole generation has been exposed to such material from an early age?

Sexting is increasingly seen as normal behaviour by adolescents, with approximately half having sent sexually explicit images of themselves and two thirds having received them.[10] Is this an example of young people expressing their freedom or just another example of normalizing deviance? Increasingly children are left vulnerable to accessing degrading material of a violent and pornographic nature, which also leaves them vulnerable to risky behaviours.[11]

This is the first generation who will be exposed to such material from an early age, and the effects on social and emotional development is ominous. Use of such material is associated with greater depressive symptoms, poorer quality of life, more mental and physical-health diminished days, and lower health status.[12] Teen sexting is significantly associated with symptoms of depression, impulsivity and substance use.[13] Nevertheless, a furore seems to arise when schools encourage girls to 'protect their integrity', for example by dressing more modestly and not sending explicit images of themselves. Increasingly, boys in particular are treating girls with scant respect and abusing them by posting images in the public domain that were sent in private. Nevertheless, some with a more liberal social agenda see sexting as adolescents being who they are[14] but surely this is more a case of them shaping their character for what they will become.

As a society we can have what want but what, in the fullness of time, will come with it? Are adolescents really expressing who they are when they act in this way or are they just being swept along by a misplaced desire to conform to peer culture, or to be cool, daring or popular? Do girls have absolutely no idea that such actions leave them vulnerable? What aspect of boys' nature is constantly being incited by the physical and virtual environments their minds are immersed in these days? Are boys just being swept along by a debased male culture and an increasing addiction to degrading material? Is this really evidence of a liberated community? From an adult perspective, are we derogating our responsibility to protect and guide children by leaving them to sip the sweet nectar of pleasure, but all the while falling headlong into one massive pitfall? If such things continue unfettered then the problems we are currently dealing with may be insignificant compared to what we will see in the future.

Gambling

Even when families go to watch what should be innocent sporting events these days, they are bombarded with advertising for sports betting. Sports betting advertising is tightly controlled in some countries like the United States but, in the name of advertising freedom, restrictions on such advertising were relaxed in Australia and soon there was saturation exposure at major sporting events.[15] It has had its desired effect from the sports betting perspective because four years later over 75 per cent of children and 95 per cent of adults believe that betting is a normal part of sport,[16] and spending on sports betting is increasing 30 per cent annually.[17] The next generation are being groomed in a way that no previous generation has been. Governments now have a conflict of interest, parents seem not to be taking up the issue and the industry certainly won't regulate itself. Is this just another example of a freer society or the normalization of deviance? In the United States, clamouring for a slice of the US$400 billion funds that go to illegal sports betting sites, governments are increasingly pressured to liberalize laws in this area.[18]

Media violence

Now even free-to-air television in 'child-friendly hours' is increasingly impacted upon by news stories of horrific events. The child takes these things in as normal without any real intellectual filters to understand or process them. Reviews of the research show that the effects of violent media on children include that:

1. **Prolonged exposure leads to being more likely to display aggressive behaviour.**
2. **Some children develop an appetite for viewing violent material.**
3. **It leads to immediate distress and fear.**
4. **Many children retain longer-term recurrent disturbing memories.**
5. **It can contribute to beliefs that aggression is an acceptable and effective behaviour.**
6. **It induces fear and the belief that the world is an unsafe place.**
7. **It can desensitize children to real violence.**[19]

Parents are often fighting a losing battle to protect their children from the ubiquitous presence of violent television, movies and video games. The rare things that are still open to active censorship are quite extreme, like child pornography and inciting terrorism, but even then the Internet makes such material only a few clicks away.

The importance of limits

There may well be a need to set limits and develop strategies for how to use technology rationally and safely. Unwanted Internet material can be blocked but it is hard, if not impossible, to quarantine it entirely. With modern freedom of access being what it is, and schools and parents normalizing the overuse of IT, this is only going to get harder. Maybe discipline and clear guidelines are needed and limits need to be set? Maybe we need to stop normalizing the abnormal and see it for what it is?

Children need to learn limits, not so much to limit their potential, but to find out how much of something is enough and what should be avoided altogether. It is the job of adults and society to do that for them by the laws, regulations and customs we adopt. Setting such limits requires consistency over time. Experiments on self-restraint mentioned previously illustrate that when young children have the ability to delay gratification they are much more likely to be successful and happy in their later life. Children need to learn focus, reason, self-restraint, equanimity, resilience and balance from the adults around them and, hopefully, what is modelled in the popular media children's minds are fed with.

Developmentally, the prefrontal cortex or executive functioning and attention regulation region of the brain is the last area to wire itself in and it does this mostly during late adolescence to early adulthood. It happens slower in males than females, which explains a lot about the poor and impulsive behaviour of a lot of male adolescents and young adults. The child needs adults to model executive functioning for them up until the time that they can do it for themselves. Before that time, their decisions and behaviours will be not so much the product of a conscious and reasonable decision-making process, but rather a product of the environment in which they have been brought up.

In days past, children were seen and not heard, but children are much louder and more boisterous than previously, although much of that could be the attempt of children to get the attention of unmindful, distracted and multitasking adults. Children have become much more used to getting their way early on in their upbringing, which is hard to rein in later in life. They can become quickly conditioned to it and expect it. Children are swamped with choice these days. They more often get to decide what they want to eat and drink — sweets, sweet drinks and fast food, for example — rather than eat what is put in front of them. Many get unfettered online and social media access even at night or at school. Poor behaviour and language are increasingly tolerated, disrespect to elders is more commonplace and is increasingly reported. Children increasingly decide how or if they want to learn. Is this a recipe for freedom or disorder?

Two kinds of love

Discipline, self-restraint and a healthy environment are important in many ways. Programmes in health-promoting schools[20] are aimed at things like promoting physical activity and limiting food choices to more healthy options.[21] Promoting healthy options at the school canteen or removing vending machines is sometimes seen as overbearing or a form of oppression, but being oppressed by diabetes, obesity, arthritis, cancer and heart disease is far worse. Life skills and healthy habits need to be fostered in early development and to ignore such responsibilities at home or school could be seen as failing in our duty of care to children and adolescents.

It is generally because parents and teachers love their children that they don't want to deny them anything, whereas discipline can be seen as cruel and uncaring. The difference between the two largely depends on what the love and discipline are motivated by and how they are delivered. The reality may be that all love with no discipline is far crueller for the child in the long run. Old-fashioned discipline could be very dismissive, oppressive and harsh, but now we have almost gone to the other extreme. What seems to be more prevalent these days is a mass experiment in a lack of restraint for children as if restraint or discipline in some way harms the child. Discipline can be, and historically often was, meted out in a very harsh and brutal way leaving some children bearing emotional and even physical scars. But is it more loving to the child to withhold discipline or limits? Yes, if our idea of happiness is getting what we want on demand. The superficial happiness and short-lived approval that comes from an appeased child is no doubt gratifying but it soon becomes a subtle and evermore restrictive trap for parents and child alike. This kind of love becomes synonymous with desire and approval. No, withholding discipline is not loving if we have a notion of happiness being dependent on self-mastery and our interest is in the child's long-term wellbeing and freedom.

The importance of attention

In days gone by, education was often a rather dry affair with many things being learned by rote. In many Western countries, education now increasingly resembles entertainment. Constant stimulation is required in order to maintain the attention of a student at school or university. Students are less and less inclined to learn things they see as 'boring' despite the fact that literacy and numeracy levels are falling. The report on Australian literacy and numeracy at the end of 2013, *PISA 2012: How Australia Measures Up*, found that rather than improving, Australia's performance had dropped significantly over the last decade.[22] Is this the product of children no longer having to be constrained to learn the 'boring' things they once had to learn? Is it a product of a freer approach to education? Is it a product of the inability of modern students to sustain attention? Is it a product of the distracted environment within which most children are raised these days? Probably all of the above.

The environment provided for a child has an enormous effect on their ability to sustain attention and learn. Studies show that the ability to sustain attention at preschool is highly predictive of educational achievement later on.[23] The more screen time a child has in early development, the more likely it is to have attentional problems in later life.[24] More screen time is also associated with poorer cognitive functioning.[25] Two hours a day is the recommended maximum but most children these days have at least twice that amount. It is not just the amount of screen time but the type of screen time that has a detrimental effect. One study found that just nine minutes of watching a fast-paced cartoon (*SpongeBob SquarePants*) was enough to reduce the executive functioning of four-year-olds in every way it could be measured.[26] Children may enjoy it, but it is a shame when 'entertainment' is having a negative effect on their development.

Of course, for most adolescents the fixation on smartphones and social media is increasing but the greater the amount of social media use, the poorer the academic performance.[27] We are literally breeding a generation of distracted, disengaged and multitasking youth. As one leading Stanford researcher, Clifford Nass, said of multitasking:

> **These are kids who are doing five, six, or more things at once all the time ... It turns out multi-taskers are terrible at every aspect of multitasking! They get distracted constantly. Their memory is very disorganized. Recent work we've done suggests that they're worse at analytic reasoning. We worry that it may be we're creating people who may not be able to think well, and clearly.[28]**

Social or antisocial media?

Evidence suggests that the greater the use of social media, the greater the risk of depression, as illustrated by a study on young adults in the United States that found the quarter who used social media the most, compared to those who used it the least, had triple the rate of depression.[29] The greater the use of social media, the poorer the nutrition and the greater the chance of skipping breakfast and consuming sweetened and energy drinks.[30] There is also the potential for children and adolescents to be bullied with the social media that is meant to connect them. Furthermore, unfettered access to screens, computers and smartphones is associated with poorer sleep and mental health, particularly in the young.[31,32]

Some studies estimate that at least a quarter of young people are now addicted to their mobile devices[33] whereas others suggest it may be one third.[34] This is associated with all the symptoms of addiction like tolerance, withdrawal, inability to modify behaviour and impaired relationships with peers.[35] One US study on young people found that the amount of texting was inversely related to the amount of fulfilment within relationships.[36]

Just because a young person is reliant on something and doesn't want to have their use of it limited in any way doesn't mean that it is good for them. Parents and teachers are less likely to restrain children's use of such media either because it keeps them quiet or because there are unquestioned assumptions that it makes them happy and enhances learning. The unlimited access to the online world through the unfettered use of computers comes at other costs as well. For example, a child having access to a computer in the bedroom is associated with higher computer use at night which, in turn, is associated with behavioural problems, and poorer sleep and mental health.[37] It is better to remove, or at least shut down at night, the electronic media in children's bedrooms.[38]

Thankfully, many families and some schools are developing more rational policies around the healthy use of mobile devices like smartphones — for example, not having them in the classroom, limiting time on the devices, not using them close to bedtime, not having them in the bedroom and not giving children access to them until they are at least seven or eight years old. To the addicted child this is seen as tyranny, but the aim is for the child to engage with the real world and have a life independent of the device while still being able to benefit from all that it has to offer. The aim is to have a real life and not just a virtual one. As a remedy, the mental discipline of mindfulness is increasingly being taught in schools. Research shows it helps to improve attention, self-awareness and executive functioning, and has important implications for child and adolescent mental health,[39–41] resilience, academic performance,[42,43] behaviour and self-control.[44–47]

Education and creativity

Another important topic is the relationship between creativity, education, intellectual conformity and dogma. Education comes from a Latin word 'educare' which means 'to draw out'. It is not about 'stuffing in' — that is indoctrination. Often what's stuffed in during formal education is more like a stopper put in the neck of the bottle that is human creativity.

There are many notable examples of gifted people who excelled in innovation and creativity but, unfortunately, viewed their education as being more of an impediment than an inspiration. The scientific genius Einstein and the English statesman Churchill are cases in point.

> **The only thing that interferes with my learning is my education.**
>
> *Albert Einstein*[48]

> **Schools have not necessarily much to do with education, they**

are mainly institutions of control, where basic habits must be inculcated in the young. Education is quite different and has little place in school.

Winston Churchill [49]

At school, students are grounded in some basic skills such as reading, writing and arithmetic. There is also socialization and learning about how to get on with others in a school environment. Then there is knowledge conveyed in subjects like history, languages, physics or biology. Most content taught in schools and universities, however, tends to get taught as fact rather than opinion or theory. This creates the illusion of certainty for teacher and student alike, but it potentially becomes a straitjacket the young mind puts on from an early age and from which it may never extract itself. We often feel uncomfortable with uncertainty so we pretend that we are certain of things about which we know very little. It creates the illusion of safety and surety, but has within it the seeds of anxiety and resistance to change. Junior doctors, for example, who never learn to be comfortable with uncertainty are far more likely to have burnout and low resilience compared to those who are comfortable with uncertainty.[50]

Mindsets

'Mindset' is a term popularized largely through a book of the same name by Carol Dweck, an educator from the United States.[51] Mindsets have implications for how (or if) we learn, how we deal with stress and our ability to persevere in the face of adversity. There are basically two mindsets described — the fixed and growth mindsets. We all have both of these traits to a greater or lesser extent. We might have a growth mindset about some things and a fixed mindset about others.

The fixed mindset is associated with a belief of having a fixed ability — 'you either have it or you don't.' When a child with a fixed mindset is confronted by a challenge, it is not seen as interesting or an opportunity to learn but as potential for failure. This is associated with a threat to self-esteem and is to be avoided. Such a child would rather stay with easy tasks they are familiar with in order to remain successful and receive continued praise. A child with such a mindset is also more likely to cheat when unable to do something in order to be perceived as successful and to hide their inability. Such a child's attention tends to be on negative, default ideas about themselves like, 'I can't do this. This is too hard. You probably think I'm stupid. I want to be somewhere else.' This means that the attention doesn't engage effectively with the task or what the teacher is saying so there is little opportunity for learning to take place. It is a lose-lose-lose situation — stress, no learning, no enjoyment and so forth. It is tempting to not challenge such a child, even gently, because of not wanting to cause them any discomfort. Such kindness may be crueller in the long run.

The growth mindset, on the other hand, is associated with an intrinsic belief that ability in any given task is not fixed and can be developed if the child wishes to put in the necessary time and effort. When confronted by challenge, a child with a growth mindset is more likely to welcome it seeing it as potential for learning and growth. They desire to extend themselves and be challenged. The attention is on the task or what the teacher is saying, not on themselves and thoughts about failing. What follows is discovery, learning, confidence and enjoyment.

There is a paradox in helping children to develop a growth mindset. One thing that doesn't help is praising children all the time whether they deserve it or not. Constantly tiptoeing around children's sensitivities increases them and fosters the kind of self-esteem that is puffed up on the outside but fragile and approval-seeking on the inside. It increases a child's ego rather than freeing them of it. Children don't need artificially positive assessments of their abilities any more than they need artificially negative ones. They simply need realistic but optimistic assessments given with care, encouragement and respect. Nor does it help praising children for results rather than effort. When a child is praised for getting something right — and there is nothing wrong with getting something right — the child wants to keep getting praise, so if they are confronted by something that is hard, such that they might get it wrong, then they become afraid and want to retreat to what they are comfortable with. If, instead, a child is praised for effort rather than results, then even if they get something wrong they will have learned something valuable along the way and also developed knowledge, experience and character. Results do matter but the paradox is that being preoccupied about future results takes the eye off the ball in the present moment. It increases anxiety and impairs performance. Being attentive to the real-time, present-moment process and being unconcerned about results helps a child to be calm and focused while actually producing better results in the end. The relaxation of being calm, engaged and focused in the present moment should not be confused with the 'relaxation' associated with apathy and disengagement.

The common trap of endless praise being given to children and the fear of challenging them undermines resilience and resourcefulness. It is important to learn how to feel comfortable with challenge rather than retreating back to what is easy and comfortable in order to protect them. The fear of making a mistake; the fear of getting hurt; the fear of being uncomfortable; we are almost paralysing children with fear these days because we, as adults, are constantly projecting our fears and anxieties onto them. We may want to make it easy for ourselves and our children but we make it hard for ourselves and may be contributing to the escalating levels of mental health problems. Helping children to learn to work with and go beyond their fears takes care and patience but it is ultimately liberating.

Dogma and mental rigidity

Information, opinion and theory are all very useful, but mainly if they are seen for what they are and are not taken for something they are not, like a true and unchanging representation of reality. When we try to make something true and certain that is not then we delude ourselves and others and we bind ourselves to dogmas and practices that may not serve us at all well. Take, for example, the 'flat earth' model of the Middle Ages or the systemic resistance to the hand-hygiene practices introduced by Florence Nightingale in the middle of the nineteenth century. When we believe we already know something we tend to confine discovery, ignore evidence and stop looking for new knowledge. It is easy to come out of our formal education with a fixed or limited view about the things we have learned, which can be hard to dispel later on. Medical education is amongst the worst offenders. One interesting study[52] explored bold statements about 'medical facts' made during grand rounds and medical conferences. Expert opinion is frequently voiced with great conviction and assimilated by junior staff as fact, never to be questioned again. Interestingly, when closely examined, only one third of such statements were evidence-based whereas in half, the available evidence contradicted the statement. When presented with the evidence, senior staff were unlikely to review evidence or alter their opinion exemplifying that changing ingrained but ill-founded medical practices generally takes generations, not years. As scientific as the medical profession generally likes to think it is, it is mired in dogma, false evidence and assumptions, conformity and convention, and even in the face of convincing scientific evidence often resists change no matter how necessary. This kind of human mentality can cause untold waste and harm.

> **All truth passes through three stages. First, it is ridiculed. Second, it is violently opposed. Third, it is accepted as being self-evident.**
>
> *Arthur Schopenhauer*[53]

The challenge is to be able to discern between those innovations that are based on wisdom and should be embraced, and those that are not based on wisdom and should be left alone. We often resist the former because it challenges accepted dogma and embrace the latter because it accords with some unquestioningly accepted ideology.

When something new, creative and useful comes along it is often resisted because it threatens the prevailing ideology and systems that have been built up around it. 'Disruptive technology' is a term defined by Clayton M. Christensen in 1995.[54] It describes things like the coming of digital photography that destroyed the market for photographic film. In medicine, the discovery by innovators like Professors Dean Ornish and George Jelinek that comprehensive mind–body-based lifestyle programmes could reverse illnesses like heart disease, prostate cancer[55] and multiple sclerosis[56]— illnesses assumed to be irreversible — has not been met with open arms. In fact, the response from the establishment has largely been quite the opposite, somewhere between ridicule and violent opposition. In another generation they will be seen as self-evidently worthwhile and many of the invasive, expensive, ineffectual and complex technologies currently being used will be seen as anachronisms.

There is nothing wrong with conformity to a prevailing view as it helps people to have a common language and a shared worldview, and it increases cohesion. But freedom of thought is a prerequisite for curiosity and discovery. We have to be able to question and leave an old assumption in order to explore something new, but that search needs to be directed by evidence and deep introspection. Like a ship of discovery, what we need is that freedom of thought that purposefully and skilfully navigates us from our familiar home to new and bountiful lands, and not that other kind of freedom of thought, which is merely a ship breaking its moorings and drifting aimlessly onto rocks or out to sea. Education has a major role to play in fostering the former and protecting us from the latter.

Curiosity

> **He who can no longer pause to wonder and stand rapt in awe, is as good as dead; his eyes are closed.**
>
> *Albert Einstein*[57]

An open mind is incurably curious and in awe of the universe it is surrounded by. Curiosity is a very natural state for a young child but their eyes are often dimmed by adults who have stopped looking. Discovery is not possible unless something wakes us up. Students' curiosity and questioning ability can be enhanced by an inspirational teacher but is unfortunately often snuffed out by education. If a student is lucky they may explore how to think and look, and not just be told what to think. To dispel false opinion we have to be awake and look afresh as if through a child's eyes.

Discovery consists of looking at the same thing as everyone else and thinking something different.

Albert Szent-Gyorgyi [58]

It is interesting to consider how to cultivate a state of mind that is more creative. One common assumption is that it is the amount of thinking we do that determines creativity, but most thinking should more rightly be called confusion or agitation and as we tend to overthink things and clutter the mind. Like a lake that is blown by the wind, its surface is broken and reflects a broken image. Another approach to creativity is contemplative — to think less and look more. We can look at what is in front of us and let a question about it come to rest in the mind. Like a lake that has a glassy, peaceful surface, it reflects truly. It allows for a creative or insightful idea to come to light. To then follow that creative insight requires attention and openness of mind. Albert Einstein was thought to be excellent at this and stories from his contemporaries speak of him sometimes silently withdrawing from a group conversation on a challenging problem they were seeking to solve. He would sit quietly with his eyes closed for a considerable amount of time until eventually they would open again and he would expound something profound.

Parallels have been found in modern studies on creativity as well. If someone is cognitively overloaded they tend to come up with automatic, predictable and non-creative responses, whereas if they help the mind to rest from thought then far more conscious and creative responses arise.[59] Helping children to settle, attend, be curious and open may therefore be an important way of fostering their innate creativity. Individually and collectively, the majority of us become dogmatic and fixed in our thinking and that is in large part why so few of us are truly creative. This narrows our ability to look with fresh eyes and to discover what others don't see. Innovators, inventors and people who take human knowledge into new realms generally have to do so in spite of prevailing beliefs and education, not because of them.

SOME THINGS TO REFLECT ON:

- As a parent or carer of children, do you to find the right balance between love and discipline? If not, is there anything you need to do about it?
- Is it really easier in the long run not to discipline a child when it needs it?
- Do you really engage your attention when you are with your children?
- What patterns of thought and behaviour do you model for your children?

SOME THINGS TO PRACTISE:

- Seek to find more balance between work and home life by defining and sticking to reasonably set limits.
- Take control of the technology in your life and, if you are the parent of young children, for your children as well.
- Practise being present with your children when you are with them.
- If possible, make it a priority to have evening meals together as a family.

CHAPTER 12

FREEDOM OF SPEECH AND PRIVACY

In many countries freedom of speech and access to information are revered, and rightly so. We do not have to look far for examples of the abuse of the right to free speech or information flow. The question is, how do we protect the right to speak those things that need to be spoken and bar the speech of things that should not be spoken? If we get that wrong then we may close down speech that informs, uplifts or liberates us and promote speech in the name of freedom that leads us into a deep and dark trap of our own making. In this chapter, we will explore how speech and information can be used for good or ill, whether they should ever be limited, and whether we are currently on a healthy trajectory.

Privacy and freedom of information

One of the most fascinating phenomena these days is to witness our collective battle to define the line where freedom of information and transparency should end and where privacy should begin. This has been brought into stark contrast by the rise of terrorism, but it has always been at issue whenever there is a real or perceived threat to public safety or prevailing power structures. Governments and law enforcement agencies want more freedom to access private information and data, and the public is oftentimes between a rock and a hard place in both wanting its safety and its privacy to be protected. For example, in what some described as 'the case of the century' in San Bernardino,[1] Apple did not want to hack one of its own phones to reveal data from a terrorist, whereas the government wanted them to do just that. Both can argue that they wish to keep us safe and free and that the other is putting our liberty at risk. Who is right and why? There is a trap at either extreme of that dipole — being watched by Big Brother at one end and a veil of secrecy that hides terrorists at the other.

Are we really more free in this information age or are the very technologies that we assumed would expand our horizons really just a complex web within which we are increasingly monitored and imprisoned? The truth probably lies somewhere in between. We all want to be able to keep private the things the world has no right to know, but that is also the cloak of invisibility under which criminals hide. Transparency, on the other hand, is the source of daylight we need to reveal injustice and corruption, but it is also the chink in the wall through which the malignant seek to monitor, control or steal.

Whistle-blowers have never fared well in society so it generally takes extraordinary courage and perseverance to blow the whistle on an injustice. But under what circumstances should a person or group blow the whistle? What information do they have the right and duty to reveal? For example, WikiLeaks is seen by many governments as a threat to safety and democracy, but for libertarians it is a powerful force for honesty, justice and transparency to keep governments honest. Strangely, an organization that champions transparency is also among the most secretive in the world.

Another issue is that with all this extra technology and information we are drowning ourselves in a sea of unnecessary data and communications. Many are plugged in and can no longer unplug. As one journalist put it:

> **Bain and Company, the consultancy, has estimated that executives in the 1970s had to deal with fewer than 1000 phone calls, telexes and telegraphs a year from people outside their company. These days, 30,000 external communications clog managers'**

inboxes annually. As Henry Mintzberg asks in his 2009 book, *Managing*, 'Might the internet, by giving the illusion of control, in fact be robbing managers of control? In other words, are the ostensible conductors becoming more like puppets?'

Andrew Hill, *Financial Times*, 5 March 2016.[2]

We created IT to unburden ourselves and make life easier, but it seems we have created an insatiable monster that invades every aspect of our lives rather than a faithful and discreet servant. In this era of computers, the Internet and social media, information is power. Whether it is criminals, government or marketers, people who control access to information, or can use it for their own purposes, have enormous influence. Even the very symbols of modern day freedom like Facebook are subtly used for manipulating emotions[3] or conducting psychological experiments,[4] something that the innocent subscriber didn't know they were signing up for. It all seems to come with such a benevolent face. Perhaps George Orwell's vision of a dystopian future outlined in the book *1984* has just come a little later than predicted.

Modernism, postmodernism and freedom of expression

Creativity is an interesting phenomenon in the modern day and another form of 'speech'. Many creations are thrown to the public now that previous generations might not have recognized as art or music. You may recall that the third of Gibbon's marks of a civilization in decline was that, 'Art becomes freakish and sensationalistic instead of creative and original.' One might wonder what his view of much modern art would be.

Once upon a time, there was a strong respect for order, proportion and harmony in music, art and literature. Modern and postmodern notions of creativity, however, driven by an insatiable thirst for 'freedom of expression', the need to shock and confront the audience, and having to be different, have increasingly embraced the idea of disorder. There are no rules of beauty or order that need to be followed, in fact, it almost seems that if there are such laws then they should be openly disobeyed. Perhaps there was a sleepy and complacent time when conformity for its own sake was seen as good, but now non-conformity is seen as good for its own sake. Among the intelligentsia, laws of harmony and beauty are not seen as inherent in nature, but more as an anachronistic social construct and an encumbrance.

Although inventive, many modern and postmodern creations seem, even to the untrained ear or eye, to disobey all musical, literary or artistic laws of harmony, rhythm, grammar, proportion, colour or form. Perhaps non-conformity with a rather staid view of the laws of beauty is breaking new and fertile ground as did the impressionists of the nineteenth century. Perhaps non-conformity with such laws is sometimes the refuge of an artist without talent. Sometimes it would seem that so long as the work is novel, confronting and barely recognizable as music, prose, poetry or art, then it is worthwhile to the avant-garde. It needs to scream individuality and not conformity. It seeks to deconstruct, not to construct. The person observing the art has to impose their own meaning on it, and sometimes it would seem that the observer has to work pretty hard. Equally, there can be a kind of order within the chaos and an appealing aesthetic within haphazardness, such as in the work of Jackson Pollock, possibly the most famous abstract artist of the twentieth century. Debate will no doubt rage as to what is or is not 'good art', whatever that may be. Perhaps we are best advised to discern that for ourselves by observing the effect it has on us mentally, emotionally and physically?

Should art imitate nature?

We often don't see the beauty around us in nature because of the presence of bias or disinterest, which either distorts it or obliterates it altogether. If we are lucky we might acknowledge the beauty of a flower, or the sleek, functional shape of a bird's wing, or the geometry of a snowflake or crystal. On the other hand, we might think that viruses are grotesque creations, but anyone who looks at an electron micrograph of them cannot but be impressed by their geometry and beautiful, if not lethal, simplicity. Nature is bursting with beauty but few have eyes open to see it. As GK Chesterton said, 'There are no uninteresting things, only uninterested people.'[5]

It could be looked at from another perspective. We would not take a postmodern attitude to the design of a car engine, the building of a bridge or the performance of a surgical procedure because it would be both dysfunctional and dangerous. Functionality relies on order through understanding and following natural laws. Perhaps the real challenge is for beauty and functionality to come together. Are art, music and literature really so arbitrary when other things are not? Great Renaissance artists like Leonardo da Vinci and Michelangelo thought not.

> **Human subtlety will never devise an invention more beautiful, more simple or more direct than does nature because in her inventions nothing is lacking, and nothing is superfluous.**[6]
>
> *Leonardo da Vinci*

> **The true work of art is but a shadow of the divine perfection.**[7]
>
> *Michelangelo*

Nevertheless, life and art would be pretty boring and uninventive if we perpetually sought to reproduce an idea of beauty honed during the Renaissance. Change will always challenge convention. The challenge is to discern when change improves us and society.

There are a lot of questions raised by the exploration into creativity. Who is to say what is beautiful and what is not? Is it subjective, is it just a matter of conformity, or are there objective measures we can use to discern beauty? Are those discerning marks merely a human invention or are they embodied in nature? Is there a risk of becoming trapped by the postmodern ideology that rejects conceptions of beauty and harmony? Is modern life the poorer for not being exposed to or aspiring to artistic creations embodying beauty? Is the freedom we associate with many contemporary literary and artistic creations really taking human creativity to new and higher levels or is it simply people unhinging themselves from all order and reason? Should we revere it, be disinterested in it or censor it? Should inspiration, beauty and/or functionality be the aim of the creative process?

Some might argue that the freedom of expression that is so highly valued now, despite the fact that it fascinates us, creates a pervasive disrespect for order, harmony and beauty, which finds its way into society's laws and customs? Plato thought it did, which is why he felt that art and literature had such an important role to play in the state. He might even argue that much of the art, music and literature now seen as being at the cutting edge of creativity are expressions of an increasingly confused, dysfunctional and disillusioned society losing its way. Who knows, but in the pursuit of self-expression, do we need to be a little more discerning in terms of what part of the self is doing the creating and what part of the self we choose to express? Will societies of the future look back on this unsettled and confused age and say that, yes, the music, literature and art of the day was an appropriate expression of those unsettled and confused times?

Censorship and food for the mind

These days censorship is mostly taken as a pejorative term as if it is opposed to freedom of speech. Censor comes from the Latin word 'censere' meaning to assess.[8] One definition of censorship is, 'The suppression or prohibition of any parts of books, films, news, etc., that are considered obscene, politically unacceptable, or a threat to security.'[9]

Is all censorship bad? We censor — at least we should censor — the food that goes in the mouth. If someone laid out healthy food, junk food and food adulterated with poison on a dining table, we wouldn't willingly and consciously put the poisonous food in our mouth unless we had a death wish. We assess or censor things all the time based on whether we think they are useful or harmful, including the things we feed the mind. If we don't like a television show or what someone has written then we don't watch or read it. A caring parent censors what a young child watches on television. We censor the thoughts we choose to listen to or give attention to.

If there are parallels between food for the body and food for the mind then perhaps we could ask a few pertinent questions and proffer a few possible answers. What is food for the mind? Ideas and sensory experience. Should we be more or less careful with the quality of food we put in the mind than we are with the food we put in the body? More careful. What is the effect of putting healthy food in the mind? Health, happiness and harmony. What is the effect of putting junk food in the mind? Mental laziness, apathy and confusion. What is the effect of putting poisonous food in the mind? Misery, destruction, conflict, hatred and death.

What then are examples of healthy food, junk food and poison for the mind? Healthy food is full of nutritional value and keeps us healthy. For the mind, it equates with that which inspires, enlightens, uplifts, harmonizes, creates happiness, and brings peace within and without. Junk food would be empty calories with little nutritional value. It makes us fat, bloated, lacking energy and ill over the long term. Junk food for the mind makes us dull, bored, disinterested, lacking in curiosity, disconnected and lowers our level of awareness. It's mostly the meaningless, time-wasting pap that passes for shallow entertainment in magazines, radio, online and television. In small doses, it might taste pleasant and probably won't harm us, but as a staple diet it's not a good long-term plan. So what is food adulterated with poison? Poison makes us ill or kills us, sometimes quickly and sometimes slowly. For the mind it is those noxious ideas that foster hatred, intolerance, division, destruction, addiction and death. It incites malfeasance. It doesn't just ignore truth, it distorts and conceals it. Whether it is hatred being spread by terrorist organizations, degrading literature or hateful things being written on social media, if we feed the mind on such ideas without an antidote it will do its work.

So, should we censor the food for the mind? Some say that all censorship is bad, but surely we should censor out the poison, especially shielding children who, like open-mouthed chicks in a nest, will take in whatever they are fed. They are so susceptible to unhealthy ideas and attitudes. Although it is commonly used as a criticism of Plato, and people argue about what is or is not moral deformity, he advocated censoring the bad and feeding the mind of the youth — especially those who have a role of protecting the community (the guardians) —with only the best.

> **We would not have our guardians grow up amid images of moral deformity, as in some noxious pasture, and there browse and feed upon many a baneful herb and flower day by day, little by little, until they silently gather a festering mass of corruption in their own soul. Let our artists rather be those who are gifted to discern the true nature of the beautiful and graceful; then will our youth dwell in a land of health, amid fair sights and sounds, and receive the good in everything; and beauty, the effluence of fair works, shall flow into the eye and ear, like a health-giving breeze from a purer region, and insensibly draw the soul from earliest years into likeness and sympathy with the beauty of reason.[10]**

What about junk food for the mind? We couldn't censor it out if we tried. Karl Marx, the famous German philosopher, economist, revolutionary and inventor of communism, said that religion was the 'opiate of the masses', but he was born in the days before television, which is the mental opiate preferred by most people these days. Encouraging moderation and helping to educate more discerning palates might help to reduce the stupefying effect of too much food for the mind with little or no nutritional value. Should we encourage healthy food for the mind? Absolutely, but perhaps too few people have a taste for it. It may not rate as well on television, go viral on the Internet or sell as many magazines. Just as whole food is not as pleasant to a palate brought up on a diet of excess sugar, fat and salt, so too is healthy food for the mind less appealing to a mind conditioned to pap, sensationalism, titillation and the banal.

There are, therefore, two challenges for feeding the mind. First is to how to make healthy food appealing. Making something truthful taste healthy and appealing is not always easy as it can easily be twisted or taken out of context. Furthermore, it often runs counter to commonly held, popular or fashionable assumptions and attitudes of the day and as a result can be poorly received. Second is how to get clarity in that grey area between what is clearly poison and what is not. Oftentimes malignant ideas are not seen as such because they are disguised. In the 1944 movie *Arsenic and Old Lace*, arsenic was hidden in sugar by two benign looking old women. The mind can be easily seduced by sweet-sounding rhetoric, half-truths and take in malicious thoughts when masked by humour. Malicious ideas can also be disguised by the conviction and force of the speaker. An artful rhetorician, like Hitler, was very good at gauging the crowd and disguising the real message in the words that the crowd wanted to hear. In such cases, it is really only the rare person who will be able to pick them for what they are, not what they seem to be. Winston Churchill, for example, was a voice in the political wilderness who heard the tyrant in Hitler as early as 1930, three years before he became German chancellor.[11]

When to censor?

So 'good' censorship is a matter of taking out the worse and leaving in the better. The problem is in deciding what is worse and what is better, and where to draw the ill-defined line with regard to what speech, art or literature is promoted, what is tolerated, what is discouraged and what is outlawed. In the West, we have a very liberal attitude to freedom of speech. Now many things are allowed into the public domain that might previously have been considered totally unconscionable. Perhaps there was a time when, because of political influences and rigid social mores, the reins of censorship were too tight and relatively harmless or potentially important things were banned. For example, it was a long time before the writings of Galileo, being counter to ill-informed church dogma, were allowed to be published. There are many examples of the distortion of history or the suppression of events for political reasons, such as happens with the denial of the historical mistreatment of indigenous people in Australia, the Nazi holocaust, or suppressing the reporting of the 1989 uprising in Tiananmen Square in China. This is perhaps the bad side of censorship where the worse is preserved and the better is left out.

But can we go too far in thinking that nothing, or at least very little, should ever be subject to censorship? Now, with the coming of the Internet, it is almost impossible to keep a check on what is out in the public domain. That unlimited 'freedom' leaves many people vulnerable especially, but not only, children and adolescents, and the consequences are not good. Regulations are being eroded in the popular media.

Some people's view is that freedom of speech means being able to say whatever you want, whereas others contend that there are limits. Surely at some point speech has to be censored if it is harmful to individuals or communities in some way. How can we claim to have a right to free speech when that speech ignores our basic duty of care to others? So where do we draw the line? What constitutes harm? Should we be more circumspect about our public utterances or do we, as the writer and wit George Bernard Shaw suggests, have a duty to use speech that is seditious, blasphemous and outrageous?

> **It is necessary for the welfare of society that genius should be privileged to utter sedition, to blaspheme, to outrage good taste, to corrupt the youthful mind, and generally to scandalize one's uncles.[12]**

Charlie Hebdo

A genius will push the envelope. New ways of thinking will challenge entrenched attitudes but can we go too far? Is all pushing of the envelope good? As a case in point, the French satirical magazine, *Charlie Hebdo*, was a relatively unknown operation until it came to prominence as the focus of a terrorist attack in 2015. The magazine is certainly seen by many as seditious, blasphemous and outrageous, and it included many searing and inflammatory cartoons ridiculing religion. The case of *Charlie Hebdo* raises interesting points. The murder of *Charlie Hebdo* staff by Muslim extremists was a crime, pure and simple. Murder is not excusable because of offense taken to satirical cartoons and the worldwide reaction afterwards was no doubt passionate. But amidst the outrage over the murders, the public and politicians seemed to ignore any concerns raised by the *Charlie Hebdo* approach to public discourse. After the shootings, *Charlie Hebdo* staff were held up as martyrs to the cause of free speech, but does that mean that they were right in printing the cartoons they published over a prolonged period of time? These cartoons were extremely offensive even to the most moderate Muslims. Admittedly, similarly offensive cartoons had been produced about Christianity, although they produced a vocal but not violent response. As GK Chesterton, the English poet, journalist and philosopher said, 'To have a right to do a thing is not at all the same as to be right in doing it.'[13]

It is one thing to parody some of the silly or hypocritical things said and done by some people in the name of religion, but it is another thing to abuse or denigrate something many hold sacred such as the image of the Prophet, whose wisdom and conduct is a model for others to follow.

The confusion over defending free speech on the one hand and wanting to close it down on the other seems not to be one that the community has yet come to grips with yet, as illustrated by the case of an Australian satirical cartoonist, Bill Leak. He published a controversial cartoon in a national newspaper. The cartoon was intended to raise attention of and debate about the important social issue of child neglect within indigenous communities but it created a Twitter storm of criticism as being racist. Leak was reported by an Australian senator to the Press Council for censure, a senator who had previously vigorously defended the freedom of the press in the case of *Charlie Hebdo*.[14] Another senator said in response, 'You might have found that cartoon offensive — of course it was offensive — but what do we say, "Je suis, Charlie", but ban Bill Leak?'[15]

How do we draw a reasonable line and yet retain freedom of the press? Surely the freedom of the press is not there to denigrate others. Perhaps there are three kinds of humour. One that is uplifting and liberating. It helps us to stand back and look at the funny side of ourselves and humanity. It unifies us because we are all in the same boat. There is another kind of humour that is a little more edgy in that it is satirical but not malicious. It makes a statement and sheds light on something that needs to be said or addressed. There is certainly a useful role that satire and parody can play and it can be a useful instrument for reflection and change. The third type of humour is somewhat more malicious. It is aimed at putting someone or something down. It laughs at someone or a group that the protagonist doesn't like and seeks to incite, hurt or denigrate them. It is often aimed at turning others against the individual or group, generally a minority, that are the object of the humour. This type of humour commonly distorts the position or views of 'the other' in order to parody them. It incites anger and ridicule, and increases divisions between people in society. It is worth considering whether much of what passed for humour in the Charlie Hebdo cartoons falls into this third category. Is the aggressive, liberal social agenda trying to marginalize, silence or destroy opposition to that agenda?

Whether such images can or should be censored, or whether it is up to the good taste of the community to patronize or not patronize such magazines can be debated. The point is, for what purpose should we use speech in all its forms? The pen, and indeed the spoken word, is mightier than the sword, but just as a sword can be wielded by a brute or by a noble knight, so too can speech be wielded by a bigot hiding behind a protective veil of free speech, or by someone more noble in defence of truth, honour, respect and with compassion for others. Consider, for example, the way that the Dalai Lama gently uses humour with respect and understanding, even to people of lesser patience and tolerance who might otherwise be considered as enemies.

Political correctness

> **Everyone is in favour of free speech. Hardly a day passes without its being extolled, but some people's idea of it is that they are free to say what they like, but if anyone else says anything back, that is an outrage.**
>
> *Winston Churchill*[16]

The power wielded by an overly reactive mob, too quick to take offence and unable to engage in meaningful debate, can be extraordinary. It seems almost as if the mob has to make everyone bow down and kneel at its feet, as if to say, 'make a tearful, unreserved apology, swear allegiance to our ideology and never let it happen again'. Take the example of two respected Yale academics, Nicholas and Erika Christakis, who were made to resign their college appointments not because they criticized or abused any minority group — quite the opposite — but simply because they suggested in an email that people should be allowed to wear what they saw fit on Halloween, and if someone doesn't like what someone is wearing then they should either not look or engage them in respectful discussion as to why they object. Some students felt this was not fostering a safe college environment and a social-media storm ensued. Once begun, it took on a life of its own. Following the collective outrage, any attempt to engage in a thoughtful discussion on the issues was howled down by the assembled activists. As a journalist, Conor Friedersdorf, wrote in *The Atlantic*:

> **When Yale's history is written, they [the Christakises] should be regarded as collateral damage harmed by people who abstracted away their humanity. Yale activists felt failed by their institution and took out their frustration on two undeserving scapegoats who had only recently arrived there. Students who profess a belief in the importance of feeling safe at home marched on their house, scrawled angry messages in chalk beneath their bedroom window, hurled shouted insults and epithets, called for their jobs, and refused to shake their hands, even months later, all over one email. And the couple's ultimate resignation does nothing to improve campus climate.[17]**

This seems to have more in common with the Spanish Inquisition than it does with a civil society. Its main by-products are fear and paranoia. Defining what is or is not harmful or denigrating is easier said than done. Some people are offended by things that other people find artistic or humorous and so, in the name of freedom, much of what is seen as provocative and even offensive is vigorously defended. People of a religious persuasion can be offended by something that is blatantly sacrilegious. For example,

Andre Serrano's artwork titled *Piss Christ* depicts a plastic crucifix of Christ within a container of Serrano's own urine.[18] It is no doubt aimed at producing offence or 'taking the piss' literally and metaphorically. These days, like low-hanging fruit, religion is an easy target in an increasingly secular and irreligious political and social climate. The defenders of the artwork can portray it as provocative rather than offensive. It can be defended as raising debate rather than making a derogatory statement.

Today, traditional authority figures — like men, politicians, lawyers and religious people — have lost much of their moral authority and so there is little or no political correctness when it comes to offending them. In fact, there is almost an expectation and a duty among the young, artists and intelligentsia to offend them. Offensive material or jokes aimed in their direction are hidden behind the intellectual justification of freedom of speech and artistic expression that would never be aimed at, for example, women, the disabled, gays or racial minorities, who can be offended by statements far less critical or not even critical at all. The issue is not how to justify the vilification of minority groups or the vulnerable, but ask why the same level of respect is not given to all?

Socially militant individuals and lobby groups, perhaps feeling vindicated by pointing to historical injustices, have been incredibly well organized and effective at taking the moral high ground vacated by former figures of authority and use language very effectively. For example, words like 'freedom', 'inclusivity', 'tolerance' or 'anti-bullying' are wonderful but are often used in such a way as to imply that if a person holds a different view on a given issue then they are necessarily anti-freedom, exclusive, intolerant and promoting bullying. No doubt this is one of the many rhetorical devices and strategies learned in courses on social activism — how to push a social agenda and vanquish opposition. It is very forceful and makes it difficult for even simple light-hearted remarks to be made, let alone a diversity of views to be equally respected and aired in the media and elsewhere. Freedom of speech is not always a level playing field, especially where vocal and well-organized ideologically driven social agendas are in play. This is probably not a new phenomenon.

The fine line between tolerance and intolerance

Inclusivity and tolerance are interesting words, and how they can be used is even more interesting. For example, in the name of inclusivity and tolerance many schools now ban the religious aspects of celebrations like Easter[19] or take Christ out of Christmas,[20] despite the fact that, whether a person chooses to believe or not, these are parts of our cultural and religious heritage. This doesn't mean that everyone has to profess to something they don't believe in, but these are important cultural, historic and symbolic events in the calendar. It would be strange to go to a foreign country and expect the locals there to ban their own festivals and traditions in the name of inclusivity and tolerance of the recent arrival. Real inclusivity and tolerance would surely recognize and welcome the contribution of other cultures, rather than to exclude one's own, unless of course the actual aim of the so-called inclusivity and tolerance in the first place was a rhetorical device used to expunge cultural and religious traditions by those who don't subscribe to them rather than to foster true tolerance and inclusivity. It may not even be that people from other cultures and religions are offended but that politically correct or irreligious locals are getting offended on their behalf. Now we risk uprooting ourselves from our cultural heritage. What will we have in its place when our cultural heritage and traditions are gone?

At the same time, schools and workplaces are less able to choose not to include 'progressive' causes even when they are opposed to the ideology of the school or workplace. Is this really freedom or a sticky ideological trap? Do we risk imposing one vocal and liberal ideology on all members in society whether they want it or not? Is this really the freedom of choice that was the original catchcry justifying its inclusion in the first place? Is dissenting opinion to certain currently popular agendas actually being closed down in a way very reminiscent of what is done in dictatorships not noted for their freedom?

Is much of our adherence to political correctness also creating conformity to new social norms of thought, speech and conduct that have little to do with real virtue and concern for others, or does it have more to do with a pervasive fear of being caught out and called out for not ascribing to some new social order or norm? It is not uncommon to see offenders being sent off for 'education' in a way reminiscent of citizens in cold-war Russia who, not subscribing to communism, were sent off for 're-education'. It is not uncommon to see overreactions and penalties that far exceed the so-called offence. Just a passing joke by a public figure can create a Twitterstorm to such an extent that a person's career could be in jeopardy. A case in point is the reaction to Nobel laureate Tim Hunt's impromptu speech at a Korean lunch for female scientists. He made what was meant to be a light-hearted and self-deprecating remark.

> **It's strange that such a chauvinist monster like me has been asked to speak to women scientists. Let me tell you about my trouble with girls. Three things happen when they are in the lab: you fall in love with them, they fall in love with you, and when you criticise them they cry. Perhaps we should make separate labs for boys and girls? Now, seriously, I'm impressed by the economic development of Korea. And women scientists played, without doubt an important role in it. Science needs women, and you should do science, despite all the obstacles, and despite monsters like me.[21]**

His remarks were taken out of context and tweeted by a woman in the audience who took offence. This led to a Twitterstorm of reaction, which was widely taken up by the media.[22] Unfortunately, the apparent freedom that social media provides also seems to be a trap for the unthinking. Sadly, the reaction was so uninformed, malicious and extreme that he was forced to resign from the University College London's Faculty of Life Sciences and from the Royal Society's Biological Sciences Awards Committee. Despite the fact that many notable women scientists quickly came out to support Professor Hunt, the damage to his career, feelings and reputation had been done. It is a significant concern that many who portray themselves as fighting for liberation from oppression are so oppressive and vicious in the way they do it, but that is perhaps a result of an ideological position driven by anger and bitterness, set on war, not peace. Perhaps many of the advocates of tolerance and inclusivity should practise a little more of the gentleness, patience and compassion that they want from others?

The key factor may reside in discerning the motivation behind a person's words. No doubt a person can intentionally use derogatory language aimed at denigrating someone else and falsely say that it was humorous or used with innocent and good intentions. Equally, there are examples of people using a word or making a statement with no harmful intent and yet they have had their reputation and motives put under the most intense pressure. Some inadvertent slips of the tongue have motivations impugned on them and are taken out of context to the point that the offender is vehemently criticized. Commonly they are reduced to tears in passionate public apologies and pleas to be accepted back into the fold. But will the vociferous, aggressive and vehement calling out of people really make us all live happily and harmoniously together or will it surreptitiously create an atmosphere of fear and even fuel and subvert bitterness, conflict and resentment that will surely surface one day? When the pendulum swings back one day, as it may well do, we may see a form of oppression far worse than what went before.

Although often courting controversy, true statespersons and instruments of healthy change like Winston Churchill, Martin Luther King Jr., Mahatma Gandhi, Nelson Mandela, the Dalai Lama, Aung San Suu Kyi and Malala Yousafzai are rare. Their speech always demonstrates good grace, humour, patience, tolerance and compassion even to their detractors, while never losing sight of the cause for which they are so passionately fighting. They are an example to us all about how speech should be used for liberation and unity.

SOME THINGS TO REFLECT ON:

- What do you censor in your life?
- Do you ever use the written or spoken word in a malicious way? If so, what is the effect on yourself or those at whom your words are directed?
- How do you draw the line as to what you should or shouldn't say? Is it because of your innate beliefs or because you are conforming to an accepted norm?
- What is the effect of not speaking those things that you feel should be spoken?

SOME THINGS TO PRACTISE:

- Try as much as you are able to align what you think with what you say and what you do.
- Practise speech that uplifts people and abstain from speech, even in the mind, that denigrates people.

EPILOGUE

We are reaching the end of our exploration into the nature of freedom and how to foster it in our personal lives and society. As a civilization, we are at a very interesting juncture of our shared history. The choices we make today, the ruling philosophy we ascribe to, the direction in which we head, will undoubtedly lay the foundations for our shared history for the centuries to follow.

If the current trajectory is wise of giving ever greater license to individual freedoms, unhooking society's customs and laws from natural laws, breaking down long-held traditions and institutions, prioritizing pleasure over reason, becoming an increasingly secular society, and preferring the wisdom of the individual to the wisdom accumulated over millennia, then we can expect to be happier, freer and more fulfilled than at any time in history. We will literally throw off the shackles of uninformed dogma, outdated customs and religious superstition as we boldly and confidently stride into a new kind of society where the individual can be and do anything they want.

If, on the other hand, this trajectory, although well meaning, is unwise, ill-informed and based on an ignorance of human nature, then we will doubtless find the opposite of what we expect. We will sink to the lowest common denominator and have what we want — freedom unfettered by reason and law — but we will also have what comes with it — the tyranny of self-inflicted illnesses, addiction, conflict, disorder, injustice and misery. If this is indeed the law of human nature and society then ignorance of the law will be no excuse. One day, history will no doubt record that the sign-posts were everywhere to be read but we ignored them in one massive act of self-deception. If this is so then the following words will not be so much an insight into the fallen civilizations of times past, but a prescient prophecy for a great civilization soon to fall.

> **A great civilization is not conquered from without until it has destroyed itself from within.**
>
> *William and Ariel Durant*[1]

Perhaps, as wisdom traditions have long told us, true freedom lies in knowing where the limits are. We should not limit that which is unlimited — the human spirit or consciousness mired though it may be in the physical body. But we should limit that which is limited. The kind of freedom that seeks pleasure without restraint and the unhindered assertion of personal desire is no doubt sweet and tempting, but the very fact that all the world's great wisdom traditions have sounded similar cautions should give us pause to reflect. Wisdom has long maintained that true happiness comes not from pleasure and true freedom comes not from unfettered desire — quite the opposite. They are hard won by taming our lower nature with discipline guided by love, courage and reason. If this is in truth the path to personal liberation then it also follows that this is the path to our collective happiness and freedom. The kind of freedom that is informed by wisdom and knows where reasonable limits are is the surest way for us to fly far from the seductive, sweet allure of 'the freedom trap'.

Endnotes

Chapter 1

1. From 'Proverbs of Hell': www.poets.org/poetsorg/poem/proverbs-hell
2. www.inspirationalstories.com/proverbs/tibetan-goodness-speaks-in-a-whisper-evil-shouts/
3. www.notable-quotes.com/b/browning_robert.html
4. www.walden.org/Library/Quotations/The_Henry_D._Thoreau_Mis-Quotation_Page
5. Thoreau H, Walden. Quoted in McKinney, MJ, 2007, *Grammardog Guide to Walden*, Grammardog LLC, Christoval, Texas.
6. www.c-c-n.org/wisdom-traditions

Chapter 2

1. www.americanrhetoric.com/speeches/mlkihaveadream.htm

Chapter 3

1. Cabell, JB, 1926. *The Silver Stallion*. Robert M. McBride & Co. New York.
2. Miller M, Rahe R, 1997. Life changes scaling for the 1990s. *J Psychosom Res.*, 43(3): 279–92.
3. Murray C, Lopez A, 1996, The Global Burden of Disease, World Health Organization, Geneva.
4. Ustun TB, Ayuso-Mateos JL, Chatterji S, et al. Global burden of depressive disorders in the year 2000. *Br J Psychiatry*. 2004;184: 386–92.
5. Mathers CD, Loncar D. Projections of global mortality and burden of disease from 2002 to 2030. *PLoS Med*, 2006 Nov;3(11):e442.
6. Rey J. The epidemiological catchment area study: Implications for Australia. *MJA*, 1992;156: 200–3.
7. Rutz W. Rethinking mental health: A European WHO perspective. *World Psychiatry*, 2003;2(2): 125–7.
8. Mathers CD, Vos ET, Stevenson CE, Begg SJ. The Australian Burden of Disease Study: Measuring the loss of health from diseases, injuries and risk factors. *Med J Aust*, 2000;172(12):592–6.
9. www.aic.gov.au/media_library/publications/tandi_pdf/tandi052.pdf
10. www.abs.gov.au/AUSSTATS/abs@.nsf/2f762f95845417aeca25706c00834efa/d2c9296f8d9c01b1ca2570ec000e2f5f!OpenDocument
11. https://afsp.org/about-suicide/suicide-statistics/
12. Centers for Disease Control and Prevention (CDC) Data & Statistics Fatal Injury Report for 2014: www.cdc.gov/injury/wisqars/fatal_injury_reports.html
13. www.ons.gov.uk/peoplepopulationandcommunity/birthsdeathsandmarriages/deaths/bulletins/suicidesintheunitedkingdom/2014registrations
14. www.washingtonpost.com/wp-srv/world/suiciderate.html; www.google.com.au/webhp?sourceid=chrome-instant&ion=1&espv=2&ie=UTF-8#q=suicide%20rates%20in%20germany

15. www.abs.gov.au/ausstats/abs@.nsf/Lookup/by%20Subject/3303.0~2015~Main%20 Features~Intentional%20self-harm:%20key%20characteristics~8
16. Turner EH, Matthews AM, Linardatos E, et al. Selective publication of antidepressant trials and its influence on apparent efficacy. *N Engl J Med*, 2008 Jan 17;358(3):252–60.
17. Kirsch I, Deacon BJ, Huedo-Medina TB, Scoboria A, Moore TJ, et al. Initial severity and antidepressant benefits: A meta-analysis of data submitted to the Food and Drug Administration. *PLoS Medicine*, 2008 Feb;5(2):e45 doi:10.1371/journal.pmed.0050045
18. Fournier JC, DeRubeis RJ, Hollon SD, et al. Antidepressant drug effects and depression severity: A patient-level meta-analysis. *JAMA*, 2010 Jan 6;303(1):47–53.
19. Jureidini JN, Doecke CJ, Mansfield PR, Haby MM, Menkes DB, Tonkin AL. Efficacy and safety of antidepressants for children and adolescents. *BMJ*, 2004;328(7444): 879–83.
20. Vitiello B, Swedo S. Antidepressant medications in children. *N Engl J Med*, 2004;350(15):1489–91.
21. Turner EH, Matthews AM, Linardatos E, Tell RA, Rosenthal R. Selective publication of antidepressant trials and its influence on apparent efficacy. *N Engl J Med*, 2008 Jan 17;358(3):252–60.
22. BMJ 2015; 351:h4973. www.bmj.com/content/351/bmj.h4973/rr
23. Kasser T. Materialistic values and goals. *Annual Review of Psychology*, 2016;67:489–514. doi: 10.1146/annurev-psych-122414-033344
24. www.drugabuse.gov/drugs-abuse/emerging-trends
25. https://en.wikipedia.org/wiki/Turn_on,_tune_in,_drop_out
26. www.drugabuse.gov/publications/mdma-ecstasy-abuse/what-does-mdma-do-to-brain
27. www.abs.gov.au/ausstats/abs@.nsf/2f762f95845417aeca25706c00834efa/738d23457b86de fbca2570ec000e2f5c!OpenDocument
28. Looze Md, Raaijmakers Q, Bogt TT, et al. Decreases in adolescent weekly alcohol use in Europe and North America: Evidence from 28 countries from 2002 to 2010. *Eur J Public Health*, 2015 Apr;25 Suppl 2:69–72. doi: 10.1093/eurpub/ckv031.
29. Richter L, Pugh BS, Peters EA, Vaughan RD, Foster SE. Underage drinking: Prevalence and correlates of risky drinking measures among youth aged 12–20. *Am J Drug Alcohol Abuse*, 2015 Dec;18:1–10.
30. www.problemgambling.gov.au/facts/
31. www.egba.eu/pdf/EGBA_FS_ProblemGaming.pdf
32. Volberg, R. Gambling and problem gambling in Nevada: Report to the Nevada Council of Human Resource. 2002 March 22; 28: www.nevadacouncil.org/wp-content/ uploads/2014/08/NV-Prevalence-Study-Adults-2002.pdf
33. Thomas S, and Jackson A. Report to Beyondblue, Risk and Protective Factors: Depression and co-morbidities in problem gambling. Monash University and the University of Melbourne, 2008.
34. Dowling N, Jackson A, Thomas S, Frydenberg F. Children at risk of developing problem gambling. The Problem Gambling Research and Treatment Centre, May 2010.
35. Makary MA, Daniel M. Medical error — the third leading cause of death in the US. *BMJ*, 2016;353:i2139. doi: http://dx.doi.org/10.1136/bmj.i2139
36. www.brainyquote.com/quotes/quotes/s/samueljohn385293.html

37. Australian Bureau of Statistics. Physical activity in Australia: A snapshot, 2004–05, 2006 December 21: abs.gov.au/ausstats/abs@.nsf/Lookup/4835.0.55.001main+features12004-05
38. www.education.vic.gov.au/Documents/about/research/sovc201314.pdf
39. Hamer M, Lavoie KL, Bacon SL. Taking up physical activity in later life and healthy ageing: The English longitudinal study of ageing. *Br J Sports Med*, doi:10.1136/bjsports-2013-092993
40. Ogden CL, Carroll MD, Kit BK, Flegal KM. Prevalence of childhood and adult obesity in the United States, 2011–2012. *JAMA*, 2014 Feb 26;311(8):806–14. doi: 10.1001/jama.2014.732.
41. Magarey AM, Daniels LA, Boulton TJ. Prevalence of overweight and obesity in Australian children and adolescents: Reassessment of 1985 and 1995 data against new standard international definitions. *Med J Aust*, 2001;174(11):561–4.
42. www.nhs.uk/Livewell/loseweight/Pages/statistics-and-causes-of-the-obesity-epidemic-in-the-UK.aspx. Source: The state of food and agriculture 2013. Food and Agricultural Organization of the United Nations. www.fao.org/docrep/018/i3300e/i3300e.pdf
43. Lumey LH. Reproductive outcomes in women prenatally exposed to undernutrition: A review of findings from the Dutch famine birth cohort. *Proc Nutr Soc*, 1998 Feb;57(1):129–35.
44. Lumey LH, Stein AD. Offspring birth weights after maternal intrauterine undernutrition: A comparison within sibships. *Am J Epidemiol*, 1997 Nov 15;146(10):810–9.
45. Carter OB. The weighty issue of Australian television food advertising and childhood obesity. *Health Promot J Austr*, 2006;17(1):5–11.
46. Plourde G. Preventing and managing pediatric obesity: Recommendations for family physicians. *Can Fam Physician*, 2006 Mar;52:322–8.
47. Weiss RI, Smith JA. Legislative approaches to the obesity epidemic. *J Public Health Policy*, 2004;25(3–4):379–90.
48. www.fns.usda.gov/nslp/national-school-lunch-program-nslp
49. Daynard RA, Howard PT, Wilking CL. Private enforcement: Litigation as a tool to prevent obesity. *J Public Health Policy*, 2004;25(3–4):408–17.
50. Callahan ST, Mansfield MJ. Type 2 diabetes mellitus in adolescents. *Curr Opin Pediatr*, 2000;12(4):310–5.
51. Azzopardi P, Brown AD, Zimmet P, et al. Type 2 diabetes in young indigenous Australians in rural and remote areas: diagnosis, screening, management and prevention. *Med J Aust*, 2012 Jul 2;197(1):32–6.
52. Ling C, Groop L. Epigenetics: a molecular link between environmental factors and type 2 diabetes. *Diabetes*, 2009 Dec;58(12):2718–25. doi: 10.2337/db09-1003.
53. Wellen KE, Hatzivassiliou G, Sachdeva UM, Bui TV, Cross JR, Thompson CB. ATP-citrate lyase links cellular metabolism to histone acetylation. *Science*, 2009 May 22;324:1076–80.
54. Milagro F, Campion J, Cordero P, Goyenechea E, Gomez-Uriz AM, Abete I, Zulet MA, Martinez JA. A dual epigenomic approach for the search of obesity biomarkers: DNA

methylation in relation to diet-induced weight loss. *FASEB J*. 2011;25:1378–89.
55. Pharmaceutical Benefits Scheme. Expenditure and prescriptions twelve months 30 June 2014. www.pbs.gov.au/statistics/2013-2014-files/expenditure-and-prescriptions-12-months-to-30-june-2014.pdf
56. Kristensen MK, Christensen PM, Hallas J. The effect of statins on average survival in randomised trials, an analysis of end point postponement. *BMJ Open*, 2015;5:e007118. doi:10.1136/bmjopen-2014-007118
57. Studer M, et al. Effect of different antilipidemic agents and diets on mortality: a systematic review. *Arch Intern Med*, 2005;165(7):725–30.
58. Palmer SC, Mavridis D, Nicolucci A, et al. Comparison of clinical outcomes and adverse events associated with glucose-lowering drugs in patients with type 2 diabetes: a meta-analysis. *JAMA*, 2016 Jul 19;316(3):313–24. doi: 10.1001/jama.2016.9400.
59. Bell RJ. Screening mammography — early detection or over-diagnosis? Contribution from Australian data. *Climacteric*, 2014 Dec;17 Suppl 2:66–72. doi: 10.3109/13697137.2014.956718.
60. Morgan G, Ward R, Barton M. The contribution of cytotoxic chemotherapy to 5-year survival in adult malignancies. *Clin Oncol*, 2005;16(8):549–60.
61. News. US insurance company covers lifestyle therapy. *BMJ*, 1993;307:465.
62. Ornish D, et al. Can lifestyle changes reverse coronary heart disease? *Lancet*. 1990;336:129–33.
63. Ornish D, Scherwitz L, Billings J, et al. Intensive lifestyle changes for reversal of coronary heart disease. *JAMA*, 1998; 280: 2001–7.
64. Ornish D, Weidner G, Fair WR, et al. Intensive lifestyle changes may affect the progression of prostate cancer. *J Urol*, 2005 Sep;174(3): 1065–9; discussion 1069–70.
65. Frattaroli J, Weidner G, Dnistrian AM, et al. Clinical events in prostate cancer lifestyle trial: results from two years of follow-up. *Urology*, 2008 Dec;72(6):1319–23. doi: 10.1016/j.urology.2008.04.050
66. Ornish D, Magbanua MJ, Weidner G, et al. Changes in prostate gene expression in men undergoing an intensive nutrition and lifestyle intervention. *Proc Natl Acad Sci USA*, 2008 Jun 17;105(24): 8369–74. doi: 10.1073/pnas.0803080105
67. Ornish D, Lin J, Daubenmier J, et al. Increased telomerase activity and comprehensive lifestyle changes: a pilot study. *Lancet Oncol*, 2008 Nov;9(11):1048–57. doi: 10.1016/S1470-2045(08)70234-1.
68. Ornish D, Lin J, Chan JM, et al. Effect of comprehensive lifestyle changes on telomerase activity and telomere length in men with biopsy-proven low-risk prostate cancer: 5-year follow-up of a descriptive pilot study. *Lancet Oncol*, 2013 Sep 16. doi: pii: S1470-2045(13)70366-8. 10.1016/S1470-2045(13)70366-8
69. https://advertising.microsoft.com/en/WWDocs/User/display/cl/researchreport/31966/en/microsoft-attention-spans-research-report.pdf
70. Swing EL, Gentile DA, Anderson CA, Walsh DA. Television and video game exposure and the development of attention problems. *Pediatrics*, 2010 Aug;126(2):214–21. doi: 10.1542/peds.2009-1508.
71. Hallowell EM. Overloaded circuits: why smart people underperform. *Harvard Business*

Review, 2005 Jan;83(1):54–62, 116.

72. https://ucsdcfm.wordpress.com/2015/04/10/our-brains-are-evolving-to-multitask-not-the-ill-usion-of-multitasking/
73. Wagner FA, Anthony JC. Male-female differences in the risk of progression from first use to dependence upon cannabis, cocaine, and alcohol. *Drug Alcohol Depend*, 2007;86:191–8.
74. Hasin DS, Stinson FS, Ogburn E, et al. Prevalence, correlates, disability, and comorbidity of DSM-IV alcohol abuse and dependence in the United States: results from the National Epidemiologic Survey on Alcohol and Related Conditions. *Arch Gen Psychiatry*, 2007;64(7):830–42.
75. Slade T, Chapman C, Swift W, et al. Birth cohort trends in the global epidemiology of alcohol use and alcohol-related harms in men and women: systematic review and metaregression. *BMJ Open*, 2016;6:e011827. doi:10.1136/bmjopen-2016-011827
76. The Office of Juvenile Justice and Delinquency Prevention. Female offenders in the juvenile justice system. 1996 June. www.ncjrs.gov/pdffiles/femof.pdf
77. www.aic.gov.au/statistics/violent%20crime/assault.html
78. Mahoney T. Women and the criminal justice system. Statistics Canada. 2015 November. www.statcan.gc.ca/pub/89-503-x/2010001/article/11416-eng.htm
79. Office for National Statistics. Statistical Bulletin – focus on violent crime and sexual offences, 2011/12. 2013 February 7. webarchive.nationalarchives.gov.uk/20160105160709/http://www.ons.gov.uk/ons/dcp171778_298904.pdf
80. http://www.dailymail.co.uk/news/article-3199511/GPs-1-20-aged-girls-Pill-Thousands-young-12-contraceptive.html
81. Rashed AN, Hsia Y, Wilton L, Ziller M, Kostev K, Tomlin S. Trends and patterns of hormonal contraceptive prescribing for adolescents in primary care in the UK. *J Fam Plann Reprod Health Care*, 2015 Jul;41(3):216–22. doi: 10.1136/jfprhc-2013-100724. Epub 2014 Nov 14.
82. Grayson N, Hargreaves J, Sullivan EA. Use of routinely collected national data sets for reporting on induced abortion in Australia. AIHW cat. no. PER 30. Sydney: Australian Institute of Health and Welfare, 2005: www.aihw.gov.au/WorkArea/DownloadAsset.aspx?id=6442458945
83. www.guttmacher.org/about/gpr/2002/02/teen-pregnancy-trends-and-lessons-learned Source: National Center for Health Statistics. Births to teenagers in the United States, 1940–2000. National Vital Statistics Report, 2001; 49 (10).
84. www.happinessresearchinstitute.com/publications/4579836749
85. Uhlsa YT, Michikyanb M, Morris J, et al. Computers in Human Behavior. 2014;39:387–392. DOI: 10.1016/j.chb.2014.05.036
86. Lin LY, Sidani JE, Shensa A, et al. Association between social medial use and depression among U.S. young adults. *Depress Anxiety,* 2016 Apr;33(4):323–31. doi: 10.1002/da.22466.
87. www.carsafe.com.au/quick
88. Makary MA, Daniel M. Medical error—the third leading cause of death in the US. *BMJ*, 2016;353:i2139. doi: http://dx.doi.org/10.1136/bmj.i2139

89. www.bbc.com/news/world-us-canada-34996604
90. Lopez G. America's gun problem explained. Vox.com. 2016 Nov 28. www.vox.com/2015/10/3/9444417/gun-violence-united-states-america
91. www.gunviolencearchive.org/reports/mass-shootings/2015
92. Gilson D. 10 Pro-gun myths, shot down. Mother Jones, 2013 Jan 31. www.motherjones.com/politics/2013/01/pro-gun-myths-fact-check
93. www.mindfulness.org.au/urge-surfing

Chapter 4

1. www.wisdomquotes.com/quote/talmud-2.html
2. Plato, *The Republic*, book VIII, 563–4, trans. Benjamin Jowett. (1952) From *The Britannica Great Books of the Western World.* University of Chicago, Chicago.
3. Hardin G. The tragedy of the commons. *Science*, 1968 Dec 13;162(3859):1243–1248. doi: 10.1126/science.162.3859.1243
4. http://en.wikipedia.org/wiki/Tragedy_of_the_commons
5. Donne, J. 1624. 'Meditation XVII, Devotions upon Emergent Occasions'.
6. www.searchinsideyourself.com.au/
7. Vaughan, D. 1996. *The Challenger Launch Decision: Risky technology, culture, and deviance at NASA*. University of Chicago Press, Chicago.
8. www.consultingnewsline.com/Info/Vie%20du%20Conseil/Le%20Consultant%20du%20mois/Diane%20Vaughan%20(English).html
9. *The Age*, August 4, 2016.
10. 'Woman selfish for giving birth at 62, AMA president says', ABC News. 2016 Aug 03. http://www.abc.net.au/news/2016-08-03/62yo-women-labelled-'selfish'-after-giving-birth-via-ivf/7685126
11. Durant W & A. 1935. *The Story of Civilization: Our oriental heritage*. Simon & Schuster, New York. Vol. 1, p. 71.

Chapter 5

1. *Concise Oxford Dictionary*, 1976, sixth edition, Oxford University Press, Oxford.
2. www.brainyquote.com/quotes/quotes/t/tseliot109032.html
3. htttp://en.wikiquote.org/wiki/Edmund_Burke
4. Speech on receiving the Freedom Award from the National Civil Rights Museum, November 2000: http://db.nelsonmandela.org/speeches/pub_view.asp?pg=item&ItemID=NMS919&txtstr=22+November
5. www.brainyquote.com/quotes/quotes/b/buddha141546.html
6. www.youtube.com/watch?v=UTX7Cxq8aGc
7. *The Geeta*, chapter 2, verses 62–63, trans. Shri Purohit Swami. 1935. Faber and Faber, London.
8. www.verybestquotes.com/free-yourself-from-attachments-buddha-quotes/
9. Plato. Phaedo. trans. Benjamin Jowett. 1952. From *The Britannica Great Books of the Western World.* University of Chicago Press, Chicago.
10. http://quoteinvestigator.com/2014/02/01/fanatic/

11. Hafenbrack AC, Kinias Z, Barsade SG. Debiasing the mind through meditation: mindfulness and the sunk-cost bias. *Psychological Science*. 2014, 25(2):369–76.
12. http://izquotes.com/quote/301104
13. www.brainyquote.com/quotes/quotes/a/abbaeban108270.html
14. Harung H, Travis F, Blank W, Heaton D, 2009. Higher development, brain integration, and excellence in leadership. *Management Decision*, 47(6):872–94.
15 Plato. Phaedo. trans. Benjamin Jowett. (1952) From *The Britannica Great Books of the Western World*. University of Chicago Press, Chicago.
16. This and subsequent quotes from Plato. *The Republic*. 443. trans. Benjamin Jowett. 1952. From *The Britannica Great Books of the Western World*. University of Chicago Press, Chicago.
17. *The Ten Principal Upanishads*. trans. Yeats, WB and Shree Purohit Swami, 1937. Faber and Faber, London, pp. 33–4.
18. www.brainyquote.com/quotes/quotes/n/nelsonmand178789.html www.independent.co.uk/news/world/nelson-mandela-10-inspirational-quotes-to-live-your-life-by-8988290.html
19. www.goodreads.com/author/quotes/11628.Edward_Gibbon
20. Byrom, Thomas, 2001. *The Dhammapada: The sayings of the Buddha*. Belltower, New York.
21. Holmes E, 1921. *The Life of Mozart*. EP Dutton, Boston. p. 255.
22. *The Age*, 4 Jan 2016, Melbourne, p. 32.
23. Killingsworth MA, Gilbert DT. A wandering mind is an unhappy mind. *Science*, 2010 November 12;330(6006):932. doi: 10.1126/science.1192439
24. https://en.wikipedia.org/wiki/John_Philpot_Curran

Chapter 6

1. Denning A, 1949. *Freedom Under the Law*. Hamlyn Lecture Series. Stevens and Sons Ltd, London.
2. Ruskin J, 1849. *The Seven Lamps of Architecture*. Volume 1. J. Wiley, London. pp. 199–200.
3. https://en.wikipedia.org/wiki/Anarchy
4. www.brainyquote.com/quotes/keywords/anarchy.html
5. www.brainyquote.com/quotes/keywords/anarchy.html
6. Commoner B, 1971. *The Closing Circle: Nature, man, and technology*. Knopf, New York.
7. Ornish D, Weidner G, Fair WR, et al. Intensive lifestyle changes may affect the progression of prostate cancer. *J Urol*, 2005 Sep;174(3):1065–9; discussion 1069–70.
8. Frattaroli J, Weidner G, Dnistrian AM, et al. Clinical events in prostate cancer lifestyle trial: results from two years of follow-up. *Urology*, 2008 Dec;72(6):1319–23. doi: 10.1016/j.urology.2008.04.050.
9. Ornish D, Magbanua MJ, Weidner G, et al. Changes in prostate gene expression in men undergoing an intensive nutrition and lifestyle intervention. *Proc Natl Acad Sci USA*, 2008 Jun 17;105(24):8369–74. doi: 10.1073/pnas.0803080105.
10. Ornish D, Lin J, Daubenmier J, et al. Increased telomerase activity and comprehensive

lifestyle changes: a pilot study. *Lancet Oncol*, 2008 Nov;9(11):1048–57. doi: 10.1016/S1470-2045(08)70234-1.

11. Ornish D, Lin J, Chan JM, et al. Effect of comprehensive lifestyle changes on telomerase activity and telomere length in men with biopsy-proven low-risk prostate cancer: 5-year follow-up of a descriptive pilot study. *Lancet Oncol*, 2013 Sep 16. doi:pii: S1470-2045(13)70366-8. 10.1016/S1470-2045(13)70366-8.
12. www.brainyquote.com/quotes/quotes/v/voltaire106709.html
13. Palmer SC, Mavridis D, Nicolucci A, et al. Comparison of clinical outcomes and adverse events associated with glucose-lowering drugs in patients with type 2 diabetes: a meta-analysis. *JAMA*. 2016 Jul 19;316(3):313-24. doi: 10.1001/jama.2016.9400.
14. Elwood P, Galante J, Pickering J, Palmer S, Bayer A, et al. Healthy lifestyles reduce the incidence of chronic diseases and dementia: evidence from the Caerphilly cohort study. *PLoS One*, 2013;8(12):e81877. doi:10.1371/journal.pone.0081877.
15. Ford ES, Bergmann MM, Kröger J, et al. Healthy living is the best revenge: Findings from the European prospective investigation into cancer and nutrition—Potsdam Study. *Arch Intern Med*, 2009;169(15):1355–62.
16. Hamer M, Lavoie KL, Bacon SL. Taking up physical activity in later life and healthy ageing: the English longitudinal study of ageing. *Br J Sports Med*. doi:10.1136/bjsports-2013-092993.
17. https://en.wikipedia.org/wiki/United_States_Declaration_of_Independence
18. Calaprice A, 2002. *Dear Professor Einstein: Albert Einstein's letters to and from children*. Prometheus Books, New York. Pp. 127–9.
19. Jammer M, 1999. *Einstein and Religion: Physics and theology*. Princeton University Press, Princeton, p. 93.
20. www.quoteinvestigator.com/2011/12/16/spirit-manifest/
21. Kiecolt-Glaser J, Newton T. Marriage and health: his and hers. *Psychological Bulletin*, 2001;127(4):472–503.
22. Ryan SM, Jorm AF, Toumbourou JW, Lubman DI. Parent and family factors associated with service use by young people with mental health problems: a systematic review. *Early Interv Psychiatry*, 2015 Dec;9(6):433–46. doi: 10.1111/eip.12211.
23. Lim MM, Wang Z, Olazábal DE, Ren X, Terwilliger EF, Young LJ. Enhanced partner preference in a promiscuous species by manipulating the expression of a single gene. *Nature*, 2004 Jun 17;429(6993):754–7.
24. Young LJ, Wang Z. The neurobiology of pair bonding. *Nat Neurosci*, 2004 Oct;7(10):1048–54.
25. Snowdon CT, Pieper BA, Boe CY, Cronin KA, Kurian AV, Ziegler TE. Variation in oxytocin is related to variation in affiliative behavior in monogamous, pairbonded tamarins. *Horm Behav*, 2010 Sep;58(4):614–8. doi: 10.1016/j.yhbeh.2010.06.014.
26. www.wwf.org.au/what-we-do/oceans/great-barrier-reef
27. http://en.wikipedia.org/wiki/The_Burning_Season_(1994_film)
28. www.mdba.gov.au/managing-water/salinity
29. Colten HR, Altevogt BM, 2006. *Sleep Disorders and Sleep Deprivation: An unmet public health problem*. Institute of Medicine (US) Committee on Sleep Medicine and Research.

National Academies Press, Washington: www.ncbi.nlm.nih.gov/books/NBK19961/

30. Davis MP, Goforth HW. Long-term and short-term effects of insomnia in cancer and effective interventions. *Cancer J*, 2014 Sep–Oct;20(5):330-44. doi: 10.1097/PPO.0000000000000071.
31. Lange K, Cohrs S, Skarupke C, Görke M, Szagun B, Schlack R. Electronic media use and insomnia complaints in German adolescents: gender differences in use patterns and sleep problems. *J Neural Transm* (Vienna), 2015 Nov 17. [Epub ahead of print]
32. Wu X, Tao S, Zhang Y, Zhang S, Tao F. Low physical activity and high screen time can increase the risks of mental health problems and poor sleep quality among Chinese college students. *PLoS One*, 2015 Mar 18;10(3):e0119607. doi: 10.1371/journal.pone.0119607.
33. Thompson DF, Ramos CL, Willett JK. Psychopathy: clinical features, developmental basis and therapeutic challenges. *J Clin Pharm Ther*, 2014 Oct;39(5):485–95. doi: 10.1111/jcpt.12182.
34. www.goodreads.com/work/quotes/1651617-the-art-of-happiness-a-handbook-for-living
35. Hofmann SG, Sawyer AT, Witt AA, Oh D. The effect of mindfulness-based therapy on anxiety and depression: a meta-analytic review. *J Consult Clin Psychol*, 2010 Apr;78(2):169–83.
36. Hölzel BK, Carmody J, Evans KC, et al. Stress reduction correlates with structural changes in the amygdala. *Soc Cogn Affect Neurosci*, 2010 March;5(1):11–7.
37. Barrett B, Hayney MS, Muller D, et al. Meditation or exercise for preventing acute respiratory infection: a randomized controlled trial. *Ann Fam Med*, 2012;10:298–9.
38. Krasner M.S., Epstein R.M., Beckman H., et al. Association of an educational program in mindful communication with burnout, empathy, and attitudes among primary care physicians. *JAMA*, 2009:302(12), 1284–93. doi: 10.1001/jama.2009.1384.
39. Simic G, Babic M, Borovecki F, Hof PR. Early failure of the default-mode network and the pathogenesis of Alzheimer's disease. *CNS Neurosci Ther*, 2014 Apr 8. doi: 10.1111/cns.12260.
40. Epel ES, Puterman E, Lin J, Blackburn E, et al. Wandering minds and aging cells. *Clinical Psychological Science*, 2012. doi: 10.1177/2167702612460234.
41. www.brainyquote.com/quotes/quotes/w/winstonchu101776.html
42. Taylor SE, Klein LC, Lewis BP, Gruenewald TL, Gurung RA, Updegraff JA. Biobehavioral responses to stress in females: tend-and-befriend, not fight-or-flight. *Psychol Rev*, 2000 Jul;107(3):411–29.
43. Blackstone W, Lee T, Hoyenden JE, Ryland A., 1829. *Commentaries on the Laws of England*. S Sweet, Ldondon: https://books.google.com.au/books?id=1BY0AQAAMAAJ
44. *The Commentaries on the Laws of England* is an influential eighteenth-century treatise on the common law of England by Sir William Blackstone, originally published by the Clarendon Press at Oxford, 1765–1769. en.wikipedia.org/wiki/Commentaries_on_the_Laws_of_England
45. en.wikipedia.org/wiki/The_Corporation_(film)
46. www.brainyquote.com/quotes/authors/w/warren_buffett.html

Chapter 7

1. Whitehead AN, 1929. *Process and Reality: An essay in cosmology*, pt. II, ch. 1, sec. 1. MacMillan, New York.
2. Popper K, Ryan A, Gombrich EH, 2013. *The Open Society and Its Enemies*. Princeton University Press, Princeton.
3. This and subsequent quotes from Plato, *The Republic*, book VIII. trans. Benjamin Jowett, 1952. From *The Britannica Great Books of the Western World*, University of Chicago Press, Chicago.
4. ibid.
5. ibid.
6. ibid.
7. ibid.
8. ibid.
9. ibid.
10. www.vectors.umwblogs.org/2012/02/16/the-matrix-a-complex-modern-adaptation-of-platos-allegory-of-the-cave/
11. www.sparknotes.com/film/matrix/section1.rhtml
12. From *The Rubaiyat of Omar Khayyam* by Omar Khayyam, trans. Edward FitzGerald.
13. ibid.

Chapter 8

1. *The Shorter Oxford English Dictionary on Historical Principles*. 1992. Oxford University Press, Oxford. pp. 2557–8.
2. www.sanskrit.inria.fr/MW/238.html
3. Samples B, 1976. *Metaphoric Mind: A celebration of creative consciousness*. Jalmar Press, Fawnskin. p. 26.
4. www.goodreads.com/quotes/423568-i-believe-in-intuition-and-inspiration-imagination-is-more-important
5. Whittle S, Allen NB, Lubman DI, Yücel M. The neurobiological basis of temperament: towards a better understanding of psychopathology. *Neurosci Biobehav Rev*, 2006;30(4):511–25.
6. Whittle S, Yap MB, Yücel M, et al. Prefrontal and amygdala volumes are related to adolescents' affective behaviors during parent-adolescent interactions. *Proc Natl Acad Sci USA*, 2008 Mar 4;105(9):3652–7. doi: 10.1073/pnas.0709815105.
7. Whittle S, Yücel M, Fornito A, et al. Neuroanatomical correlates of temperament in early adolescents. *J Am Acad Child Adolesc Psychiatry*, 2008 Jun;47(6):682–93. doi: 10.1097/CHI.0b013e31816bffca.
8. Visser TA, Ohan JL, Whittle S, et al. Sex differences in structural brain asymmetry predict overt aggression in early adolescents. *Soc Cogn Affect Neurosci*, 2013 Mar 12. [Epub ahead of print]
9. Arch JJ, Landy LN, Brown KW. Predictors and moderators of biopsychological social stress responses following brief self-compassion meditation training. *Psychoneuroendocrinology*, 2016 Mar 17;69:35–40. doi: 10.1016/j.psyneuen.2016.03.009.

10. Feliu-Soler A, Pascual JC, Elices M, et al. Fostering self-compassion and loving-kindness in patients with borderline personality disorder: a randomized pilot study. *Clin Psychol Psychother*, 2016 Jan 28. doi: 10.1002/cpp.2000.
11. Mrazek MD, Mooneyham BW, Mrazek KL, Schooler JW. Pushing the limits: Cognitive, affective, and neural plasticity revealed by an intensive multifaceted intervention. *Front Hum Neurosci*. 2016; 10:117. doi: 10.3389/fnhum.2016.00117.
12. Sato W, Kochiyama T, Uono S, et al. The structural neural substrate of subjective happiness. *Scientific Reports*, 2015; 5: 16891 DOI: 10.1038/srep16891
13. Kurth F, Luders E, Wu B, Black DS. Brain gray matter changes associated with mindfulness meditation in older adults: an exploratory pilot study using Voxel-based morphometry. *Neuro*, 2014; 1(1): 23–6. Published online 2014 Nov 12. doi:10.17140/NOJ-1-106
14. Allan, J, 1903 (reprinted 2007). *As a Man Thinketh*. Dover Publications Inc., New York.
15. Mischel W, Ebbesen EB, Raskoff Zeiss A. Cognitive and attentional mechanisms in delay of gratification. *Journal of Personality and Social Psychology*, 1972;21(2):204–18. doi:10.1037/h0032198. ISSN 0022-3514.
16. Mischel W, Shoda Y, Rodriguzez ML. Delay of gratification in children. *Science*, 1989;244:933–8. doi:10.1126/science.2658056.
17. Ayduk ON, Mendoa-Denton R, Mischel W, Downey G, Peake PK, Rodriguez ML. Regulating the interpersonal self: Strategic self-regulation for coping with rejection sensitivity. *Journal of Personality and Social Psychology*, 2000;79(5):776–92. doi:10.1037/0022-3514.79.5.776.
18. Schlam TR, Wilson NL, Shoda Y, Mischel W, Ayduk O. Preschoolers' delay of gratification predicts their body mass 30 years later. *The Journal of Pediatrics*, 2013;162:90–93. doi:10.1016/j.jpeds.2012.06.049. PMC 3504645.
19. Shoda Y, Mischel W, Peake PK. Predicting adolescent cognitive and self-regulatory competencies from preschool delay of gratification: Identifying diagnostic conditions. *Developmental Psychology*, 1990;26(6):978–86. doi:10.1037/0012-1649.26.6.978.
20. McClelland MM, Acock AC, Piccinin A, Rhea SA, Stallings MC. Relations between preschool attention span-persistence and age 25 educational outcomes. *Early Child Res Q*, 2013 Apr 1; 28(2): 314–24. Published online 2012 Aug 3. doi: 10.1016/j.ecresq.2012.07.008
21. Ford ES, Bergmann MM, Kröger J, et al. Healthy living Is the best revenge: findings from the European prospective investigation Into cancer and nutrition — Potsdam Study. *Arch Intern Med*, 2009;169(15):1355–62.
22. Elwood P, Galante J, Pickering J, Palmer S, Bayer A, et al., 2013. Healthy lifestyles reduce the incidence of chronic diseases and dementia: Evidence from the Caerphilly Cohort Study. *PLoS One*, 8(12): e81877. doi:10.1371/journal.pone.0081877.
23. NCD Risk Factor Collaboration (NCD-RisC). Trends in adult body-mass index in 200 countries from 1975 to 2014: A pooled analysis of 1698 population-based measurement studies with 19·2 million participants. *Lancet*, 2016;387(10026):1377–96. doi: 10.1016/S0140-6736(16)30054-X.
24. Carlier N, Marshe VS, Cmorejova J, Davis C, Müller DJ. Genetic similarities between compulsive overeating and addiction phenotypes: A case for 'food addiction'? *Curr*

Psychiatry Rep, 2015 Dec;17(12):96. doi: 10.1007/s11920-015-0634-5.

25. Gillespie D, 2008. *Sweet Poison: Why sugar makes us fat.* Penguin, Melbourne.
26. www.vichealth.vic.gov.au/media-and-resources/media-releases/study-shows-bottle-shops-concentrated-in-poor-areas-of-victoria
27. www.google.com.au/search?q=HI_Background_Paper_latest.pdf&rls=com.microsoft:en-AU&ie=UTF-8&oe=UTF-8&startIndex=&startPage=1&gfe_rd=cr&ei=YG5QWPDRIs_u8wfqmbLYDQ&gws_rd=ssl
28. http://gawler.org/adept-changing-habit/
29. Hassed C, 2014. *Playing the Genetic Hand Life Dealt You.* Michelle Anderson Publishing, Melbourne.
30. Bygren LO, Kaati G, Edvinsson S. Longevity determined by paternal ancestors' nutrition during their slow growth period. Acta Biotheor. 2001 Mar;49(1):53–9.
31. Richardson A, Austad SN, Ikeno Y, Unnikrishnan A, McCarter RJ. Significant life extension by ten percent dietary restriction. *Ann N Y Acad Sci*, 2016 Jan;1363:11–7. doi: 10.1111/nyas.12982.
32. Mathers JC. Impact of nutrition on the ageing process. *Br J Nutr*, 2015 Jan;113 Suppl:S18–22. doi: 10.1017/S0007114514003237.
33. Soare A, Weiss EP, Pozzilli P. Benefits of caloric restriction for cardiometabolic health, including type 2 diabetes mellitus risk. *Diabetes Metab Res Rev*, 2014 Mar;30 Suppl 1:41–7. doi: 10.1002/dmrr.2517.
34. Pembrey ME, Bygren LO, Kaati G, et al. ALSPAC Study Team. Sex-specific, male-line transgenerational responses in humans. *Eur J Hum Genet*, 2006 Feb;14(2):159–66.
35. Peña CJ, Bagot RC, Labonté B, Nestler EJ. Epigenetic signalling in psychiatric disorders. *J Mol Biol.* 2014 Apr 5. pii: S0022-2836(14)00174-0. doi: 10.1016/j.jmb.2014.03.016.
36. Vassoler FM, Sadri-Vakili G. Mechanisms of transgenerational inheritance of addictive-like behaviors. *Neuroscience*, 2013 Aug 3. pii: S0306-4522(13)00658-1. doi: 10.1016/j.neuroscience.2013.07.064.
37. Brake WG, Zhang TY, Diorio J, et al. Influence of early postnatal rearing conditions on mesocorticolimbic dopamine and behavioural responses to psychostimulants and stressors in adult rats. *Eur J Neurosci*, 2004 Apr;19(7):1863–74.
38. Kjaer TW, Bertelsen C, Piccini P, et al. Increased dopamine tone during meditation-induced change of consciousness. *Brain Res Cogn Brain Res*, 2002 Apr;13(2):255–9.
39. Bowen S, Chawla N, Collins SE, et al. Mindfulness-based relapse prevention for substance use disorders: a pilot efficacy trial. *Subst Abus*, 2009 Oct–Dec;30(4):295–305.
40. Bowen S, Witkiewitz K, Clifasefi SL, et al. Relative efficacy of mindfulness-based relapse prevention, standard relapse prevention, and treatment as usual for substance use disorders: a randomized clinical trial. *JAMA Psychiatry*, 2014 May;71(5):547–56.
41. Maynard BR, Wilson AN, Labuzienski E, Whiting SW. Mindfulness-based approaches in the treatment of disordered gambling: A systematic review and meta-analysis. *Research on Social Work Practice*. Published online October 16, 2015. doi: 10.1177/1049731515606977.
42. Hamer M, Lavoie KL, Bacon SL. Taking up physical activity in later life and healthy ageing: The English longitudinal study of ageing. *Br J Sports Med*, doi:10.1136/

bjsports-2013-092993.

43. Chen ST, Siddarth P, Ercoli LM, et al. Modifiable risk factors for Alzheimer disease and subjective memory impairment across age groups. *PLoS One*, 2014 Jun 4;9(6):e98630. doi: 10.1371/journal.pone.0098630. eCollection 2014.
44. Entringer S, Epel ES, Kumsta R, et al. Stress exposure in intrauterine life is associated with shorter telomere length in young adulthood. *Proc Natl Acad Sci USA*, 2011;108(33):E513-8.
45. Kroenke CH, Epel E, Adler N, et al. Autonomic and adrenocortical reactivity and buccal cell telomere length in kindergarten children. *Psychosom Med*, 2011 Sep;73(7):533–40.
46. Tomiyama AJ, O'Donovan A, Lin J, et al. Does cellular aging relate to patterns of allostasis? An examination of basal and stress reactive HPA axis activity and telomere length. *Physiol Behav*, 2012 Apr 12;106(1):40–5. doi: 10.1016/j.physbeh.2011.11.016.
47. Epel ES, Blackburn EH, Lin J, et al. Accelerated telomere shortening in response to life stress. *Proc Natl Acad Sci USA*, 2004;101(49):17312–5.
48. Verhoeven JE, Révész D, Epel ES, et al. Major depressive disorder and accelerated cellular aging: results from a large psychiatric cohort study. *Mol Psychiatry*, 2013 Nov 12. doi: 10.1038/mp.2013.151.
49. Lin J, Dhabhar FS, Wolkowitz O, et al. Pessimism correlates with leukocyte telomere shortness and elevated interleukin-6 in post-menopausal women. *Brain Behav Immun*, 2009 May;23(4):446–9.
50. Brydon L, Lin J, Butcher L, et al. Hostility and cellular aging in men from the Whitehall II cohort. *Biol Psychiatry*. 2012 May 1;71(9):767–73. doi: 10.1016/j.biopsych.2011.08.020.
51. Prather AA, Puterman E, Lin J, et al. Shorter leukocyte telomere length in midlife women with poor sleep quality. *J Aging Res*, 2011;2011:721390. doi: 10.4061/2011/721390.
52. Chae DH, Nuru-Jeter AM, Adler NE, et al. Discrimination, racial bias, and telomere length in African-American men. *Am J Prev Med*, 2014 Feb;46(2):103–11. doi: 10.1016/j.amepre.2013.10.020.
53. Ahola K, Sirén I, Kivimäki M, et al. Work-related exhaustion and telomere length: A population-based study. *PLoS One*, 2012;7(7):e40186. doi: 10.1371/journal.pone.0040186.
54. Parks CG, DeRoo LA, Miller DB, et al. Employment and work schedule are related to telomere length in women. *Occup Environ Med*, 2011 Aug;68(8):582–9. doi: 10.1136/oem.2010.063214.
55. Hill TD, Ellison CG, Burdette AM, Taylor J, Friedman KL. Dimensions of religious involvement and leukocyte telomere length. *Soc Sci Med*, 2016 Apr 28. pii: S0277-9536(16)30206-4. doi: 10.1016/j.socscimed.2016.04.032.
56. Krauss J, Farzaneh-Far R, Puterman E, et al. Physical fitness and telomere length in patients with coronary heart disease: Findings from the Heart and Soul Study. *PLoS One*, 2011;6(11):e26983. doi: 10.1371/journal.pone.0026983.
57. Puterman E, Lin J, Blackburn E, et al. The power of exercise: Buffering the effect of chronic stress on telomere length. *PLoS One*, 2010 May 26;5(5):e10837.
58. Lin J, Epel E, Blackburn E. Telomeres and lifestyle factors: Roles in cellular aging. *Mutat Res*, 2012 Feb 1;730(1–2):85–9. doi: 10.1016/j.mrfmmm.2011.08.003.

59. Valdes AM, Andrew T, Gardner JP, et al. Obesity, cigarette smoking, and telomere length in women. *Lancet*. 2005;366:662–4.
60. Crous-Bou M, Fung TT, Prescott J, Julin B, Du M, Sun Q, Rexrode KM, Hu FB, De Vivo I. Mediterranean diet and telomere length in Nurses' Health Study: Population based cohort study. *BMJ*. 2014; 349:g6674. Published online 2014 December 2. doi: 10.1136/bmj.g6674.
61. Boccardi V, Esposito A, Rizzo MR, Marfella R, Barbieri M, Paolisso G. Mediterranean diet, telomere maintenance and health status among elderly. *PLoS One*, 2013; 8(4): e62781. Published online 2013 April 30. doi: 10.1371/journal.pone.0062781.
62. Farzaneh-Far R, Lin J, Epel ES, Harris WS, Blackburn EH, Whooley MA. Association of marine omega-3 fatty acid levels with telomeric aging in patients with coronary heart disease. *JAMA*. 2010 Jan 20;303(3):250–7.
63. Kiecolt-Glaser JK, Epel ES, et al. Omega-3 fatty acids, oxidative stress, and leukocyte telomere length: A randomized controlled trial. *Brain Behav Immun*, 2013 Feb;28:16–24. doi: 10.1016/j.bbi.2012.09.004.
64. O'Callaghan NJ, Toden S, Bird AR, et al. Colonocyte telomere shortening is greater with dietary red meat than white meat and is attenuated by resistant starch. *Clin Nutr*, 2012 Feb;31(1):60–4. doi: 10.1016/j.clnu.2011.09.003.
65. Zhang X, Lin S, Funk WE, Hou L. Republished: Environmental and occupational exposure to chemicals and telomere length in human studies. *Postgrad Med J*, 2013 Dec;89(1058):722–8. doi: 10.1136/postgradmedj-2012-101350rep.
66. Carlson LE, Beattie TL, Giese-Davis J, Faris P, Tamagawa R, Fick LJ, Degelman ES, Speca M. Mindfulness-based cancer recovery and supportive-expressive therapy maintain telomere length relative to controls in distressed breast cancer survivors. *Cancer*, 2014 Nov 3. doi: 10.1002/cncr.29063.
67. Ornish D, Lin J, Chan JM, et al. Effect of comprehensive lifestyle changes on telomerase activity and telomere length in men with biopsy-proven low-risk prostate cancer: 5-year follow-up of a descriptive pilot study. *Lancet Oncol*, 2013 Sep 16. doi:pii: S1470-2045(13)70366-8. 10.1016/S1470-2045(13)70366-8.
68. Frattaroli J, Weidner G, Dnistrian AM, et al. Clinical events in prostate cancer lifestyle trial: Results from two years of follow-up. *Urology*, 2008 Dec;72(6):1319–23. doi: 10.1016/j.urology.2008.04.050.
69. Ornish D, Magbanua MJ, Weidner G, et al. Changes in prostate gene expression in men undergoing an intensive nutrition and lifestyle intervention. *Proc Natl Acad Sci USA*, 2008 Jun 17;105(24):8369–74. doi: 10.1073/pnas.0803080105.
70. Ornish D, Lin J, Daubenmier J, et al. Increased telomerase activity and comprehensive lifestyle changes: A pilot study. *Lancet Oncol*, 2008 Nov;9(11):1048–57. doi: 10.1016/S1470-2045(08)70234-1.

Chapter 9

1. www.mindandlife.org
2. James W. 1956. *The Dilemma of Determinism*, republished in *The Will to Believe*. Dover Books, New York. p. 149.

3. Freud S. Letter to Pfister, 10 September 1918. www.freudarchives.org/PDFS/finding_aid.pdf
4. www.freud.org.uk/education/topic/10567/subtopic/10570/
5. Letter to Wilhelm Fliess, Feb. 1, 1900. *The Complete Letters of Sigmund Freud to Wilhelm Fliess 1887–1904.* 1986. Harvard University Press, Cambridge.
6. www.iep.utm.edu/freud
7. http://statusmind.com/clever-quotes-892/
8. Jung CG, 1959. *Archetypes of the Collective Unconscious.* Routledge & Kegan Paul, London.
9. www.brainyquote.com/quotes/quotes/c/carljung146686.html
10. www.goodreads.com/quotes/549821-there-is-no-coming-to-consciousness-without-pain-people-will
11. Jung C. Two Essays on Analytical Psychology. www.azquotes.com/quote/610215
12. Jung C. Letters Vol. II, pp. 546–7, quoted in Robinson D, 2005. *Conscience and Jung's Moral Vision: From id to thou.* Paulist Press, New York.
13. Jung C. Letters Vol. II, pp. 182–3, quoted in Adler G ed., 1976. *Letters of CG Jung, volume 2; 1951–1961.* Routledge & Kegan Paul, London.
14. Jung CG, 1969. *On the Nature of the Psyche.* Trans RFC Hull. Routledge, New York. p. 110.
15. Skinner BF, 1974. *About Behaviorism.* Knopf, New York.
16. www.simplypsychology.org/freewill-determinism.html
17. Skinner BF, 1972. *Beyond Freedom and Dignity.* Bantam Vintage, New York. p. 17.
18. Frankl V. *Man's Search for Meaning, Part One: Experiences in a concentration camp.* Beacon Press, Boston. pp. 56–7.
19. ibid.
20. ibid.
21. www.youtube.com/watch?v=-7rY-7q8Pzw
22. ibid.
23. Seligman MEP, Maier SF. Failure to escape traumatic shock. *Journal of Experimental Psychology*, 1967;74(1):1–9. doi:10.1037/h0024514.
24. Seligman M, 2002. *Authentic Happiness: Using the new positive psychology to realize your potential for lasting fulfillment*, Free Press, New York. p. xiv.
25. www.picturequotes.com/habits-of-pessimism-lead-to-depression-wither-achievement-and-undermine-physical-health-the-good-quote-252181
26. Seligman M, 1990. *Learned Optimism.* Pocket Books, New York. p. 211.
27. ibid.
28. Seligman M, 2007. *The Optimistic Child: A proven program to safeguard children against depression and build lifelong resilience.* Houghton Mifflin, Boston. p. 32.
29. Seligman M, 2011. *Flourish: A visionary new understanding of happiness and well-being.* Free Press, New York. p. 20.
30. Poulin MJ, Brown SL, Dillard AJ, Smith DM. Giving to others and the association between stress and mortality. *Am J Public Health*, 2013 Sep;103(9):1649–55. doi: 10.2105/AJPH.2012.300876.

31. Gotink RA, Chu P, Busschbach JJ, Benson H, Fricchione GL, Hunink MG. Standardised mindfulness-based interventions in healthcare: An overview of systematic reviews and meta-analyses of RCTs. *PLoS One*, 2015 Apr 16;10(4):e0124344. doi: 10.1371/journal.pone.0124344. eCollection 2015.
32. Kuyken W, Warren FC, Taylor RS, et al. Efficacy of mindfulness-based cognitive therapy in prevention of depressive relapse: an individual patient data meta-analysis from randomized trials. *JAMA Psychiatry*. Published online April 27, 2016. doi:10.1001/jamapsychiatry.2016.0076
33. Kabat-Zinn J, 2001. *Meditation for Everyday Life*. Piatkus Books, London.
34. www.brainyquote.com/quotes/quotes/j/jonkabatz526303.html
35. www.quotes.net/quote/14653
36. Kabat-Zinn J, 2013. *Full Catastrophe Living: How to cope with stress, pain and illness using mindfulness meditation*. Piatkus Books, London.
37. Zilverstand A, Parvaz MA, Moeller SJ, Goldstein RZ. Cognitive interventions for addiction medicine: Understanding the underlying neurobiological mechanisms. *Prog Brain Res*, 2016;224:285-304. doi: 10.1016/bs.pbr.2015.07.019.
38. www.everyday-mindfulness.org/20-beautiful-quotes-about-mindful-living/
39. Bowen S, Chawla N, Collins SE, et al. Mindfulness-based relapse prevention for substance use disorders: A pilot efficacy trial. *Subst Abus*, 2009 Oct–Dec;30(4):295–305.
40. Gotink RA, Chu P, Busschbach JJ, Benson H, Fricchione GL, Hunink MG. Standardised mindfulness-based interventions in healthcare: An overview of systematic reviews and meta-analyses of RCTs. *PLoS One*, 2015 Apr 16;10(4):e0124344. doi: 10.1371/journal.pone.0124344.
41. Modesto-Lowe V, Farahmand P, Chaplin M, Sarro L. Does mindfulness meditation improve attention in attention deficit hyperactivity disorder? *World J Psychiatry*, 2015 Dec 22;5(4):397–403. doi: 10.5498/wjp.v5.i4.397.
42. Veehof MM, Trompetter HR, Bohlmeijer ET, Schreurs KM. Acceptance- and mindfulness-based interventions for the treatment of chronic pain: A meta-analytic review. *Cogn Behav Ther*, 2016 Jan 28:1–27. [Epub ahead of print]
43. de Souza IC, de Barros VV, Gomide HP, Miranda TC, Menezes Vde P, Kozasa EH, Noto AR. Mindfulness-based interventions for the treatment of smoking: A systematic literature review. *J Altern Complement Med*, 2015 Mar;21(3):129–40. doi: 10.1089/acm.2013.0471.
44. www.oxforddictionaries.com/definition/english/persona
45. www.myersbriggs.org/my-mbti-personality-type/mbti-basics/the-16-mbti-types.htm
46. www.2knowmyself.com/a_b_c_d_personality_type
47. Briley DA, Tucker-Drob EM. Genetic and environmental continuity in personality development: A meta-analysis. *Psychological Bulletin*, 2014;140(5):1303–31. doi:10.1037/a0037091
48. Sng AA, Janca A. Mindfulness for personality disorders. *Curr Opin Psychiatry*, 2016 Jan;29(1):70–6.
49. Chafos VH, Economou P. Beyond borderline personality disorder: The mindful brain. *Soc Work*, 2014 Oct;59(4):297–302.

50. Kramer U, Pascual-Leone A, Berthoud L, et al. Assertive anger mediates effects of dialectical behaviour-informed skills training for borderline personality disorder: A randomized controlled trial. *Clin Psychol Psychother*, 2015 Apr 10. doi: 10.1002/cpp.1956.
51. www.authentichappiness.sas.upenn.edu/testcenter
52. www.psychologytoday.com/blog/what-matters-most/201402/boosting-happiness-one-the-best-exercises-you-can-do

Chapter 10

1. John 8: 1–11.
2. Francis Collins, Head of the Human Genome Project. Cited in Kaku M, 1997. *Visions: How science will revolutionise the 21st century*. Anchor Books, New York.
3. *The Concise Oxford Dictionary*, 1976. Oxford University Press, Oxford.
4. www.gov.uk/government/uploads/system/uploads/attachment_data/file/470179/Sugar_reduction_The_evidence_for_action.pdf
5. www.philosophybasics.com/branch_virtue_ethics.html
6. *The Geeta*, Chapter 2, verses 62–63, trans. Shri Purohit Swami. 1935. Faber and Faber, London.
7. www.goodreads.com/quotes/8912-i-am-fond-of-pigs-dogs-look-up-to-us
8. Tooley M. Abortion and Infanticide. *Philosophy & Public Affairs*, 1972;2(1):37–65.
9. Tooley M, 1983. *Abortion and Infanticide*. Clarendon Press, Oxford.
10. www.elise.com/quotes/einstein_-_a_human_being_is_part_of_the_whole
11. Finer LB, Zolna MR, Declines in unintended pregnancy in the United States, 2008–2011, *New England Journal of Medicine*, 2016, 374:843–52.
12. Daugirdaitė V, van den Akker O, Purewal S. Posttraumatic stress and posttraumatic stress disorder after termination of pregnancy and reproductive loss: A systematic review. *J Pregnancy*. 2015;2015:646345. doi: 10.1155/2015/646345.
13. Coleman PK. Abortion and mental health: Quantitative synthesis and analysis of research published 1995–2009. *Br J Psychiatry*, 2011 Sep;199(3):180–6. doi: 10.1192/bjp.bp.110.077230.
14. Fergusson DM, Horwood LJ, Boden JM. Does abortion reduce the mental health risks of unwanted or unintended pregnancy? A re-appraisal of the evidence. *Aust NZ J Psychiatry*. 2013 Sep;47(9):819–27. doi: 10.1177/0004867413484597.
15. Steinberg JR, McCulloch CE, Adler NE. Abortion and mental health: Findings from The National Comorbidity Survey-Replication. *Obstet Gynecol*, 2014 Feb;123(2 Pt 1):263–70. doi: 10.1097/AOG.0000000000000092.
16. Appleby L. Suicide during pregnancy and in the first postnatal year. *BMJ*, 1991 Jan 19;302(6769):137–40.
17. Gissler M, Hemminki E, Lonnqvist J. Suicides after pregnancy in Finland, 1987–94: Register linkage study. *BMJ*, 1996;313:1431–4.
18. Gissler M, Karalis E, Ulander VM. Decreased suicide rate after induced abortion, after the Current Care Guidelines in Finland 1987–2012. *Scand J Public Health*, 2015 Feb;43(1):99–101. doi: 10.1177/1403494814560844.
19. Thorp J, Hartman K, Shadigan E. Long-term physical and psychological health

consequences of induced abortion: Review of the evidence. *Obstet Gynecol Surv*, 2003;58:67–79.

20. www.law.cornell.edu/supremecourt/text/410/113
21. Schuklenk U, Smalling R. Why medical professionals have no moral claim to conscientious objection accommodation in liberal democracies. *J Med Ethics*, 2016 Apr 22. pii: medethics-2016-103560. doi: 10.1136/medethics-2016-103560.
22. www5.austlii.edu.au/au/legis/vic/consol_act/alra2008209/s8.html
23. Kost K, Forrest JD. Intention status of US births in 1988: Differences by mothers' socio-economic and demographic characteristics. *Fam Plann Perspect*, 1995;27:11–7.
24. Finer LB, Zolna MR. Unintended pregnancy in the United States: Incidence and disparities, 2006. Contraception. 2011 Nov;84(5):478–85. doi: 10.1016/j.contraception.2011.07.013.
25. Stewart FH, Trussell J. Prevention of pregnancy resulting from rape: A neglected preventive health measure. *American Journal of Preventive Medicine*, 2000;19(4):228–9. doi:10.1016/S0749-3797(00)00243-9.
26. www.guttmacher.org/fact-sheet/unintended-pregnancy-united-states
27. Guttmacher Institute, Facts on induced abortion in the United States. 2011 August: www.guttmacher.org/pubs/fb_induced_abortion.html
28. https://en.wikiquote.org/wiki/Abortion_(pre-Reformation)
29. www.wma.net/en/30publications/10policies/g1/WMA_DECLARATION-OF-GENEVA_A4_EN.pdf
30. https://history.nih.gov/research/downloads/ICME.pdf
31. ibid, pp132–3.
32. www.bioethics.org.au/Resources/Online%20Articles/Other%20Articles/Euthanasia%20practices%20in%20the%20Netherlands%20-%20Brian%20Pollard's%20third%20Document.pdf
33. Keown J. Further reflections on euthanasia in the Netherlands in the light of The RemmelinkReport and the van der Maas study in euthanasia, in Gormally L (ed). Euthanasia, Clinical Practice and the Law. (1994). Oxford:The Linacre Centre. p 219–40.
34. Jochemsen H, Keown J. Voluntary euthanasia under control? Further empirical evidence from The Netherlands. *J Med Ethics*, 1999 Feb;25(1):16–21.
35. van der Maas PJ. Euthanasia, physician-assisted suicide, and other medical practices involving the end of life in the Netherlands, 1990–1995. *New England Journal of Medicine*, 1996;335:1699.
36. van der Wal G. Evaluation of the notification procedure for physician-assisted death in the Netherlands. *New England Journal of Medicine*, 1996;335:1706.
37. Dierickx S, Deliens L, Cohen J, Chambaere K. Comparison of the expression and granting of requests for euthanasia in Belgium in 2007 vs 2013. *JAMA Intern Med*, 2015 Oct;175(10):1703–6. doi: 10.1001/jamainternmed.2015.3982.
38. Kim SY, De Vries RG, Peteet JR. Euthanasia and assisted suicide of patients with psychiatric disorders in the Netherlands 2011 to 2014. *JAMA Psychiatry*, 2016 Feb 10. doi: 10.1001/jamapsychiatry.2015.2887.
39. Snijdewind MC, Willems DL, Deliens L, Onwuteaka-Philipsen BD, Chambaere K. A

study of the first year of the End-of-Life Clinic for Physician-Assisted Dying in the Netherlands. *JAMA Intern Med*, 2015 Oct;175(10):1633–40. doi: 10.1001/jamainternmed.2015.3978.

40. Van der Wal G. Euthanasia and assisted suicide. *Medisch Contact*, 1991;46:212–14.
41. Chapple A, Ziebland S, McPherson A, Herxheimer A. What people close to death say about euthanasia and assisted suicide: A qualitative study. *J Med Ethics*, 2006 Dec; 32(12): 706–710. doi: 10.1136/jme.2006.015883.
42. Medical Decisions About the End of Life, I. Report of the Committee to Study the Medical Practice Concerning Euthanasia. II. 1991. The Study for the Committee on Medical Practice Concerning Euthanasia, The Hague.

Chapter 11

1. www.youtube.com/watch?v=nojWJ6-XmeQ
2. Maloney EA, Ramirez G, Gunderson EA, Levine SC, Beilock SL. Intergenerational effects of parents' math anxiety on children's math achievement and anxiety. *Psychol Sci*, 2015 Aug 7. pii: 0956797615592630. [Epub ahead of print]
3. Byles JE, Vo K, Forder PM, et al. Gender, mental health, physical health and retirement: A prospective study of 21,608 Australians aged 55–69 years. *Maturitas*, 2016 May;87:40–8. doi: 10.1016/j.maturitas.2016.02.011.
4. Kiecolt-Glaser J, Newton T. Marriage and health: His and hers. *Psychological Bulletin*, 2001;127(4):472–503.
5. Orth-Gomér K, Wamala SP, Horsten M, et al. Marital stress worsens prognosis in women with coronary heart disease: The Stockholm Female Coronary Risk Study. *JAMA*. 2000 Dec 20;284(23):3008–14.
6. Carels RA, Sherwood A, Blumenthal JA. Psychosocial influences on blood pressure during daily life. *International Journal of Psychophysiology*, 1998;28:117–29.
7. www.mybudget360.com/cost-of-living-2014-inflation-1950-vs-2014-data-housing-cars-college
8. Resnick MD, Bearman PS, Blum RW, et al. Protecting adolescents from harm: Findings from the National Longitudinal Study on Adolescent Health. *JAMA*, 1997 Sep 10;278(10):823–32.
9. Grubbs JB, Volk F, Exline JJ, Pargament KI. Internet pornography use: Perceived addiction, psychological distress, and the validation of a brief measure. *J Sex Marital Ther*, 2015;41(1):83–106. doi: 10.1080/0092623X.2013.842192.
10. Lee M, Crofts T, McGovern A, Milivojevic S. Sexting among young people: Perceptions and practices. *Trends & Issues in Crime and Criminal Justice*, 2015 Dec:508. www.aic.gov.au/publications/current%20series/tandi/501-520/tandi508.html
11. Noll JG, Shenk CE, Barnes JE, Haralson KJ. Association of maltreatment with high-risk internet behaviors and offline encounters. *Pediatrics*, 2013 Feb;131(2):e510–17. doi: 10.1542/peds.2012-81.
12. Weaver JB 3rd, Weaver SS, Mays D, et al. Mental- and physical-health indicators and sexually explicit media use behavior by adults. *J Sex Med*, 2011 Mar;8(3):764–72. doi: 10.1111/j.1743-6109.2010.02030.x.

13. Temple JR, Le VD, van den Berg P, et al. Brief report: Teen sexting and psychosocial health. *J Adolesc*, 2014 Jan;37(1):33–6. doi: 10.1016/j.adolescence.2013.10.008.
14. *The Age*. 20 August 2016. p. 3.
15. Thomas S, Lewis S, Duong J, McLeod C. Sports betting marketing during sporting events: A stadium and broadcast census of Australian Football League matches. *Australian and New Zealand Journal of Public Health*, 2012;36(2):145–152. doi: 10.1111/j.1753-6405.2012.00856.x.
16. Pitt H, Thomas S, Bestman A, Stoneham M, Daube M. 'It's just everywhere!' Children and parents discuss the marketing of sports wagering in Australia. *Australian and New Zealand Journal of Public Health*, 2016;40:48–56.
17. www.qgso.qld.gov.au/products/reports/aus-gambling-stats/aus-gambling-stats-32nd-edn.pdf
18. Cornwell R. US considers a change in the law to allow gambling on sports. *Independent*, 30 November 2014: www.independent.co.uk/voices/comment/us-considers-a-change-in-the-law-to-allow-gambling-on-sports-9893158.html
19. www.psychology.org.au/Assets/Files/effects_of_violent_media_on_children.pdf
20. www.ahpsa.org.au/
21. www.healthyactive.gov.au/internet/healthyactive/publishing.nsf/Content/schoolcommu_resourcekit.pdf/$File/schoolcommu_resourcekit.pdf
22. www.acer.edu.au/ozpisa/pisa-2012
23. McClelland MM, Acock AC, Piccinin A, Rhea SA, Stallings MC. Relations between preschool attention span-persistence and age 25 educational outcomes. *Early Child Res Q*, 2013 Apr 1; 28(2): 314–324. Published online 2012 Aug 3. doi: 10.1016/j.ecresq.2012.07.008.
24. Swing EL, Gentile DA, Anderson CA, Walsh DA. Television and video game exposure and the development of attention problems. *Pediatrics*, 2010 Aug;126(2):214–21. doi: 10.1542/peds.2009-1508.
25. Hoang TD, Reis J, Zhu N, et al. Effect of early adult patterns of physical activity and television viewing on midlife cognitive function. *JAMA Psychiatry*, 2015:1. doi: 10.1001/jamapsychiatry.2015.2468.
26. Lillard AS, Peterson J. The immediate impact of different types of television on young children's executive function. *Pediatrics*. Published online: 2011 September 12. doi: 10.1542/peds.2010-1919.
27. Posso A. Internet usage and educational outcomes among 15-year-old Australian students. *International Journal of Communication*, 2016;10:3851–76. doi: 1932-8036/20160005.
28. Dretzin R, Rushkoff D. Digital nation: Life on the virtual frontier. February 2010: www.pbs.org/wgbh/pages/frontline/digitalnation/
29. Lin LY, Sidani JE, Shensa A, et al. Association between social medial use and depression among US young adults. *Depress Anxiety*, 2016 Apr;33(4):323–31. doi: 10.1002/da.22466.
30. Sampasa-Kanyinga H, Chaput JP, Hamilton HA. Associations between the use of social networking sites and unhealthy eating behaviours and excess body weight in

adolescents. *Br J Nutr*, 2015 Dec 14;114(11):1941–7. doi: 10.1017/S0007114515003566.

31. Harbard E, Allen NB, Trinder J, Bei B. What's keeping teenagers up? Prebedtime behaviors and actigraphy-assessed sleep over school and vacation. *J Adolesc Health*, 2016 Apr;58(4):426–32. doi: 10.1016/j.jadohealth.2015.12.011.
32. Demirci K, Akgönül M, Akpinar A. Relationship of smartphone use severity with sleep quality, depression, and anxiety in university students. *J Behav Addict*, 2015 Jun;4(2):85–92. doi: 10.1556/2006.4.2015.010.
33. Halayem S, Nouira O, Bourgou S, et al. The mobile: A new addiction upon adolescents. *Tunis Med*, 2010;88:593–596.
34. https://digitalaustralia.ey.com/
35. Sansone RA, Sansone LA. Cell phones: The psychosocial risks. *Innov Clin Neurosci*, 2013 Jan;10(1):33–7.
36. Angster A, Frank M, Lester D. An exploratory study of students' use of cell phones, texting, and social networking sites. *Psychol Rep*, 2010;107:402–4.
37. Parent J, Sanders W, Forehand R. Youth screen time and behavioral health problems: the role of sleep duration and disturbances. *J Dev Behav Pediatr*, 2016 Feb 17.
38. Allen SL, Howlett MD, Coulombe JA, Corkum PV. ABCs of SLEEPING: A review of the evidence behind pediatric sleep practice recommendations. *Sleep Med Rev*, 2015 Sep 1;29:1–14. doi: 10.1016/j.smrv.2015.08.006.
39. Biegel et al. Mindfulness-based stress reduction for the treatment of adolescent psychiatric outpatients: A randomized clinical trial. *Journal of Consulting and Clinical Psychology*, 2009;77(5):855–66. http://dx.doi.org/10.1037/a0016241.
40. Kuyken W, Weare K, Ukoumunne OC, et al. Effectiveness of the Mindfulness in Schools programme: A non-randomised controlled feasibility study. *British Journal of Psychiatry*, 2013 June 20;1–6. doi: 10.1192/bjp.bp.113.126649.
41. Kurth F, Luders E, Wu B, Black DS. Brain gray matter changes associated with mindfulness meditation in older adults: An exploratory pilot study using Voxel-based morphometry. *Neuro*. 2014; 1(1): 23–26. Published online 2014 Nov 12. doi: 10.17140/NOJ-1-106
42. Ramsburg JT, Youmans RJ. Meditation in the higher-education classroom: Meditation training improves student knowledge retention during lectures. *Mindfulness*, 2013. doi: 10.1007/s12671-013-0199-5.
43. Zenner C, Herrnleben-Kurz S, Walach H. Mindfulness-based interventions in schools: A systematic review and meta-analysis. *Front Psychol*, 2014 Jun 30;5:603. doi: 10.3389/fpsyg.2014.00603.
44. Singh NN, Lancioni GE, Winton ASW, Karazsia BT, Singh J. Mindfulness training for teachers changes the behavior of their preschool students. *Research in Human Development*, 2013;10(3):211–33.
45. Kilpatrick LA, Suyenobu BY, Smith SR, et al. Impact of mindfulness-based stress reduction training on intrinsic brain connectivity. *Neuroimage*, 2011 May 1;56(1):290–8.
46. Hölzel BK, Carmody J, Vangel M, et al. Mindfulness practice leads to increases in regional brain gray matter density. *Psychiatry Res*, 2011 Jan 30;191(1):36–43.
47. Tang YY, Tang R, Posner MI. Brief meditation training induces smoking reduction. *Proc*

Natl Acad Sci USA, 2013 Aug 20;110(34):13971–5. doi: 10.1073/pnas.1311887110.
48. www.brainyquote.com/quotes/quotes/a/alberteins110208.html
49. http://quotes.liberty-tree.ca/quote_blog/Winston.Churchill.Quote.57BB
50. Cooke GPE, Doust JA, Steele MC. A survey of resilience, burnout, and tolerance of uncertainty in Australian general practice registrars. *BMC Medical Education*, 2013;13:2. doi:10.1186/1472-6920-13-2.
51. Dweck C, 2006. *Mindset: The new psychology of success*. Ballantine Books, New York: http://mindsetonline.com/whatisit/about/
52. Linthorst G, Daniels J, Van Westerloo D. The majority of bold statements expressed during grand rounds lack scientific merit. *Medical Education*, 2007;41(10):965–7.
53. www.brainyquote.com/quotes/quotes/a/arthurscho103608.html
54. https://hbr.org/1995/01/disruptive-technologies-catching-the-wave
55. http://deanornish.com/ornish-lifestyle-medicine/
56. Jelinek G, 2010. *Overcoming Multiple Sclerosis: An evidence-based guide to recovery*. Allen & Unwin, Sydney.
57. www.brainyquote.com/quotes/quotes/a/alberteins121255.html
58. www.goodreads.com/quotes/72272-discovery-consists-of-looking-at-the-same-thing-as-everyone
59. Baror S, Bar M. Associative activation and its relation to exploration and exploitation in the brain. *Psychol Sci*, 2016 Jun;27(6):776–89. doi: 10.1177/0956797616634487.

Chapter 12

1. Lichtblau E, Bennerfeb K. Apple fights order to unlock San Bernadino gunman's iPhone. *New York Times*. 17 February 2016: www.nytimes.com/2016/02/18/technology/apple-timothy-cook-fbi-san-bernardino.html?_r=0
2. www.ft.com/cms/s/0/5d3ae2fe-e159-11e5-9217-6ae3733a2cd1.html#axzz467hh7Y5y
3. Booth R. Facebook reveals news feed experiment to control emotions. *The Guardian*, 30 June 2014: www.theguardian.com/technology/2014/jun/29/facebook-users-emotions-news-feeds
4. Rushe D. Facebook sorry — almost — for secret psychological experiment on users. *The Guardian*, 2 October 2014: www.theguardian.com/technology/2014/oct/02/facebook-sorry-secret-psychological-experiment-users
5. www.goodreads.com/quotes/17762-there-are-no-uninteresting-things-only-uninterested-people
6. www.brainyquote.com/quotes/quotes/l/leonardoda402461.html
7. www.brainyquote.com/quotes/quotes/m/michelange108740.html
8. www.oxforddictionaries.com/definition/english/censor
9. www.oxforddictionaries.com/definition/english/censorship
10. Plato, *The Republic*, book III, 401. trans. Jowett B, 1952. From *The Britannica Great Books of the Western World*. University of Chicago Press, Chicago.
11. www.scottmanning.com/content/churchills-earliest-warning-about-hitler/
12. www.goodreads.com/quotes/430071-it-is-necessary-for-the-welfare-of-society-that-genius

13. Chesterton GK, 2014. *The GK Chesterton Collection*. Catholic Way Publishing, London.
14. www.facebook.com/senatordinatale/posts/747633638661566
15. Kerin L. Bill Leak defends controversial cartoon against 'sanctimonious Tweety Birds'. ABC news. 6 August 2016: www.abc.net.au/news/2016-08-05/bill-leak-defends-controversial-cartoon/7693244
16. Speech to the House of Commons, 13 October 1943: http://izquotes.com/quote/326376
17. Stapleton S. The perils of writing a provocative email at Yale. *The Atlantic*, 26 May 2016: www.theatlantic.com/politics/archive/2016/05/the-peril-of-writing-a-provocative-email-at-yale/484418/
18. https://en.wikipedia.org/wiki/Piss_Christ
19. https://au.news.yahoo.com/a/31179123/sydney-public-school-principal-bans-the-word-easter-in-annual-easter-hat-parade/#page1
20. http://www.theaustralian.com.au/opinion/christmas-carol-ban-is-out-of-tune-with-society/news-story/3065c467b3c77fc54cd7a6fab03982fa
21. https://en.wikipedia.org/wiki/Tim_Hunt
22. Ratcliffe R. Nobel scientist Tim Hunt: Female scientists cause trouble for men in labs. *The Guardian*. 10 June 2015: www.theguardian.com/uk-news/2015/jun/10/nobel-scientist-tim-hunt-female-scientists-cause-trouble-for-men-in-labs

Epilogue

1. Durant A, Durant W, 1944. *The Story of Civilization*, vol III 'Caesar and Christ'. Simon & Schuster, New York.

INDEX

A

abortion 37–8, 49, 179, 181–3
academic performance, social media 203
addiction
  antithesis of freedom 142–3
  attachment to 73
  chain of habit 29
  craving sweet rewards 139
  to gamblings taxes 28
  genetic predisposition 142–3
  increasing problem 25–8
  lack of restraint 137–8
  legitimizing causes of 43–4
  meditation to overcome 143
  mobile devices 204–5
  part of modern life 136
addictive substances *see* drugs
ADEPT, changing unhealthy habits 140
advertising, regulation 139–40
affluence, effects of 29
ageing
  and lifestyle 143–5
  position on euthanasia 189
alcohol 27, 36
anarchy 87–90
anger 163, 177
apartheid 14–15
appetitive element, psyche 78–80
aristocracy 114, 115–17
art
  imitating nature 216–18
  increasingly shocking 215–16
Assange Julian 40
assumptions 47
atheism, more militant 63
attachment, to possessions 71–2
attention, importance of 203
attention span 34–5
Aung San Suu Kyi 70, 124
autonomy 54, 169–72
Avon Longitudinal Study 142
awareness 160–1

B

beauty products 61
Bentham, Jeremy 166
Bhagavad Gita (Hindu text) 71, 177
bias
  forms of 72
  seen as truth 47
Blackstone, Sir William 107–8
Blake, William 4
body
  how did we get it 186
  worship of 61
Boethius 70
borderline personality disorder 135, 163
Botticelli, Sandro 114
boundaries
  importance of limits 200–2
  science and technology 133
boys, disrespecting girls 198–9
brain
  development in males 134
  three main regions 133–4
    see also prefrontal cortex
Brandeis, Louis D 89
Browning, Robert 5
Buddha 69, 71, 82
Buffett, Warren 109
Bunyan, John 67
Bygren, Lars 141

C

Cabell, James Branch 22
cancer
  longer survival 33
  management 92
  prostate 145
capitalism 103
carnivorous plants 3–4
cartoons
  'racist' 223
  satirical 222–3
cave allegory 126–8
censorship
  definition 218–21
  distortion of history 221
  'good' 221–2
  humour in the press 222–4
certainty, illusion of 206
change
challenging convention 215–18
social conventions 104–5
see also social change
Charlie Hebdo (magazine) 222–4

chemical network, genetic levers 141
chemicals, exposure to 144
chemotherapy, survival benefit 33
Chesterton, GK 223
children
  effect of screen time 203
  family engagement 196–7
  fewer limits 201
  food choices 31
  modelling parents 194–5
  multitasking 203–4
  obesity 30
  protecting from harm 197–200
  and self-restraint 193–4, 200–1
  too much praise 207–8
choice
  in adversity 157
  freedom of 58, 155–6
  individual 53–4, 54
  normalization 170
  paradox of 35–6
  pro-choice or none 182–3
  and rights 176
cholesterol-lowering drug 32
Christakis, Nicholas and Erika 225
chronic illnesses 30, 31–4
Churchill, Winston 72, 103, 178, 206, 221, 224
civilizations
  marks of decline 80–2, 215
  rise and fall 62–3
The Closing Circle (book) 91
clothes consciousness 61
cohabitation 96–7
collective interest 54
collective unconscious 151
Collins, Francis 172
common good 54
Commoner, Barry 91, 97
communism 50, 103
compassion
  law of 103
  power of 159
computer use, unfettered 204–5
concentration camp experience 154–5
condom advertisement 193–4
conformity 53–4, 227–8
connection, Commoner's first law 99
conscience 102
conscientous objection
to abortion 49
to war 53
conscious mind 151
consequences
  actions without 59
  virtue ethics 176
consumerism 24–5, 80–1
contraception 37–8, 183–4
corporations, as 'persons' with rights 108
counter-cultural movement, 1960s 59
courage, facing adversity/death 69–70
creativity 205–11, 215–16
crime
  form of anarchy 88–9
  organized 106–7
  against ourselves 105–7
  underlying causes 40–41
  young women 36
crisis, living on the edge 55–6
cruelty 101
culture, imposition on others 48–9
curiosity 210–11
cyber-crime 40

D

da Vinci, Leonardo 217
Dalai Lama 70, 100, 224
deaths
  due to medical errors 29
  'good' or bad care 188
  suicide 23–4
  US shootings 41
Declaration of Independence (US) 25
The Decline and Fall of the Roman Empire (book) 80
democracy
  apparent openness 50–1
  decline of 123–4
  described 115
  examined 119–21
  imposing 50
  parallels with Plato's 124–6
  rise of 49–51
  tyranny pendulum 51
demonstrations 50
Denning, Lord Alfred 87
deontology 165–9, 176
depression
  escalating problem 23–4
  social media use 39, 204–5
derogatory language 228–9
determinism 148–9, 153–4
deviance from the norm 57–8
Devotions upon Emergent Occasions (essay) 55
dialectical behaviour therapy (DBT) 163
discipline
  inner 69

lack of 84–5
self-mastery 82–5
withholding 202
disease-free lifestyle, best chance for 137–8
'disruptive technology' 209
distraction 34–5
divine will
social control 94–5
universal laws 96
doctors
abortions 49, 182–3
unquestioned 169
'doctrine of double effect' 187–8
dogma 208–10
Donne, John 55
dopamine 143
drugs
experimenting with 58
normalized 25–6
profusion of 25
Durant, William and Ariel 62–3, 232
duties 174–6
Dweck, Carol 206

E

East meets West 51–3
eating, appetite control 79
Eban, Abba 73
ecology, four laws of 91–4
economic injustice 15–16
ecstasy, serotonin production 26
education, and creativity 205–11
Einstein, Albert 96, 132, 180, 205, 210, 211
elders, respect for 59–60
Eliot, TS 34, 67
emotive element, psyche 77–8
energy production 41
enlightenment 68
environment
influence on behaviour 139
overcoming 154
environmental crisis 41–2, 98–9
envy 177
Epictetus 155
epigenetics 141–5
equality
vs sameness 102–5
of the sexes 103–5
ethics, understanding 165
euthanasia 186–90
excess
of liberty 51, 121
life of 119–20
love of 93
a right to 175
as a virtue 60
executive function, prefrontal cortex 133–4
exercise, regular 30

F

Facebook, unplugging from 38–9
families, modern 196–7
family income 196
fanatic, definition 72
fantasy 163–4
fear
of ageing 189
of death 190
projected from parents 208
response to 78
fear of missing out (FOMO) 35–6
Federer, Roger 84
feminist ideology 48
fixed mindset 206–7
foetus, status of 184–5
food for the mind 218–24
Frankl, Viktor 154–6
free will 152
freedom
within a democracy 119
different philosophies 65–6
explained 66
of expression 215–18
ideas of 5–6
of information 213–15
knowing the limits 231–2
with meditation 85
obedience to law 87
of others 12
in praise of 18
of the press 223
slow diminution of 6–7
of speech 222, 226–7
of thought 210
through non-attachment 70–3
ultimate 149
see also inner freedom; outer freedom
Freedom Under the Law (lecture series) 87
Freud, Sigmund 149–50
functional reserve 55–6
functionality, and beauty 217

G

gambling
addiction to 42–3
legitimizing 43–4

gambling addiction 27–8, 199
Gandhi, Mahatma 70, 124
gender roles 103–5
genetic determinism, freedom from restraint 141–5
genetic engineering 109–10
Gibbon, Edward 80
global financial crisis (GFC) 15–16, 42, 108–9
globalization, meaning 68
gluttony 176
God-given principles
  natural laws 165–6
  social control 94–5
  universal laws 96
government
  'good' paternal 173
  of the individual 53–4
  secularization 52
government forms
  aristocracy 114, 115–17
  democracy 115, 119–21
  oligarchy 115, 116
  timocracy 114, 117
  tyranny 115, 122–3
government regulation, public health 31
grandparents, effect on grandchildren's health 141–2
greed 54, 176
growth mindset 207–8
gun control 40–1

H

Halloween clothing 225
happiness
  hedonic attitude to 158
  main dispositions to 81
  short-term 137
health
  best chance for 137–8
  government regulation 31
  lifestyle-related illnesses 136–8
  materialist society 24–5
  modern illnesses 5
  natural law 91–4
  underlying lifestyle issues 92
healthcare, problems of 29
heaven *vs* hell 12–13
hedonic calculation 167
hedonism 80–2, 158
hell *vs* heaven 12–13
heroes, literary 67
Hildegard of Bingen 70
Hill, Andrew 214–15
Hippocratic oath 184–5
Hitler
  as 'protector' 124
  rhetoric 221
homeostasis 92
homosexuality 48
human nature, law of 100
human rights/duties 174–6
humanism 95
human-made law 107–10
humour
  self-deprecating 228–9
  three kinds 223
Hunt, Tim 228

I

immigration, clash of cultures 53
immune system 167
impermanence 74
inclusivity 227–9
independence 55
indigenous cultures
  ecological laws 91
  system of law 90
  type 2 diabetes 32
individual
  choice 54
  rule of the 53–4
individualism 158
individuality 180
indoctrination 205–6
infanticide 179
information technology (IT) *see* technology
injustice, economic 15–16
inner freedom
  can change way of being 74–5
  through discipline 69–70
'instinctuality' 152
institutions, disbanded 59–60
interdependence 55
Internet 40
intolerance 227–9
IVF treatment, age of mother 57

J

James, William 148–9
Jesus Christ 69–70
Johnson, Samuel 29
Jung, Carl 150

K

Kabat-Zinn, Jon 159
Killingsworth, Matthew 85

kindness 159
King, Billie-Jean 74
King Jr., Martin Luther 14–15, 70
knowledge, kinds of 131–3

L

law
- breakdown in 89
- human-made 107 10
- obedience to 87
  - *see also* natural law

law-makers, most learned? 110
Leak, Bill 223
'learned helplessness' 156
liberalization, process of 52
liberation
- historical struggle for 13–18
- of women 17

'liberation ideology' 48–9
libertarian view 171
liberty
- excess of 51, 121
- freedom from restraint 87–9

lie detectors, stress response 100
life
- definition of its beginning 184–5
- as a journey 67

life expectancy 34
lifestyle, and ageing 143–5
lifestyle habits, life expectancy 34
lifestyle-related illnesses
- lack of restraint 137–8
- love of excess 93
- medical approach to 92–3
- modern life 29–30, 136
- type 2 diabetes 32–3
- Western living 32

limits, importance of 200–2
love, two kinds 202
lust 177

M

'mad cow disease' 99–100
malignant ideologies 172
Mandela, Nelson 70, 78, 124
marriage
- modern 196
- natural law 96–7

Marx, Karl 220
mastery, achieving 83–4
materialism 24–5, 63–4, 80–1, 126–7
McCarthyism 50
media violence 200
medicine
- art of 92
- biomedical approach 32–3

meditation
- to overcome addiction 143
- training the mind 85

Mediterranean diet 144
'me-generation' 158
men
- gender differences 103–5
- modern 196
- reduced health risks 138
- stress response 103

mental health 23–4
mental rigidity 208–10
mental traps 163–4
Michelangelo 217
Mill, John Stuart 166
mind, law governing 101–2
mind–body-based lifestyle programmes 209–10
mindfulness
- explained 159–62
- lengthening telomeres 144–5
- prostate cancer 144–5
- taught in schools 205

mindfulness meditation 85, 101–2
mindfulness-based intervention 135
mindsets 206–8, 210
modelling, teaching by 194–5
modernism 215–18
monkey, trapped 70–1
monogamy 97
morality 152
More, Thomas 70
morphine, high doses 187–8
Mother Teresa 70
Mozart, abilities of 83
multitasking 35

N

natural law
- consequences of ignoring 98–102
- God-given 165–6
- health and ecology 91–4
- human psychology and society 94–7
- physical laws 90–1

natural order, breakdown 120
nature, art imitating 216–18
Nazism 16, 121
necessity 149
negative psychology 149–50, 158
neuroplasticity 135–6

neuroscience of wellbeing 133–6
non-attachment
  freedom through 70–3
  mental 80
non-conformity of art 216
normalization
  adolescents' behaviour 198
  of choices 170
  democracy in decline 125
  of deviance 57–8
  drug use 25–6
nutrition, poor 29, 30–1

O

obesity
  modern phenomenon 30–1
  prevalence of 138
  statistics 30
  sweet cravings 139
oligarchy 115, 116, 118
open mind 210
optimism *vs* pessimism 22
organized crime 106–7
outer freedom
  can change situation 74–5
  liberty or licence 68–9

P

Pallas and the Centaur (painting) 114
parents
  challenges for 195–7
  'good' 173
  teaching by modelling 194–5
paternalism 169, 172–4
Pembrey, Marcus 142
pendulum, democracy/tyranny 51
personality, definition 162
personality disorders 163
personality traits 162–3
personhood 178–80
pessimism *vs* optimism 22
Pied Piper 172
Pilgrim's Progress (book) 67
Pinker, Steven 89
Piss Christ artwork 226
pitfall plants 3–4
Plato
  attachment 71
  cave allegory 126–8
  censorship 219–20
  on democracy 119, 120–1, 122–4
  democracy in decline 124–5
  excess of liberty 51
  forms of government 114–23
  inner freedom 75
  philosophers as kings 123–4
  psyche and government 113
  reason/wisdom 77
  self-mastery/justice 75–6
  tyranny 82, 122–3
  on virtues 176
pleasure
  interpretations of 119
  pursuit of 60–1
  a sweet trap 77
political correctness 224–9
political systems
  imposition of 48–9
  tyrannical 16
Pollard, Brian 187
pollutants, exposure to 144
pornography 198–9
positive psychology 156–7, 158
possessions
  mental objects 72
  physical 71
postmodernism 215–18
power, abuse of 169–70
praise
  common trap of 208
  results *vs* effort 207–8
prefrontal cortex
  executive function 133–4
  late development 201
pregnancies, unwanted 37–8
pride 177
privacy 213–15
progress, positive aspects 21–2
prostitution, legitimizing 43–4
protections, forms of 22–3
psyche
  appetitive element 78
  balance of elements 76–7
  emotive element 77–8
  harmonious 177
  reason/wisdom 77–8
psychology
  early focus 149–50
  how we study it 147–8
  negative 149–50, 158
  positive 156–7, 158
psychotherapy, conventional approaches to 161–2

R

racism 12, 14–15, 102

reason, from rule of 60–1
reasoning element, psyche 77–8
regulation *vs* restraint 139–40
'relaxation response' 143
religion
  decline 62–4
  inflammatory cartoons 222–3
religious beliefs, imposition of 48–9
religious celebrations, banned 227
religious oppression 17–18
resilience 158
restraint
  lack of restraint 68–9
  vs regulation 139–40
revolutions
  periods of anarchy 89–90
  against tyranny 49–50
rhetoric, sweet sounding 221
rights 174–6
Rubaiyat of Omar Khayyam (poems) 126
rules, both absolute and flexible 167
Ruskin, John 87–8

S

sacred images
  denigrated 223
  'Piss Christ' artwork 226
sameness *vs* equality 102–5
Schopenhauer, Arthur 209
science
  dangerous potential 132–3
  form of knowledge 131–3
  a new religion 131
  rule of 62–4
screen time, long-term effects 203
secularization of government 52
sedentary life 29–30
self, rule of 169–72
self-expression, freer 59–60
self-harm, right to choose 105–6
self-interest, an isolating trap 12
self-mastery
  balance of psyche elements 76–82
  brain functions 134
  discipline 82–5
  harnessing abilities 83–4
  and justice 75–6
self-mutilation, physical 58
self-reflection 151
self-restraint
  children learning 193–4, 200–1
  development of 136
Seligman, Martin 156–9
serotonin production 26
'seven deadly sins' 176
sex
  as marketing tool 80–1
  underage 37–8
sexting 198–9
sexually transmitted diseases (STDs) 37
Shakespeare, William 74, 78, 173
shared-resource systems 54
Shaw, George Bernard 222
shootings 40–1
Singer, Peter 179, 185
single parenthood 57
skin colour 102
Skinner, BF 152–4
slavery
  entrenched 13–14
  in tyranny 122
sleep, laws related to 100
sloth 176–7
smoking
  laws related to 105
  war against 26
Snowden, Edward 40
social activism, words and strategies 226
social change
  1950s 37
  1960s 59
  East meets West 52
social control, God-given principles 94–5
social isolation 38–9
social media
  academic performance 203
  and depression 39, 204–5
  over-reliance on 39
  social effects of 204–5
  storms caused by 225, 228
  virtual relationships 38
social norms, new 228
socialism 103
society, natural law 94–7
Socrates 69
Sparta, government 117
sports betting 199
statistics
  euthanasia 187, 188
  Facebook users 39
  gambling addiction 27
  obesity 30, 138
  shootings 40–1
  suicide rates 23–4
  teen pregnancies 37–8
  type 2 diabetes 32

- unwanted pregnancies 183–4
- violent crime 36
- women's alcohol abuse 36

stimulants, serotonin production 26
The Story of Civilization (book) 62–3
stress response
- lie detectors 100
- men *vs* women 103

subjugation 11–12
'sugar taxes' 175–6
suicide
- after abortion/childbirth 181–2
- rates 23–4
- right to choose 106

'sunk-cost' bias 72
Swami Nirmalananda 72
Szent-Gyorgyi, Albert 211

T

talent, harnessing 83–4
technology
- computer time 204–5
- dangerous potential 133
- discerning use of 145–6
- hasty adoption 109
- threat to civil liberties 40
- too much information 214–15
- tyrannical master 197
- unplugging from 38–9

television, 'opiate of the masses' 220
telomeres 143–5
The Ten Principal Upanishads (Hindu texts) 76–7
terrorism, cancer-like 42–3
The Talmud (Jewish text) 48
Thoreau, Henry David 7
thought patterns 135–6
thoughts
- censored 218–24
- not reality 160–1

three people; three paths 65–6, 85–6
timocracy 114, 117
tolerance 227–9
Tooley, Michael 179
traditions, discarded 59–60
'tragedy of the commons' 54
transcendence 73–5
transgenerational genetics 141–2
type 2 diabetes 32–3
tyranny 51, 115, 122–3

U

unconscious mind 151
underage sex 37–8
uniformity, architectural 53
United States Declaration of Independence 94–5
utilitarianism 58, 165–9, 167

V

Vaughan, Diane 57
vices 176–7
violence, media 200
virtual reality 145–6
virtue
- sustainable life rule 88–9
- true 177

virtue ethics 176
Voltaire 92

W

wars, necessary evil 3
wealth, growing disparity 81
welfare safety net 173
wellbeing, neuroscience of 133–6
Western world
- cultural evolution 51–3
- imposing democracy 50
- reaching tipping point 81

whistle-blowers 214
Whitehead, Alfred North 113
WikiLeaks 214
wisdom, explained 132
wise leaders, poor treatment of 124–5
women
- alcohol abuse 36
- 'equality' of 36
- gender differences 103–5
- liberation of 17
- modern, liberated 195
- stress response 103

words
- power of 226
- self-deprecating humour 228–9

worry 163
wrath 177

Y

Yousafzai, Malala 70
youth-worshiping culture 59–60